INSIDERS'GUIDE®

New York

Neighborhoods

Third Edition

*A Food Lover's
Walking, Eating, and
Shopping Guide to Ethnic Enclaves
throughout New York City*

Eleanor Berman

Drawings by John Coburn

W9-APJ-004

INSIDERS'GUIDE®

GUILFORD, CONNECTICUT
AN IMPRINT OF THE GLOBE PEQUOT PRESS

The prices and rates listed in this guidebook were confirmed at press time. We recommend, however, that you call establishments before traveling to obtain current information.

Interior text design by Lana Mullen and Deborah Nicolais
Map design by M.A. Dubé

ISSN 1547-9870
ISBN 0-7627-3028-5

Manufactured in the United States of America
Third Edition/First Printing

Contents

NIGHT
NEW YORK CITY JOHN COBURN
1999

$\mathcal{P}reface$

This is a book that I started in order to satisfy my own curiosity. It is dedicated to people like me who want to explore the wonderful ethnic neighborhoods and foods of Manhattan and the boroughs but want to feel comfortable about getting around.

One of my great pleasures as a Manhattanite has been sampling New York's diverse restaurants. Greek, Italian, Afghan, Indian, Chinese, Vietnamese, and Thai restaurants are all within 4 blocks of my apartment building, and the variety is one of the things I love about the city.

But I've been aware that there are other neighborhoods offering more authentic experiences of other lands, places where people have chosen to maintain their ethnic flavors even while becoming part of the city's "melting pot." I had visited some of these communities in Manhattan, but I wanted to venture further into the boroughs, and I couldn't find a single source to lead the way. Walking tours gave me history but no information on food; food books didn't give me walking tours. Nobody gave me detailed maps of shopping in the boroughs or told me where to go once I got off the subway in an unfamiliar neighborhood. Nor did they tell me what to order in a Korean restaurant where the waiter doesn't speak English or what to buy in a Polish bakery or a Chinese market.

So I decided to explore on my own, taking formal walking tours where they were available, as a start, but basically walking the streets and finding my way around. As I explored, the scope of the book began to grow. I started with a focus on food and shopping but soon realized that it was a shame to walk around a fascinating neighborhood without knowing some of the history and seeing the landmarks, from some of the city's oldest homes to magnificent churches and synagogues.

I wanted to know more about the foods of different nationalities. Thus I have incorporated some of my background reading into this book—not as an expert guide, to be sure, but as an introduction, including definitions of some of the basic foods that I hope will be helpful. I've combed restaurant reviews and quizzed neighborhood residents to come up with a list of recommendations.

We have created easy-to-follow maps for each chapter. A dotted line shows the suggested walking route. Each point of interest is indicated with a number in a square; restaurants are marked with letters in a circle.

This past year of wandering has been full of rewards for me. The areas I've visited are not Disneyland, with kitschy fake architecture, nor are they a miniature Athens or Bombay. For the most part they are middle-class working neighborhoods with modest housing, yet most are maintained with care and pride and are a pleasure to see. Outside Manhattan, the low-rise buildings are a welcome change, almost like visiting another city. Shopkeepers have been patient with my questions and generous with samples, and everyone has been warm to me, clearly an outsider. I have admired the love of language, culture, and cuisine that has motivated the people of each neighborhood to maintain their traditional ways even as they have adopted new ones.

The boroughs are no longer such a mystery to me. I've learned that I can get to Astoria or Jackson Heights, Atlantic Avenue or Williamsburg within minutes of Midtown Manhattan, that the Brooklyn shore is the best place in the city on a warm summer day, that some of the most interesting historic districts are not in Manhattan. And I have found that I had long overlooked treasures in my own backyard; half a dozen lovely small ethnic churches have stood on the side streets of my Manhattan neighborhood, unnoticed as I passed by.

I've gained five pounds on Italian sausage and cheese, Lebanese lamajuns, Polish babka and kielbasa, Indian samosas, Russian pirogis, Greek olives, and Latin American churros—and loved every bite.

Most of all I've gained a new sense of the people and places that add up to a world-class city.

I hope this book will lead you to do your own exploring, to share in the fun and make your own discoveries. I can almost guarantee that you'll wind up with a fuller sense of the city and new regard for its many diverse parts.

What sums up my last year of getting to know New York neighborhoods? That's easy. *I love New York.*

Rates for Restaurants

$	most entrees less than $12
$$	most entrees between $12 and $20
$$$	most entrees more than $20

The Mixing Bowl

Afghanistan to Zimbabwe: Name a country and you'll likely find its cuisine and some of its flavor in New York.

One of the city's greatest assets is the many nationalities that come together here, making for a delicious ethnic stew. With a sense of adventure, you can travel from Odessa to Athens, Bombay to Sicily, Lima to Hong Kong, without ever leaving New York.

WHO CAME WHEN AND WHERE

From its beginnings New York City has been a mixing bowl where many nationalities come together. According to the *Encyclopedia of New York*, in 1643, when the population was about 500, eighteen languages were spoken in the city. The nationalities have changed over the years, but the stream of newcomers searching for opportunity in a new land has never ceased. New Amsterdam became New York as the English displaced the Dutch. Early in the nineteenth century, difficult economic conditions in Northern and Western Europe led many Irish and Germans to leave their homelands for the plentiful jobs in New York, a growing seaport and manufacturing center. Many first settled in the crowded tenements of the Lower East Side of Manhattan. As they prospered and moved uptown, their places were taken by Russian and Polish Jews and southern Italians, who arrived in record numbers in the late 1880s, fleeing persecution or hard economic times in their native countries. The building of bridges and subways to the boroughs spread the immigrant population to Brooklyn, Queens, and the Bronx.

By 1920 nearly 40 percent of New Yorkers were foreign-born. A national sentiment against the changing mix in the United States caused laws to be passed in 1924 putting quotas on immigration, and for a while the numbers of newcomers dwindled.

When these laws were negated in 1965 by the Hart-Cellar Act, which ended discrimination based on national origin, new groups quickly arrived. These included Greeks, Eastern European refugees from Communist regimes, and many immigrants from the Caribbean. Asians, freed for the first time from rigid restrictions, began coming in large numbers. Civil wars and poverty in Central and South America brought waves of newcomers from Colombia, Peru, Uruguay, Ecuador, Argentina, and Brazil in the early 1970s. By the mid-1990s more than one hundred nationalities were part of the city's makeup.

Newcomers typically want to become Americans, but they also don't want to lose their own cultures. They tend to cluster together in neighborhoods where everyone knows their language, their history, their customs, their music, and, most of all, their foods. Even after they move up and out, they often return to the old neighborhoods to shop.

Thus ethnic neighborhoods flourish in New York, from Midtown Manhattan to the fringes of the other boroughs, still untouched by gentrification, allowing New Yorkers to feel like tourists without leaving home. Turn a corner in Herald Square and you will find a slice of Seoul. Travel to Astoria in Queens and you'll encounter the largest Greek population outside of the homeland. Brighton Beach in Brooklyn has become "Odessa by the Sea," and Greenpoint is a "Little Poland." Italian enclaves can be found from the Bronx to Brooklyn, and the #7 Train to Queens has been dubbed the International Express.

TIPS FOR REWARDING EXCURSIONS

Each neighborhood described in the pages ahead has its own language and shops—and restaurants offering a chance to sample authentic cuisines, usually unchanged to suit the tastes of tourists. I often note supermarkets, which are fun to explore because they show the variety of foods available, but even more rewarding are the family-owned small shops, where you can ask questions and perhaps sample a few kinds of homemade cheese or sausage. Most storeowners take delight in introducing an interested stranger to their country's foods and take pride in offering the foods they have made.

Can you find many of these foods in your own neighborhood? Probably. The difference, as one storekeeper told me, lies in the "TLC," the loving care that goes into the making and the pride in the stocking of quality merchandise from the home country.

Another happy difference is in cost. Though the foods are of high quality, these are not high-income neighborhoods, and the stores price their products accordingly.

In restaurants you'll do well to ask the waiters' advice; they like showing off their native foods as well. Be adventurous and try something new—a Peruvian stew or a Sicilian pasta made with sardines, a Moroccan tagine or a serving of Jewish gefilte fish—any dish that you've never experienced before.

To make the most of each excursion, read something about the cuisines and spices you are about to experience. You'll get a small introduction here, but pick up a cookbook as well. A visit to a neighborhood will be more fun if you choose a recipe to make at home so that you can look for the ingredients while you are shopping.

Think about planning on company after an excursion as well. It will give you an excuse to stock up on cheeses and sausages and olives, on Indian sweets or Lebanese pizzas, and all the other wonderful foods you'll find in abundance.

Every neighborhood outlined here is easy to reach and safe to wander in, and you shouldn't feel constrained to stick to the routes mentioned. Making your own discoveries is part of the adventure. Just remember that this is the real world, not a movie set, and these are city neighborhoods, not necessarily pretty or quaint. Many of the neighborhoods formed under rumbling elevated subway tracks, where rents are cheaper. Though one ethnic group predominates, none of these neighborhoods is entirely made up of one nationality. One of the fascinations is seeing that you can walk from Korea to China or India to Argentina within a block.

These neighborhoods are populated with people who have everyday needs and wants beyond their ethnic identity, so intermingled with the baklava and babkas and kielbasas, you'll find banks, drugstores, nail salons, Chinese restaurants, maybe even a McDonalds, just like any other city block.

The most rewarding excursions I found are those beyond Manhattan. The minute the subway comes above ground in Brooklyn or Queens, showing you a miniature skyline in the distance, you feel like you are headed for an adventure far from your everyday routine. The languages you hear, the signs in Cyrillic script or Greek or Arabic, the foods, the clothing, the handicrafts, and the colors allow you to share a tiny taste of life in another land—and to gain a new appreciation for the wonderful richness each group adds to life in New York.

Brooklyn

It is the borough of brownstones and churches, of New York City's largest Hasidic Jewish population, and of its most colorful Russian enclave. Come and discover the city's last working fishing fleet, its largest Polish neighborhood, and its most inviting beaches.

The Middle East on Atlantic Avenue

The unexpected mixture of antiques and ethnic foods helps make Atlantic Avenue one of Brooklyn's most intriguing enclaves. This Middle Eastern shopping hub is also enhanced by the attractive surrounding brownstone neighborhoods of Brooklyn Heights, Cobble Hill, and Boerum Hill, making this a great area for exploring.

THE HISTORY

Atlantic Avenue, which extends to the shoreline of the East River, has a long history as a commercial street. During the Civil War years from 1860 to 1864, shipping activity along the Brooklyn waterfront constituted an important part of the supply line to Union troops. Afterward the avenue emerged as a center of shipping-related commerce. Many of the nineteenth-century commercial buildings from this prosperous era remain, their storefronts built with large expanses of glass to display merchandise.

Syrians and Lebanese, motivated by the wish to escape economic hardship and Ottoman conscription plus a thirst for new opportunities, began to migrate to New York in the 1870s.

The majority of the early arrivals were Christians. Many began as peddlers. Eventually they prospered enough to establish their own businesses in groceries and imports, supplying Middle Eastern communities throughout the country.

The first large Middle Eastern settlements in New York were in Lower Manhattan, but they were displaced in 1940 by the construction of the Brooklyn–Battery Tunnel. Atlantic Avenue, which already had a few Syrian businesses, became the new heart of the Middle Eastern community. From the turn of the century until the 1960s, New York's well-established Syrian–Lebanese community was the largest and most important in the United States.

Another big influx of newcomers began when immigration quotas were lifted in 1965. Many Lebanese arrived after 1975, when civil war broke out in their homeland. This group was drawn more from the professional classes, and many did not choose to live in the old neighborhoods. Nevertheless, Atlantic Avenue remains a major hub for Middle Eastern food shopping and dining.

How to Get There

By subway: Take the M, N, or R Train to Court Street; the #2, 3, 4, or 5 Train to Borough Hall; or the A, C, or F Train to Jay Street/Borough Hall. Follow the flow of traffic on one-way Court Street, walking south about 4 blocks and turning right onto Atlantic Avenue.

By car: Exit the Manhattan or Brooklyn Bridge at Adams Street, turn right onto Tillary Street, and take a left onto Court Street to Atlantic Avenue.

A Shopping / Walking Tour

The number of Middle Eastern establishments seems to be dwindling, but you can still have a delicious inexpensive meal here or pick up wonderful foods to take home, followed by a pleasant stroll for antiquing or exploring the appealing nearby neighborhoods of Cobble Hill and Brooklyn Heights.

Damascus Breads & Pastry (1), 195 Atlantic Avenue, (718) 625–7070, is the place to buy savory meat and spinach pies as well as tempting pastries, including pistachio or walnut baklava, the shredded-wheat confections called bird's nests, and "lady fingers"— not the sponge-cake variety, but phyllo layers with raisins and walnuts. The pita bread is carried at fine stores all over the city.

The biggest store on the block is **Sahadi Importing Co., Inc. (2),** 187 Atlantic Avenue, (718) 624–4550. This business was started in 1895 and was launched in this location in 1948 by the great-uncle of the current proprietors. It is reason enough for a trip to Atlantic Avenue. Recently expanded to provide a more varied selection, the store has everything and anything in the way of Middle Eastern foods—two dozen kinds of olives, more than one hundred cheeses, honeys, oils, dried fruits, and nuts. Grains, beans, herbs, spices, sesame seeds, sumac, fava beans, ground ginger, and coffees are sold in bulk from barrels. A big take-out counter sells hummus, stuffed grape leaves, babaghanouj, tabouli salad, couscous salad, and many other foods.

Another good shopping stop is **Atlantic Fruit and Vegetables (3),** 181 Atlantic Avenue, (718) 596–4624, which is not necessarily Middle Eastern but offers a great selection of salad greens, fruits, and vegetables at good prices.

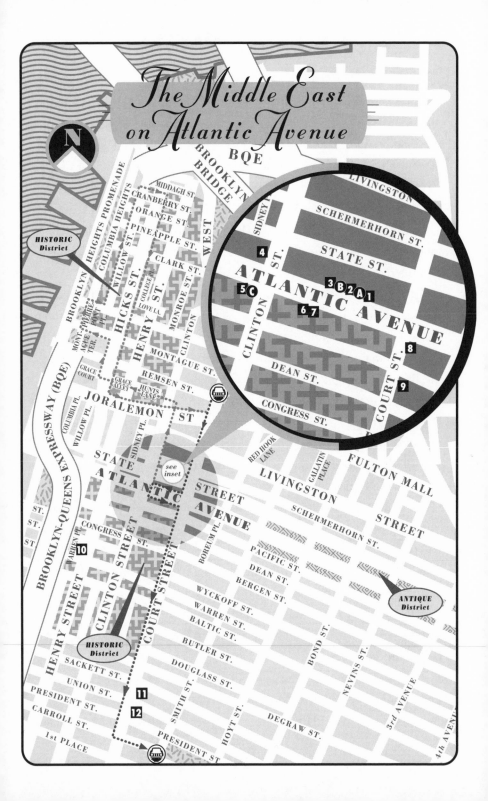

Just across Clinton Street is **Two for the Pot (4)**, 200 Clinton Street, (718) 855–8173, a haven for lovers of coffee or tea. Though the shop is small, it stocks over 200 kinds of bulk and packaged teas, custom-blended coffees, plus a variety of herbs and spices. For utensils you might need in the kitchen, cross the street and visit **A Cook's Companion (5)**, 152 Atlantic Avenue, (718) 852–6901. This block between Clinton and Henry Streets is becoming a restaurant row, with cuisines of all kinds. On the corner is Tripoli (see page 15), the most elegant of the Middle Eastern restaurants.

If you want to combine this trip with a stroll through the beautiful brownstones of Brooklyn Heights, detour right onto Clinton; stroll along some of the side streets like charming Grace Court; and turn down Montague Street, the main thoroughfare of the neighborhood, to the Brooklyn Heights Promenade, offering one of the most spectacular views of the Lower Manhattan skyline. Continue walking on streets such as Pierrepont, Willow, and Cranberry to see some of the oldest homes in the area. Truman Capote wrote *Breakfast at Tiffany's* and *In Cold Blood* in the basement of 70 Willow Street, and playwright Arthur Miller once owned the property at 155 Willow.

If you prefer to continue on Atlantic, head back up the street. You can pick up anything you may still need at the **Oriental Pastry & Grocer (6)**, 170 Atlantic Avenue, (718) 875–7687. The windows are filled with intriguing Middle Eastern artifacts, and the stock inside includes a dozen kinds of rice, dried fruits, and beans. Pastries, spinach and meat pies, cookies filled with walnuts, dates, and pistachios, and four kinds of baklava are all baked on the premises.

Another good source for foods of all kinds (and another fine window display) is **Malko Karkanni Brothers (7)**, 174 Atlantic Avenue, (718) 834–0845.

The Arab influence continues around the corner on Court Street. The **Garden of Fragrances (8),** 141 Court Street, (718) 625–6340, carries all kinds of scents for men and women, from Chanel #5 and Michael Jordan to Egyptian, Tunisian, and Arabian fragrant oils. Jasmine, myrrh, and musk are some of the most popular Middle Eastern scents that you may want to sample.

To find classic recipes for your Middle Eastern ingredients, walk on to **Rashid Sales Company (9),** 155 Court Street, (718) 852–3295, where you will find cookbooks in English—*Arabic Cooking Step by Step* and *The Lebanese Cookbook* are typical titles—along with a large stock of Arabic books. The shop, established in 1934, also calls itself the oldest and largest source of Arabic music in the city.

You are now into the heart of the pleasant, upscale neighborhood of Cobble Hill, where Court Street offers a variety of spots for dining and shopping. Turn to the right on any block between Pacific and

Kane Streets to see the handsome row houses of the Cobble Hill Historic District. Most of these homes were built in the mid-1800s. In 1997 a row house on Congress Street sold for a record amount, more than $1 million. One charming complex is **Warren Place (10),** an enclosed court between Warren and Baltic Streets begun in 1876. Though small, the attached homes provided amenities rare at the time—ample natural light, air, privacy, and a courtyard where children could play safely.

If you continue farther along Court Street, past DeGraw Street, you'll find yourself in the Carroll Gardens neighborhood—and in the midst of another of Brooklyn's ethnic pockets, a host of venerable Italian food shops. Explore if you like, picking up crusty Italian breads at **Caputo's Bake Shop (11),** 329 Court Street, (718) 875–6871; or homemade sausages at **Esposito's Pork Store (12),** 357 Court Street, (718) 875–6863.

When you've had enough shopping, turn left up Carroll Street and walk 1 block to Smith Street, where you can take the F Train back to Manhattan.

Middle Eastern Cuisine

Middle Eastern cuisine has much in common with Greek and Turkish food, in the use of lamb and dishes such as stuffed grape leaves and grilled kebabs as well as phyllo-dough pastries and yogurt. The difference lies in the spices. Many dishes have a sweet flavor— foods are often cooked with cinnamon, dried fruits and nuts, and sometimes rose water. The most common flavorings are turmeric, dill, mint, parsley, tahini (a sesame-seed paste), cumin, saffron, nutmeg, and sumac. (Most cooks make up their own seasonings, personal blends of six or seven spices; you can find mixtures of this kind in

Antiques Antics

Antiques shoppers will want to walk past Court Street and go 2 blocks farther up Atlantic Avenue to Smith Street, the beginning of "antiques row," which extends almost to Fourth Avenue. Here you can pick up furniture of all kinds and unusual collectibles, from candlesticks to china, at more than thirty shops.

For more contemporary tastes, look into two shops sharing space at 369 Atlantic Avenue: Breukelen, (718) 246–0024, is filled with handcrafted home accessories; Bark, (718) 625–8997, has fine bed linens. Melting Pot, 492 Atlantic Avenue, (718) 596–6849, offers handcrafted batik clothing.

Farther on, a West Indian and African influence is found at Zawadi Gift Shop, 519 Atlantic Avenue, (718) 624–7822, and at Lewis Gallery, 525 Atlantic Avenue, (718) 624–8372, which specializes in African-American and African-inspired crafts and art. Two eating places in this section of the avenue are popular: Bedouin Tent, 405 Atlantic Avenue, (718) 852–5555, specializes in Middle Eastern "pitzas" made with pita dough. Brawta Caribbean Cafe, 347 Atlantic Avenue, (718) 888–5515, gets high marks for Jamaican specialties such as jerk chicken and roti. Unusual fruit drinks go well with the spicy food.

Each year on the third Sunday in September, all facets of life on Atlantic Avenue come together for the annual Atlantic Antic, a lively street fair that fills the avenue from the harbor to Fourth Avenue with foods of all kinds, Arab bands and belly dancers, and West Indian marchers.

**A TYPICAL
MIDDLE-EASTERN MEAL**

*Appetizers (Mezze):
hummus, babaghanouj,
stuffed grape leaves*

*Shish kebab (lamb or
chicken) or
a Moroccan tagine stew*

Baklava

various Atlantic Avenue stores.) Flat pita pockets are served with meals; these breads can be slit open and filled with various spreads.

Moroccan cuisine seems more sophisticated, perhaps reflecting the subtle influence of the French, who occupied Morocco for so long. The best-known dishes are the tagines—gently simmered stews cooked with fruits, nuts, and complex spice combinations. Tagines are named for the traditional clay pot with a cone-shaped cover in which they are cooked.

A MIDDLE-EASTERN SAMPLER

Atlantic Avenue menus offer many of the following foods:

Babaghanouj: mashed eggplant in sesame-seed paste (tahini).

Baklava: layers of phyllo dough soaked in honey.

Couscous: ground semolina wheat. The word is also used on menus to denote a meat or vegetable stew served over couscous.

Falafel: fried balls of ground chickpeas.

Glaba: sautéed lamb with a choice of okra, artichokes, or string beans, served with rice.

Hummus: mashed chickpeas with sesame-seed paste (tahini), garlic, and lemon juice.

Kafta: ground lamb.

Kebab: meat grilled on a skewer.

Kibbeh: ground lamb flavored with cinnamon and pine nuts.

Laban: sliced cucumbers with spiced yogurt.

Lamajun: a Lebanese version of pizza; pita dough topped with a savory layer of ground lamb blended with onions, tomatoes, and spices.

Mezze: a selection of appetizers.

Pastella: Moroccan chicken pie, filled with chunks of chicken, roasted almonds, raisins, and spices.

Tabouli: a salad of bulgar wheat, parsley, tomatoes, and onions, flavored with mint and other spices.

Tagines: Moroccan-style meat stews, usually lamb, made with fresh zucchini, carrots, fruits, nuts, and a special sauce.

Tahini: a sesame-seed paste.

RECOMMENDED 🍽 RESTAURANTS

Caravan Restaurant (A) ($), 193 Atlantic Avenue, (718) 488–7111. This pleasant cafe has a varied menu offering curries along with Middle Eastern lamb and chicken standards and special menus for vegetarian fare and Moroccan specialties. Yemeni specials are sometimes featured. The Atlas Barber Dinner for four gives the chance to sample several Moroccan dishes inexpensively. The restaurant often features belly dancers on Saturday night.

Fountain Cafe (B) ($), 183 Atlantic Avenue, (718) 624–6764, is an attractive little place with table service and a take-out menu. It is especially popular for the generous number of vegetarian platters and sandwiches. And it does have a fountain in the rear, albeit a tiny one.

Tripoli (C) ($), 156 Atlantic Avenue, (718) 596–5800, is an attractive restaurant with sea-themed murals and a two-level interior decorated like the deck of a ship. The specialties are Lebanese, such as sumki hara (sautéed fish fillets in a spicy sauce made with chopped

almonds and walnuts); Ma'ani (Tripoli lamb sausage made with wine, pine nuts, and spices); and caussa b'leben (squash stuffed with ground lamb, rice, and pine nuts in a yogurt sauce cooked with mint). Meatless dishes include an eggplant stew with potatoes and onions in tomato sauce and lentils cooked with rice and onions and served with a yogurt salad. You can make a meal of the twenty mezze (appetizers) on the menu.

The Little Italy of Bensonhurst

In many ways, this is the real "Little Italy" of New York. Unlike Manhattan's Little Italy or Arthur Avenue in the Bronx, Bensonhurst is more than a shopping and dining center. It is a neighborhood of homes, almost like an Italian village in Brooklyn.

If you diverge from the main shopping street for half a block, you will see that the residents have re-created many of the things they loved about Italy, planting grape arbors and fig trees in their backyards. They have christened 18th Avenue, their main shopping street, Christoforo Columbo Boulevard. Many buildings are festooned with Italian flags and red, white, and green banners, emphasizing the message of pride in Italy and the Italians.

Most of the patrons enjoying espresso and biscotti in the coffee shops are not tourists, but people from the neighborhood. The many wedding shops along the avenue cater to local families, who follow the old world custom of lavish marriage preparations.

When you visit Bensonhurst's markets, you have the feeling that you are among choosy residents who really know Italian food.

THE HISTORY

Bensonhurst was part of the Dutch settlement called New Utrecht. It retained its farmlands and Dutch character into the nineteenth century. The Dutch Reformed Church, dating from 1828, still stands on 18th Avenue and 73rd Street, serving a congregation founded in 1677.

In 1783 patriotic citizens put up a liberty pole in front of the church and flew an American flag to celebrate the evacuation of the British from Brooklyn. George Washington visited the church in 1790. The liberty pole has been replaced several times, but it still stands.

This large neighborhood once bordered on Gravesend Bay; its proximity to the water and improvements in public transportation inspired its first residential development, in the late 1880s. A developer named James Lynch bought large parcels of farmland from the Benson family and created a suburban community known as Bensonhurst-by-the-Sea. Lynch planted 5,000 shade trees and designed villas that attracted middle-class families and wealthy weekenders headed for the

How to Get There

By subway: Take the N Train to 18th Avenue,
forty-five to fifty minutes from 42nd Street.

By car: Take the Belt Parkway to Bay Parkway and
follow Bay Parkway to 86th Street; 18th
Avenue is 4 blocks to the northwest.

Bensonhurst Yacht Club. Most of the seaside area is now considered part of Bath Beach rather than Bensonhurst.

Things changed again in 1915, when the subway reached Bensonhurst, bringing in new residents. Italians and Jews from Manhattan's Lower East Side discovered a more pleasant lifestyle in Bensonhurst, and the population zoomed. Two- and three-family homes and low-rise apartments were built to house them.

In the 1950s Bensonhurst was transformed by the arrival of thousands of immigrants from southern Italy, especially Sicily, who prospered and sent for their families. By 1980 nearly 80 percent of the residents in the neighborhood were Italian, making for a homogeneous community where everyone seems to know everybody else. Family and church are central to most; several generations may even live on the same block.

... *A Shopping Tour* ...

When you emerge from the subway, you are at 64th Street and 18th Avenue, close to the start of the shopping area. Turn right on 18th Avenue, where the numbers begin to get larger, and walk down one side of the street to 73rd Street and back on the other; by then you'll have found most of the cream of the stores.

Detour anywhere the spirit moves you to look at the side streets where people live. If you visit here in winter, these blocks have an eerie look, as the ubiquitous fig trees are wrapped in black tar paper to protect them from the cold.

You'll know you've made the right turn when you pass a Citibank with a sign in the window reading QUO, NOI PARLIAMO ITALIANO. And if you want sustenance to get you through your walk, you'll soon see the most highly recommended stop for pizza, Da Vinci Pizzeria (see page 25).

Berta 67 (1), 6708 18th Avenue, (718) 256–0291, is a favorite spot to find gifts for bridal showers, which are major events in the life of young Italian brides-to-be. These are often multicourse lunches or dinners, with ninety to one hundred people attending. If the crystal and knickknacks don't seem to be particularly Italian, look around. There are shelves packed with oil and vinegar cruets in all shapes and forms, dozens of varieties of pasta bowls, and every conceivable kind of espresso pot.

Trunzo Brothers Meat Market (2), 6802 18th Avenue, (718) 331–2111, is the best-known store in Bensonhurst, now in the sixth generation of one family. Though meats are still a specialty, it has grown into an Italian supermarket. The windows tell the story— packed with jars of olives and red peppers, fat Italian cheeses and ham, and with signs proclaiming HOMEMADE SAUSAGES MADE DAILY.

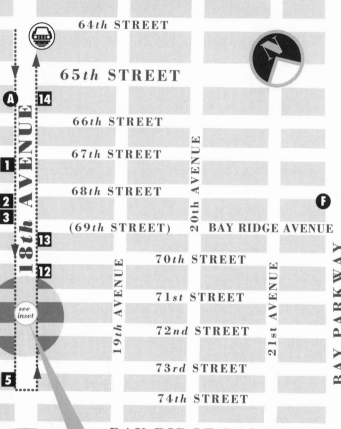

Bensonhurst

64th STREET

🚇

65th STREET

A **14**

18th AVENUE

66th STREET

1 67th STREET

2
3 68th STREET

13 (69th STREET) BAY RIDGE AVENUE

20th AVENUE

12 70th STREET

17th AVENUE

see inset 71st STREET

72nd STREET

19th AVENUE

21st AVENUE

73rd STREET

5 74th STREET

BAY RIDGE PARKWAY

76th STREET

B

71st   ST.

11
10 77th STREET

18th AVENUE

C **9**
8 78th STREET

79th STREET

D

72nd   ST. 80th STREET

4 **7**
6

E

F

BAY PARKWAY

G

There's a whole counter devoted just to sausages, sweet to pepper and onion, and a whole wall of pastas in myriad shapes. You can also take home freshly made mozzarella, broccoli rabe, stuffed peppers, pasta, grilled eggplant, and prime meats ready for the pan, like beef braciole and veal rollatine.

Mondello Pescheria (3), 6824 18th Avenue, (718) 236–3930, is the place to find absolutely fresh seafood, including Italian favorites like calamari (squid) and octopus, and baccala (dried cod).

Stop at the fruit and vegetable stands adjoining the store and extending around the corner, and marvel at the low prices for favorite Italian ingredients like broccoli rabe, eggplant, red peppers, dandelion leaves, and plum tomatoes. Prices for prime fruits are equally enticing.

The finest tiles from the mother country can be found at **Italian Tile Import (4),** 7202 18th Avenue, (718) 236–9174.

Arcorbaleno Italiano (5), 7306 18th Avenue, (718) 259–7951, is the place to find the latest in Italian movie videos and music.

Now cross the street and turn back along 18th Avenue to find more treasures. **Bridal Boutique (6),** 7217 18th Street, (718)

149–1212, is among several shops in the next few blocks specializing in wedding attire as well as offering favors, invitations, photos, gifts and everything else to do with these events so grandly celebrated in a family-oriented neighborhood.

Queen Ann Ravioli (7), 7205 18th Avenue, (718) 256–1061, has pastas large and small, fresh and dry, most made on the premises. Many frozen prepared dishes, like ravioli, manicotti, and stuffed rigatoni, will stock your freezer with treats. The gnocchi are also recommended.

Bari Pork Store (8), 7119 18th Avenue, (718) 837–1257, sells sausages hot and sweet, not to mention a fine assortment of cheeses, including some delicious Parmesan. Try some of the sausage made with parsley and cheese or peppers and onion.

Villabate Pasticceria (9), 7117 18th Avenue, (718) 331–8430, makes delicious, crusty semolina breads. The displays of cookies and cakes are artistic. If you need a hostess gift, a package of cookies tied with a red ribbon is a guaranteed pleaser. The store also sells marzipan and dried fruits.

If all that good food makes you want to sing, **SAS Italian Records (10),** 7113 18th Avenue, (718) 331–0539, is another chance to pick up music, from rock to opera.

If household goods are on your shopping list, make a stop at **Il Centro Del Corredo Italiano (11),** 7109 18th Avenue, (718) 331–1578. This is a favorite for wedding gifts, a center for imported linens, silks, and pillows.

The granddaddy of Italian bakeries is **Alba Pastry (12),** 7001 18th Avenue, (718) 232–2122. After Nicolo Alba immigrated to the United States, he opened for business in 1932, continuing a family tradition that had begun in Sicily in 1870. Alba's store is still at the original address, and his family is still in charge. Among the treats

Festive Occasions

When Bensonhurst celebrates, it does so in style. The Feast of Santa Rosalia (Santa Rosalia is the patron saint of Sicily) is a weeklong event at the end of August that is not to be missed.

According to legend, Santa Rosalia saved the city of Palermo from a plague. She clearly holds a special place in the hearts of many Sicilians, who have affectionately nicknamed her La Santuzza ("The Little Saint").

The annual celebration lights up 18th Avenue with colored lights and brings out Church auxiliaries and local food purveyors with delicious Italian food rivaling the annual San Gennaro festival in Manhattan's Little Italy— but with half the crowds.

Another festive date is Good Friday, when thousands of parishioners from neighborhood churches, carrying statues and banners, walk in a candlelight procession to a 9:00 P.M. High Mass at Our Lady of Guadalupe Church, 15th Avenue at 72nd Street.

here are tiramisu, buccellati filled with walnuts and figs, and Sicilian favorites like cassata, layers of sponge cake and creamy ricotta, iced and decorated with candied fruits. Pignoli macaroons, authentic Italian cheesecake, and spumoni cake are also recommended. All the cakes are gorgeous, and there's even a do-it-yourself kit of pastry shells and ricotta filling for cannoli. The store also does a large mail-order business.

Il Telaio (13), 6915 18th Avenue, (718) 331–7880, is another store offering gifts for brides, featuring, among other things, lacy underwear. Then you can drop into the Caffe Italia next door for a final cappuccino, a pastry, or a refreshing gelato.

One last chance for Italian ices or ice cream is **Uncle Louie G's (14)**, 6517 18th Avenue, (718) 236–7417, famous for the amazing variety of flavors served. The business started in a tiny stand by two brothers, John and Rick Russo, now has locations all over the city and is rapidly going national. The current menu, ninety flavors and counting, includes killer kiwi, peanut butter chocolate chip, and Georgian peach on the Italian ice menu. The ice cream roster, equally diverse, has an Italian accent with offerings such as Soprano Spumoni and Paulie Maple Walnuts.

Italian Cuisine

The information about Italian cuisine on page 237 applies, but Sicilians have their own specialties, influenced by the Spaniards and Arabs who invaded the area in the past. Capers, pignoli (pine) nuts, panelle (a chickpea flour), anchovies, and sardines are common ingredients. A popular pizza comes with anchovies and onions; a favorite dish is a rice ball filled with meat. Pasta consarde, virtually the national dish, is spaghetti or penne with a sauce containing sardines, fennel, capers, and pignoli nuts.

R E C O M M E N D E D ꠶ R E S T A U R A N T S

Da Vinci Pizzeria (A) ($), 6514 18th Avenue, (718) 232–5855, remains the place for crusty pizza, despite all the rivals you will pass on your stroll. Afterwards, Uncle Louie G's is ready with dessert, right across the street.

Caffe Bella Cucina (B) ($–$$), 7023 18th Avenue, (718) 234–5597, is a popular low-key local eatery serving the Sicilian pasta con sarde as well as calamari, scampi, and other Italian favorites.

Gino's Focacceria (C) ($), 7118 18th Avenue, (718) 232–9073, features Sicilian dishes as well as focaccia, served cafeteria style and for minuscule prices. You can watch a soccer match on television while you munch.

Caffe Milleluce (D) ($–$$), 7123 18th Avenue, (718) 837–7017, a bright modern cafe on the corner, is a coffee house and bar as well as a restaurant serving all the familiar Italian specialties.

More restaurants are found on Bay Parkway, 4 blocks away, and on 86th Street, another busy shopping area, though not as bountiful as 18th Avenue.

Ortobello (E) ($), 6401 Bay Parkway, corner of 64th, (718) 236–9810, is casual and cozy, a family-run restaurant serving family-style southern Italian fare. The prix fixe dinner is a great bargain.

Torre's (F) ($–$$), 6808 Bay Parkway, (718) 256–1140, is a bit more upscale, with waiters clad in tuxedos; but the prices are still moderate and the food is excellent. Two pastas worth sampling are spaghetti with anchovy rounds and Spaghetti Frank Sinatra, tossed in a light sauce embellished with sautéed scallops, clams, and black and green olives.

Tommasso's (G) ($–$$), 1464 86th Street, (718) 236–9883, is a little distance away but offers Old World ambience, ample and tasty Italian food, and live opera, making for a festive night out. The Julliard-trained owner occasionally joins in the song.

Strictly Kosher Borough Park

Borough Park is about the good life, in many senses of the phrase. It is home to the largest Orthodox Jewish population in the United States, mostly Hasidic sects clinging to the Old World ways and dress that they feel are the path to righteousness. It is also a vibrant community of large families, with a big, bustling shopping street filled with bargains, especially in children's clothes and furniture.

How to Get There

By subway: Take the M or W Train to 55th Street, about a forty-minute ride from Mid-Manhattan.

By car: Take the Brooklyn–Battery Tunnel from Manhattan to the Brooklyn–Queens Expressway. Stay in the left lane (do not follow signs to Staten Island) to the Prospect Expressway. Exit west (to the right) at Church Avenue, which becomes 14th Avenue. Look for 13th Avenue, 1 block to the right. Watch for parking on the cross streets.

The Hasidic Way of Life

The mystical branch of Judaism known as Hasidism emerged in the 1700s, largely in Poland and the Carpathian Mountains, as a protest movement against the academic emphasis in the Jewish community. At that time the only respected deeply religious men were scholars who spent all their days studying the Talmud (the book of Jewish law) and the Torah (the first five books of the Hebrew scriptures), which make up the authoritative writings of Jewish tradition and learning. Only the wealthy could afford this way of life, meaning that poorer people whose days were spent making a living were excluded from the Jewish elite.

Hasidism taught that you could be a humble woodcutter or a tailor and still be acceptable in the eyes of God as long as you followed His precepts to the letter, and did so with joy in your heart.

This meant following the Halacha—the way to God—by fulfilling commandments known as mitzvohs. There are 613 of these commandments, 248 "shalts" and 365 "shalt nots." These include wearing the payehs (forelock curls), beards, and the prayer fringes called tzi-tzis seen on men, as manifest signs of devotion. Equally important is the adherence to the food preparation and diet known as kosher. These and every other detail of daily life are taken from literal translations of

Though modestly dressed, Borough Park women have a distinct sense of style, and there are many discount clothing stores and an amazing number of shops with good-looking low-heeled shoes. Among a legion of stores selling religious articles are shops with magnificent sterling silver. Food is bountiful here, from kosher pizza, to blintzes,

passages from the Bible. One of these commandments, to mul-
tiply, has been followed quite faithfully; Hasidic families
average five to eight children.

The characteristic dress of Hasidic men—long black
coat, white shirt buttoned at the collar but with no tie, black
or fur hat—is very similar to the dress of Polish nobility of
the seventeenth century. In order to follow standards of
modesty, married women shave their heads and wear wigs or
sheitels, and often hats as well. Skirts are long and necklines
high for girls and women alike. Men and women are sepa-
rated in schools and in worship.

The Hasidic movement was spread and is still led by men
known as rebbes. A rebbe is not a rabbi trained in schools but,
rather, a charismatic leader or prophet, believed to be close to
God and to understand His will. Each rebbe has his own style
and following and remains the leader of the sect for life.
Disciples want to live near the rebbe, as he is consulted not only
on religious matters and Jewish law but on life decisions as well.

The Hasidim study avidly and pray fervently, singing
and swaying during worship. Their spirit of joy comes out
during holidays. Visit Borough Park in September, the time
of Simchat Torah, when the completion of the yearly cycle
of reading the Torah scrolls is celebrated with dancing in
the streets; or in March for Purim, when children parade in
costumes.

to half a dozen bakeries loaded with wonderful breads and pastries.

This is a much more worldly and accessible neighborhood than
the Hasidic communities in Crown Heights and Williamsburg. A visit
to Borough Park is both an education in another way of life and a
shopping bonanza.

Early Friday afternoon, when the street bustles with preparation for the Jewish Sabbath, is a colorful time for a visit. Don't bother coming on Saturday, however. From late afternoon Friday until Saturday night, everything is closed. Observant Hasidic families do not drive, turn on electricity, carry or use money, or conduct business on the Sabbath.

THE HISTORY

Like much of Brooklyn, the Borough Park neighborhood was once farmland; its residential development began when advances in transportation made it possible to commute to Manhattan. Russian Jews from the Lower East Side began moving to Borough Park as early as 1910, seeking more pleasant surroundings, and the movement grew after World War I as elevated trains made connections easier. By 1930 about half the population was Jewish—many of them Orthodox, but not of the extreme Hasidic faiths. Temple Beth El, a beautiful house of worship, was built in 1923. It became famous for its great cantor, Moshe Koussevitsky. When he sang, the synagogue overflowed with people and crowds sometimes lined the sidewalk, hoping to hear his great tenor voice. His recordings are still available in local record stores.

Young Israel, the other prominent synagogue in the neighborhood, attracted younger worshippers with modernized rituals such as services in English. The temple had a gymnasium and was part of a basketball league. As the number of Hasidic residents has grown, these congregations have dwindled, and Young Israel has merged with Beth El.

Hasidic Jews, largely from the Bobover sect from Poland, began to arrive in large numbers during the 1930s, escaping Hitler. After World War II many less Orthodox young Jewish families moved away to the suburbs. The Hasidic population grew enormously in the late 1940s and 1950s, due to several events: the inflow of World War II refugees; the 1956 uprising in Hungary; and the completion of the Brooklyn–Queens Expressway in 1957, which displaced Hasidics in Williamsburg and Crown Heights. Today the area, comprising some 90,000 people, is mostly Hasidic. More than thirty sects are represented, and there are close to 300 synagogues—some are fine, newly built temples, while others operate in modest storefronts. The Bobovers remain the largest contingent. Their

modern temple is between 15th and 16th Streets on 48th Street, which has been renamed Bobover Promenade.

Unless it is the Sabbath, wherever you go in Borough Park, yellow school buses can be seen delivering or waiting for children. Hasidic families are typically large, and children are not sent to public school, so there are more than 25,000 children attending more than fifty religious schools in the neighborhood, with separate facilities for girls and boys. Education is the largest employer in the area.

However, education ends with high school, as college is considered an invitation to worldly temptations. Young Hasidic men are expected to go to work, girls to marry and raise a family. Women are also expected to work, since men devote many hours to study and worship and financial support is often needed from wives.

... *A Walking Tour* ...

When you walk down the stairs from the elevated train tracks, turn down 13th Avenue, the buzzing main shopping street of Borough Park. You'll find two kinds of strollers here—two-legged and four-wheeled. The streets are filled with mothers pushing children in strollers, with big brothers and sisters tagging along. Stores and service businesses provide everything that residents need to live the carefully proscribed life of their Hasidic faith as well as to supply the worldly needs of clothing and furnishings for large families. The stores are numerous, with many choices beyond those listed here; this is a street meant for browsing and making your own discoveries. There are many shops with linens, shoes, children's clothing and furniture, and maternity clothes. Even more shopping is found on 16th and 18th Streets, and many people make special trips to shops such as Underworld Plaza, 1421 62nd Street near 14th Avenue, (718) 232–6804, which has a vast selection of lingerie at wholesale prices.

At every cash register you'll see a *pushka* for your change—a box for charity donations for needy families in a neighborhood that takes care of its own.

Walking down 13th Avenue, among several shops with children's clothes **Wonderland (1),** 5309 13th Avenue, (718) 435–4040, stands out, packed to the rafters with offerings including many special-occasion dresses and suits.

Borough Park

The little gallery called **All-Art Direct (2)**, 5217 13th Avenue, (718) 972–6386, is interesting for its selection of artworks depicting Jewish life in the Old Country and paintings of the great rebbes.

Look into **Cohen's Houseware & Hardware Company (3)**, 5212 13th Avenue, (718) 851–7343, to see the wide selection of dishes to serve families who must have separate sets for meat and dairy dishes and additional sets for Passover.

Everything from religious items to music to children's games to braided candles can be found across the street at **Kodesh (4)**, 5205 13th Avenue, (718) 633–8080.

Look at the lines and you'll know that **Strauss Bakery (5)**, on the corner at 5115 13th Avenue, (718) 851–7728, is one of the best in the neighborhood, a mainstay for more than thirty-five years. The challahs are warm from the oven, the chocolate or raspberry rugelach as light as air, and the bags wisely advise "try Bubby Strauss' cookies."

At the **Hosiery Boutique (6)**, also at 5115 13th Avenue, (718) 854–1230, Calvin Klein and Donna Karan are among the discounted brands. "Shabbos locks" are one of the specialties at **Perfect Locksmith (7)**, 5113 13th Avenue, (718) 435–5300. This shop supplies combination door locks for homes whose occupants are not allowed to use keys on the Sabbath.

Notions, buttons, lace, rhinestones, ribbons, flowers, and trims of all kinds are stocked across the street at **Sew Splendid (8)**, 5016 13th Avenue, (718) 437–5154, which advertises "decor-a-hat—a splendid hat trimmed at your own taste for a bargain." Hats and hat pins, wig boxes, and sewing boxes are among the offerings.

A favorite bakery on the block is **Weiss (9)**, 5011 13th Avenue, (718) 438–0407, which has a tempting display of fancy cakes.

Next comes the most unique Jewish emporium in New York, **Eichler's (10)**, 5004 13th Avenue, (718) 633–1505. Its slogan,

"The Judaica Superstore," is no exaggeration. Frames, sets of goblets and trays for the Sabbath, spice boxes used in traditional rites, thousands of books in both Hebrew and English, CDs and tapes of Jewish music of all kinds, mugs that say *Mazel Tov* ("Congratulations") and menorahs in the shape of klezmer bands, old synagogues, clowns, toy trains, Mickey Mouse, and Winnie the Pooh are just a few of the endless offerings in this big, modern store. There are stacks and stacks of yarmulkes (prayer caps) large and small, plain and fancy; piles of  prayer shawls; and a whole wall of traditional and modern mezuzahs (the tiny portion of the Torah that is displayed in a case at the door to signify the sanctity and blessing of a Jewish home). For kids there are books like *My Shabbas 1, 2, 3s* and *Torah Rhymes and Riddles*, for ladies *The Jewish Homemaker* magazine; and for scholars or those who want to learn more about the Hasidic way, a large section of books on Halacha as well as titles such as *Great Hasidic Leaders* and *The Rebbe's Advice*.

Among many stores offering handsome silver, the standout is **Grand Sterling (11),** 4921 13th Avenue, (718) 854–0623, known for its reproductions of antique designs. The shop overflows with magnificent silver frames, goblets, candlesticks, and trays.

Don't overlook **Stern's Bakery (12),** across the street and just off 13th Avenue at 1278 49th Street, (718) 633–7466, another bakery with a loyal band of fans for rye, challah, and pumpernickel baked fresh daily, as well as rich babkas.

There are many more stores of all kinds ahead, including **Mostly**

Music (13), 4805 13th Avenue, (718) 438–2766, advertising the "world's largest selection of Jewish Music" and **Candy Man (14)**, 4702 13th Avenue, (718) 438–5419, a children's favorite for its bins of penny candy and a good place to look for nuts and chocolates—all kosher—and pretty gift baskets. **Mildred's Bed and Bath Boutique (15)**, 4612 13th Avenue, (718) 435–2323, has two floors of duvets, sheets, and an extensive bath shop at discount prices. The store does a lot of mail and phone business. Farther down the street, at the edge of the neighborhood, is the **Shmura Matzoh Bakery (16)**, 1285 36th Street, (718) 438–2006, which opens only in spring in order to make Passover matzohs.

But to get a better sense of the neighborhood, turn up 48th Street, away from the shops, and walk to 15th Avenue to see **Temple Young Israel Beth El (17)**, 4802 15th Avenue, (718) 435–9020. The handsome, Moorish-inspired building was constructed in 1923. The temple is rarely open except during services, but it's worth calling ahead or walking around the side to the office to see if by chance someone is available to show you the beautiful interior.

Just across the way, taking up most of the block, is the main **Bobover Hasidic Synagogue (18)**, 48th Street between 15th and 16th Avenues, (718) 438–9791, done in marble with tall windows, columns, and rows of tall wrought-iron arches in front. Instead of pews, there are rows of desks inside, as the building is used for study as well as prayer. The temple is usually open because someone is almost always inside reading or praying, but remember that head coverings are required and that women must go upstairs.

You may want to detour for a couple of blocks down 16th Avenue to get a sense of a smaller but still thriving shopping district, with duplicates of almost every kind of store found on 13th Avenue. One interesting organization here is the Yochsin Institute, 1605 48th Street at the corner of 16th Avenue, (718) 435–4400, specializing in researching Jewish family roots. **Schick's Bakery (19),** 4710 16th Avenue, (718) 436–8020, sells to every major bakery in Manhattan; the rugelach sold in Zabars are often made here.

If you want to understand more about the Borough Park community, come back to 49th Street, walk to 14th Avenue, and ask to see the program listing at the **Boro Park YM-YWHA (20),** 4912 14th Avenue, (718) 438–5921. Separate activities and hours are scheduled for boys, girls, women, and men. Women are offered classes in washing, setting, and styling your own *sheitel* (wig) and in food decoration, as well as self-esteem workshops and classes in how to defuse tense family situations. Both sexes can take computer workshops, which are an excellent preparation for jobs for people with limited educations.

Walk back along 14th Avenue and observe the homes on the side streets. Older homes have given way to small apartment buildings with extra bedrooms to accommodate large families. They are low-rise because Hasidic Jews will not use an elevator on the Sabbath. Each building has staggered balconies to accommodate the tradition of the holiday of Succoth, when families take meals in a four-sided shelter open to the sky.

Turn right again at the corner of 53rd Street and 14th Avenue, where a former public school is now a girls' school for the Satmar sect, and take a left again to reach the subway.

You've now seen how people who fled the *shtetls*—villages in Europe where they were persecuted—have turned a corner of Brooklyn into a peaceful shtetl all their own.

Kosher Cuisine

Some general comments and a sampler of Jewish cuisine are found on pages 257–60. In Orthodox neighborhoods like Borough Park, the emphasis is on strictly kosher cuisine, which means separating meat and dairy products. Religious families keep two sets of dishes, pots, and flatware to be sure that these dishes are never mixed together. Foods without meat or dairy ingredients, such as vegetables, fish, fruits, grains, and eggs, are considered *pareve* (neither meat nor dairy) and may be eaten with either kind of dish.

Other kosher regulations require that meat come only from animals that chew their cud and have split hooves, as ordained in the Torah, which means that pork cannot be eaten. The use of chicken fat, or *schmaltz*, developed as a substitute for lard.

According to kosher tradition, fowl must be slaughtered by a *shochet*, a man trained and skilled in the precise methods taught in the Code of Jewish Law. Only fish that have both fins and scales are kosher, meaning that seafood such as shrimp, clams, and lobster are not allowed. *Glatt kosher* foods, which include vegetables and grains, are carefully inspected for purity, and are free of even the tiniest insects or other impurities. *Glatt*, the Yiddish word for "smooth," also refers to the smoothness of an animal's lungs during slaughtering, free of cysts and scabs.

Another dietary stricture in the Old Testament states that the blood of any animal is sacred to the Lord and may not be consumed by humans. The result is the practice of "koshering" meats by salting and hanging them to release blood and the practice of cooking meats for a long time to be sure that no trace of blood will be visible when eaten.

The requirement that no cooking be done on the Jewish Sabbath—

from sundown Friday until sundown on Saturday—has led to other traditional dishes that the cook can begin late Friday afternoon and leave over a very low fire for a full twenty-four-hour period, such as cholent, a slow-cooked meat stew.

R E C O M M E N D E D 🍽 R E S T A U R A N T S

There are no fancy restaurants in Borough Park, and the emphasis is on home cooking; neighborhood families are more likely to take out than eat out. But they do like variety, so places where inventive chefs have found ways to serve Kosher pizza or Chinese food are popular.

If kosher food is not your dish, however, you are only 5 blocks from the wealth of Chinese offerings on Eighth Avenue. If you have walked enough, the #9 Bus on 60th Street will get you there in no time.

Matamin Dairy Restaurant (A) ($), 5001 13th Avenue, (718) 437–2772, is a fine place to sample blintzes and other dairy dishes.

Crown Deli (B) ($), 4909 13th Avenue, (718) 853–9000, sells lots of take-out sandwiches and stuffed cabbage, but there's a small area with tables, and hot dishes are served.

Amnon Kosher Pizza (C) ($), 4814 13th Avenue, (718) 851–1759, serves pizza made with kosher cheeses. It also makes falafel, hummus, and homemade knishes.

Chef AH (D) ($), 4810 13th Avenue, (718) 972–0140, is a glatt kosher establishment with a long counter full of traditional hot foods to go. This is a good source for a roasted-chicken dinner with kugel.

Donutman (E) ($), 4708 13th Avenue, (718) 436–7318, is basically a luncheonette counter with only a few tables, but it serves a full menu and has many fans.

J on 13th (F) ($), 4703 13th Avenue, (718) 437–0300, one of the newer, more modern establishments on the block, serves a mix of sandwiches, pizza, salads, and tasty fish dishes.

Plaza Dining (G) ($$), Avenue Plaza Hotel, 4624 13th Avenue, (718) 552–3200, is housed within a new hotel. With murals on the walls and attractive lighting, it is by far the fanciest restaurant in the area, but the menu remains strictly kosher, featuring fish dishes, pastas, and salads. A sign outside recently promised Buffalo Wings and schwarma.

Kosher Delight Family Restaurant (H) ($), 4602 13th Avenue, (718) 435–8500, offers a varied menu of crepes, knishes, fish dishes, and even some Chinese food, and features special value meals for budget watchers.

Little Odessa on Brighton Beach

Welcome to "Odessa by the Sea." In the past decade thousands of Soviet Jews have made this boardwalk town their home, bringing a lively new flavor to the neighborhood. To see the influence, just look at all the signs in Cyrillic lettering, look at the throngs

How to Get There

By subway: Take the Q Train to Brighton Beach,
forty-five minutes to an hour from Midtown. (Be sure to
check current subway information. The D Train that once
served Brighton Beach has been re-routed during track construction and is no longer serving Brooklyn. It has been replaced by the Q
Train, but this may change after 2004. The Ocean Parkway station has
been out of service due to construction, but will reopen at some point.
For current schedules, phone the Travel Information Center,
718–330–1234, or check www.mta.info.)

By car: Take the Belt Parkway to exit 7S, Ocean Parkway.
Turn right onto Shore Parkway, drive about one-half
mile and turn left onto Brighton Beach
Avenue, which is under the El.

buying from street vendors and crowding the stores, and listen to the
buzz in the stores—all in Russian. Businesses even answer the telephone in Russian. Rather than trying to assimilate into American
culture, this group of Russians seems to be establishing the Old
Country on new territory. Better know what you want in the stores, as
the clerks speak little English. The restaurants, fortunately, print
translations on the menu.

A boardwalk stroll is a fine addition to the day. It can include
enjoying refreshments in a Russian cafe and, if the day is fine, bask-
ing on the beach. Keep walking and you will arrive at the New York

Aquarium and Coney Island. If you choose to walk in the opposite direction from Brighton Beach, you can visit colorful Sheepshead Bay, New York's only fishing village. The proximity of these diverse waterside communities makes this a prime excursion, one worth repeating many times.

THE HISTORY

Native Americans once summered here at the tidal basin, gathering clams and oysters, and Henry Hudson's *Half Moon* moored briefly at Brighton Beach. The first serious development did not begin until the mid-nineteenth century, when the neighborhood was named for the resort in England. The elegant Hotel Brighton went up in 1878, followed by the Brighton Beach Racetrack, which became an important center for Thoroughbred horse racing. In 1907 the Brighton Beach Baths opened—a resort with pools, tennis, mini-golf, shuffleboard, entertainment, and a day camp. It was sometimes referred to as "Brooklyn's Catskills," or the "world's largest beach resort," covering fifteen acres and having more than 13,000 members.

Antigambling sentiment helped close the racetrack, and by 1920 all the hotels were gone. Apartment buildings went up to serve the growing population, composed largely of Jews moving up from the Lower East Side and other less desirable neighborhoods in Brooklyn. It became known as "kosher Brighton Beach," with six kosher butchers tending shop along the dozen blocks of Brighton Beach Avenue.

After World War II younger families left for the suburbs, while older residents stayed behind. The neighborhood began to feel like a ghost town. By the 1970s stores were empty and crime was on the rise. It was about this time that the Soviet Union relaxed its emigration policies and Soviet Jews began coming into the neighborhood, where there were plenty of vacancies and rents were low. Many were from Odessa in the Ukraine; they were attracted by the proximity of the ocean, which reminded them of their home on the Black Sea. Beneath the elevated tracks, Russian food stores, restaurants, nightclubs, fruit stands, and bookstores brought new life to Brighton Beach Avenue.

Like all successful immigrants, some of the Russian families are prospering and moving into better areas, such as neighboring Manhattan Beach. Their places are beginning to be filled by newcomers from Asia and the Middle East. But Brighton Beach remains the center for Russian shopping and entertainment, as you can clearly see by the crowded stores.

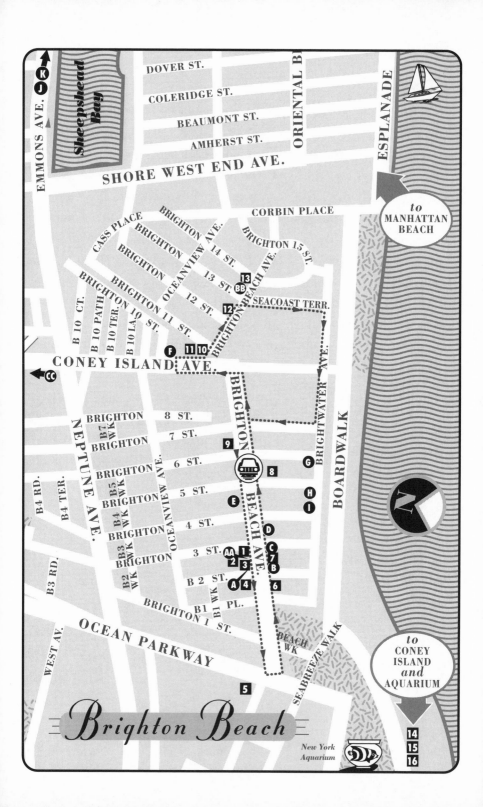

... *A Walking Tour* ...

Take the side of Brighton Beach Avenue farthest from the ocean and walk east (toward lower number streets) to get some sense of the neighborhood. Calm on weekdays, it can become a bustling mass of people on weekends, but it is always fun to watch the action—sidewalk vendors hawking their wares, shoppers jostling to get a better spot at the many tempting sidewalk displays of fruits and vegetables. The prices will both delight and depress visitors from Manhattan.

Look into **Vintage (1),** 287 Brighton Beach Avenue, (718) 769–6674, one of several Turkish merchants who come into the neighborhood to please the Russian sweet tooth with bin after bin of dried fruits, nuts, and candies.

Gastronom Jubile (2), 281 Brighton Beach Avenue, (718) 743–3900, is a supermarket and deli selling all manner of Russian products, but the best is yet to come.

M&I International Food (3), 249 Brighton Beach Avenue, (718) 615–1011, a two-story supermarket/deli/bakery, is perhaps the best known of all the area stores, and for good reason. It has been here for well over twenty years, founded by a family from Odessa, and it has grown from a tiny shop to this busy emporium filled with Russian and Eastern European foods.

You'll find miles of Russian sausage, barrels of sour pickles, and top-quality smoked fish. This is also the place to look for cheeses, cold cuts, and delicious salads such as Georgian eggplant caviar, cabbage and beets, and stuffed eggplant. Upstairs are imported jams, honey, candies, and giant pastries. Many people call in huge orders and drive to Brighton Beach just to pick them up.

You can sample their cooking at the cafeteria-style cafe on the second floor, which is open for all three meals.

Keep strolling and you'll pass **Mosvideo (4)**, 227 Brighton Beach Avenue, (718) 934–0055, with a big selection of Russian music and videos, and Classic Fur Galleria at 221 Brighton Beach, one of several shops showing lavish furs even in mid-summer. If you continue to Ocean Parkway, the end of Brighton Beach, **Art and Art Gallery (5)**, 3100 Ocean Parkway at West Brighton, (718) 714–6830, offers contemporary Russian paintings and decorative arts. No bargains to be found here, but browsers are welcome.

Coming back on Brighton Beach Avenue, cross to the other side for more shops and eating places. The **St. Petersburg Book Shop (6)**, 230 Brighton Beach Avenue, (718) 368–4128, properly adorned with photos and picture books of its namesake city, offers books and videos galore in Russian.

The aptly named **Russian Favorite Gifts Co. (7)**, 292 Brighton Beach Avenue, (718) 791–0719, offers painted enamel boxes, nesting dolls, amber jewelery, flowered shawls, and many other nice souvenirs of your visit.

Caviar Kiosk (8), ahead at 504 Brighton Beach Avenue (no phone listed), is a small outlet where you can stock up on that favorite Russian delicacy.

Cross the street again at Brighton Sixth Street for the **Ellanda Bakery (9)**, 615 Brighton Beach Avenue (no phone listed), a bright modern addition to the street with gorgeous cakes and Russian chocolates in the window. A little outdoor area in the back is a fine place for a sweet or an ice cream cone.

At Coney Island Avenue, roughly at the center of Brighton Beach Avenue, you'll spy **Mrs. Stahl's Knishes (10)**, 1001 Brighton Beach Avenue, (718) 648–0210, a landmark left over from the old Jewish neighborhood. It was under renovation at press time, which probably means new owners.

Sheepshead Bay

Come early for a day of fishing, come in the late afternoon, in time to hear the boat horns announcing their arrival with the day's catch. Crowds throng the piers, waiting to buy the freshest fish in the city, direct from the fisherman. (Beware of the fakers drawing their fish up from the water in wooden containers to take advantage of the crowds.)

This neighborhood has drawn anglers and seafood lovers since its founding in the early 1800s. At its peak, the fishing fleet numbered over fifty boats. Like neighboring Brighton Beach, Sheepshead Bay also was once home to a popular racetrack.

The track is gone but the fleet remains, moored to concrete piers along Emmons Avenue that were taken over and rebuilt by the city in the 1930s. Some sixteen to twenty boats go out regularly. If you want to go fishing, you pick a boat large or small, leaving from 7:00 A.M. to 9:00 A.M. Many offer night fishing starting at 7:00 P.M. In summer months, some of the boats offer half-day outings, as well as evening cruises around New York Harbor and the Statue of Liberty. Any time of day, a stroll along the docks is a refreshing look at a unique slice of New York.

Across the street from the start of the piers is a short strip filled with seafood restaurants. Have a cup of chowder, a platter of clams, or a shore dinner to complete your nautical day. Restaurants are listed on page 55.

The basic knish, oniony mashed potatoes in a soft flaky dough shell, was a Depression food, cheap and filling. Mrs. Stahl, an émigré from Eastern Europe, opened here in 1935, and reportedly also sold her knishes along the beachfront. Nowadays, knishes come in fifteen flavors, including kasha, cheese, apple, cabbage, cherry cheese, and blueberry. No telling what you'll find when the renovation is complete, but a hot knish and a cold cream soda are still a great nostolgic snack.

Want to see a copy of *Windows for Dummies* in Russian? Walk down a couple of doors to the **Black Sea Bookstore (11),** 3175 Coney Island Avenue, (718) 769–2878, to see a vast array of Russian books in a pleasant, old-fashioned store.

In general, this area beyond the El tracks is calmer and less congested than the scene below, but you may not think so when you enter **Golden Key (12),** 1067 Brighton Beach Avenue at Brighton 12th, (718) 743–5841. This store can be a madhouse, especially on Saturday, packed with customers vying for chicken kielbasa, spicy derma, smoked fish, farmer cheese, savory gefilte fish, garlicky eggplant spread, and all kinds of salads.

Also on this block is a sign of the growing sophistication of the residents of Brighton Beach, Brioche Cafe, serving cappuccino and espresso.

The scene is definitely refined at **Odessa Gastronome (13),** 1113 Brighton Beach Avenue, (718) 332–3223, the most upscale of the shops, located next door to the lavish Odessa night club. Cheese blintzes, cheese- or potato-filled turnovers, tempting sausages, and smoked fish are among the delicaces.

At the corner of Seacoast Terrace, you'll see condominium towers going up where the old Brighton Beach Baths once stood, a sad developement for old-timers. If you want to proceed to Sheepshead Bay from here, follow the arrows on the map.

But don't miss a stroll on the Brighton Beach boardwalk, a delightful break to sniff the salt air and enjoy a drink or a meal with an ocean view. In summer, everyone is headed for the beach, which

Aquarium for Wildlife Conservation

The Aquarium for Wildlife Conservation *is a particularly pleasant aquarium because so many of the exhibits are out of doors, including the Aquatheater, where sea lions do their tricks at feeding time. The Sea Cliffs exhibit features walruses, seals, sea otters, and absolutely adorable penguins cavorting in their pools. Beneath is a viewing area where you can watch them swimming underwater. The Sea Horse and Octopus exhibits can also be seen from underwater. The Explore the Shore, Native Sea Life, and Hudson River exhibits are educational, designed to teach about the creatures who live in nearby waters. In all there are over 600 species of marine mammals and birds, fishes and invertebrates, a total of 8,000 fascinating creatures at home here. You could easily and happily spend half a day right here.*

remains amazingly uncrowded on weekedays. Even in winter, if the weather is at all mild, there is plenty to see—older folks on benches, bundled in scarves and sweaters, and young families with strollers. Between Sixth and Fourth Streets, you'll come to a series of restaurants with outdoor cafes.

You can turn back to the subway on Sixth, or extend your day with a beautiful five-to-ten-minute stroll along the water to reach the **Aquarium for Wildlife Conservation (14),** West Eighth Street and Surf Avenue, (718) 265–FISH, www.nyaquarium.com.

Just beyond the aquarium is **Coney Island (15).** Although it is no longer the great amusement park it once was, the famous Cyclone, now a National Historic Landmark, is still giving thrills and chills at

Astroland Amusement Park, as it has since 1927. Take a ride on the venerable Wonder Wheel, West 12th between Surf Avenue and the Boardwalk. A ticket for this local landmark, well past its eightieth birthday, includes a free child's admission to the aquarium.

Walk to the end of the Steeplechase Pier at West 17th Street and you'll be 1,000 feet into the Atlantic, like standing on a ship's prow. Benches are provided for gazing out to sea.

Plan ahead and you can take in a minor league baseball game, watching the Brooklyn Cyclones in action at handsome Keyspan Park, just a few steps from the Boardwalk. The Atlantic Ocean is in view beyond the right field wall of this delightful stadium and the lights of the amusement parks are off to the left.

If the sea air has whetted your appetite, come over to Surf Avenue. Hot dogs somehow taste better when you get them at the original **Nathan's Famous (16),** Surf Avenue at Stillwell Avenue, (718) 946–2202, which has been at this stand since 1928. At Stillwell Avenue you can board a subway for the ride back to Manhattan.

Russian Cuisine

In a vast country stretching across some 5,000 miles, there are tremendous differences in climate and food from one region to another. The cuisine served in Brighton Beach is Russian with a Slavic accent, robust and filling, similar to the foods of the Ukraine, where Odessa is located, and with influences from neighboring Poland and Hungary.

Though most Russian residents of Brighton Beach are Jewish, they were denied the chance to practice their religion for so many years under Russian rule that many ties have been lost. Dishes such as blintzes resemble what is considered Jewish cuisine, but pork sausage is sold in stores and served in restaurants, and none of the local restaurants is kosher.

Most Russian cuisines do have some things in common. Menus include vegetables that grow well in cold climates, such as cabbage, beets, and potatoes. Stuffed cabbage is a popular main dish. Pickled dishes and preserves are important—reflecting the short growing season—as are smoked fish and meats. Kasha, the nutty-flavored cooked buckwheat, is a favorite side dish.

A Russian proverb says "A house without soup is an unlucky house"; and indeed, soups are a mainstay of Russian cuisine, along with bread, perhaps reflecting times in the Old Country when foods were scarce. Bread is usually eaten in thick

A TYPICAL RUSSIAN MEAL

Beet or spinach borscht

Potato or meat pirogi

Chicken or lamb stew or beef stroganoff

Blini with jam

slabs, generously buttered. Rye, a dependable crop for the fickle Russian growing season, is a familiar favorite, along with dark breads like pumpernickel. In many restaurants a round of dense, crusty white bread is brought to the table pie-cut into generous portions.

In Russia, the zakouski, a generous smorgasbord of hot and cold dishes served before the main meal, and always served with plenty of vodka, is a sign of a host's prosperity. The custom is reflected in the generous appetizers served in Russian restaurants, especially at the banquets served in Brighton Beach nightclubs. Caviar remains the special Russian delicacy; the rarest can be wildly expensive. The best way for a reasonable sampling is to order blini topped with caviar.

A RUSSIAN SAMPLER

Here are some popular dishes found on Russian menus:

Blini: crepes, served with red caviar or as dessert with preserves and sour cream.

Beef Stroganoff: strips of lean beef sautéed and served in a sour-cream sauce with onions and mushrooms; said to be named for a nineteenth-century count who was mayor of Odessa.

Borscht: Ukraine and Poland both claim this as a national dish, and there are a dozen ways to prepare it. The clear beet soup can be served hot or cold, with or without meat, but is always accompanied by sour cream.

Chicken Chakhokhbili: chicken stew with tomatoes and onions.

Kasha: buckwheat grains that can be cooked like cereal or shaped into small pancakes and fried.

Kharcho: chicken or lamb soup with walnuts.

Kvass: Russian near-beer, a cider-like concoction made with fermented grain.

Pirogi: dough pockets filled with potatoes, kasha, or meat, served as a side dish or in soups.

Pirozhki: a smaller version of pirogi made with a variety of fillings, including with jam as a dessert.

Salyanka: lamb stew with tomatoes and onions.

Shashlyk: another word for shish kebob; meat grilled in small chunks on a skewer, sometimes served flaming.

Schav: green borscht made with spinach or sorrel.

Shchi: cabbage soup fresh in summer, made with sauerkraut in winter.

Ukha: fish soup, known as the mother of Russian soups; may be "white," made with pike, whitefish or perch; "black," made with carp or rosefish; or "red," made with sturgeon or salmon. Usually served with black bread.

Vareniki: dumplings, usually stuffed with potato.

R E C O M M E N D E D 🍽 R E S T A U R A N T S

Cafe St. Petersburg (A) ($–$$), 223 Brighton Beach Avenue, (718) 743–0880, is a quiet spot serving tasty Russian items such as smoked sturgeon on thick Russian bread and whole mackerel boiled in parchment paper. Things are livelier at night when there is entertainment.

Primorski Restaurant (B) ($–$$), 282 Brighton Beach Avenue, (718) 891–3111, seems to be everyone's first recommendation for food. Some of the specialties are from the Georgian region of Russia. The setting is dramatic red and black with lots of tiny lights, even in the daytime. By night the dance floor goes into action. Appetizer salads are delicious, and chicken in walnut sauce, shashlyk, and lamb stew all come recommended. Put yourself in the waiter's hands; he knows what's good and he does speak English—albeit with an accent. Prix fixe lunches are a huge bargian.

Oceanview Cafe (C) ($), 290 Brighton Beach Avenue, (718) 332–1900, is a pleasant modern cafe serving a mix of foods, traditional vareniki and blintzes to Belgian waffles, all at low prices.

Cafe Arbat (D) ($–$$), 306 Brighton Beach Avenue, (718) 332–5050, named for a famous shopping street in Moscow, shows its allegiance with photos of the Old Country and a menu of Russian favorites. Note that the window menu is in Russian; you will definitely need to hope for an English-speaking waiter.

Gina's Cafe (E) ($–$$), 409 Brighton Beach Avenue, (718) 646–6297. Russian Rock videos on the television please younger patrons of this newer cafe, but the lengthy menu is quiete traditional, with favorites such as smoked herring with potatoes and onions and blintzes with caviar. And the waiters do speak English.

Cafe Glechik (F) ($–$$), 3159 Coney Island Avenue, (718) 616–0494, located away from the bustle of the main street, has walls decorated with hand-embroidered linen and blouses. Soups such as borscht with rice, chopped hard-boiled egg and sorrel (which turns things green), and dill-seasoned chicken soup are delicious. Hardy main courses include stuffed cabbage and a tasty beef stew in a pot, sweetened with prunes.

Winter Garden (G) ($–$$), 3152 Brighton Sixth Street at the Boardwalk, (718) 934–6666, has a Russian menu with a French accent, and a nice terrace on the boardwalk.

Cafe Tatiana (H) ($–$$), 3145 Brighton Fourth Street at the Boardwalk, (718) 646–7630, colorful tablecloths and tropical decor are the setting for good soups, salads, and dumplings or a full meal with an ocean view. Prix-fixe lunches a good value.

Cafe Volna (I) ($–$$), 3145 Brighton Fourth Street at the Boardwalk, (718) 332–0341, with a terrace adjoining Cafe Tatiana, is a full-service restaurant as well as a good place for outdoor snacks like blintzes or knishes, tasty with a glass of kvass.

R U S S I A N   N I G H T C L U B S

Brighton Beach nightclubs are where Russians come to have a boisterous good time and to celebrate special occasions. The prix fixe evening includes lavish food, lots of vodka, and a gaudy floor show. Bring a big group and have fun; just be sure to have a designated driver or arrange ahead of time for a car service to pick you up.

National (AA), 273 Brighton Beach Avenue, (718) 646–1225. Dress up and dance under the strobe lights. This is the best-known Brighton Beach nightclub. It's simply enormous, with lavish food and entertainment. The menu features fifteen appetizers, roast chicken, pork, shish kebabs, and brisket. The show starts around midnight with singers from Russia, acrobats, and dancers. Las Vegas eat your heart out.

Odessa (BB), 1113 Brighton Beach Avenue, (718) 332–3223. More of the above, maybe a tad classier. Bring a crowd and go with the flow.

Rasputin (CC), 2670 Coney Island Avenue (at Avenue X), (718) 332–8333, is away from the action on Brighton Beach Avenue, but if you are taking a car anyway, this is one of the livelier choices, a gaudy two-tiered space with a skylight and a French/Russian menu. The action goes on way into the night.

SHEEPSHEAD BAY RESTAURANTS

Lundy's (J), 1901 Emmons Avenue at Ocean Avenue, (718) 743–0022. Not the original Lundy's, which was billed as the biggest restaurant in the world, but a scaled-down version in the original pink terra-cotta building, still with the look of the past and with the same long wooden oyster bar. Seafood of every kind comes steamed, grilled, fried, or baked. The giant lobster tank tells you the favorite entree.

Randazzo's Clam Bar (K), 2023 Emmons Avenue between Ocean Avenue and East 21st Street, (718) 615–0010. The clam bar and adjoining cafe are classics in the neighborhood—and wait until you taste the chowder!

Polish Pleasures in Greenpoint

Shops laden with kielbasas and babkas and cafes offering potato pancakes and pirogi beckon visitors to the largest Polish enclave in New York. According to the 1990 U.S. Census, 80 percent of the area's 156,000 residents were Polish; later estimates have counted nearly 200,000 Polish residents. So it's no surprise that even some of the Korean greengrocers have learned to speak Polish.

Greenpoint itself is an orderly, low-rise neighborhood of carefully tended row houses, with a profusion of fine churches of all denominations. A unique industrial past has left many historic landmarks as well.

THE HISTORY

It was industry that built Greenpoint, a neighborhood bordered by the East River and Newtown Creek (the narrow body of water that separates this part of Brooklyn from Queens). As a major early shipbuilding center, it was the birthplace of the famous ironclad Civil War ship the *Monitor*, constructed at the Continental Iron Works, which stood at West and Calyer Streets. It was launched in 1862, the same year the historic battle took place with the Confederate ship *Merrimack*. Streets such as Java and India recall the waterfront trade in coffee and spices that once flourished.

By 1860 Greenpoint and neighboring Williamsburg also had become known for the "five black arts"—printing, pottery, petroleum and gas refining, glassmaking, and ironmaking.

How to Get There

By subway: Take the L Train from 14th Street
to Lorimer Street, walk the underground passage to the
connecting Metropolitan Avenue Station, change to the G
Train and go one stop to Nassau Avenue. From uptown take the
E, F, or R Train to Queens Plaza and change to the Brooklyn-bound
G Train to Nassau Avenue.

By car: Take the Brooklyn–Queens Expressway to McGuinness
Boulevard, continue north for 1 mile, and turn left onto Greenpoint
Avenue to Manhattan Avenue. Or, via Queens, take the
Queensborough Bridge, turn right onto Jackson Avenue, and fol-
low signs for the Pulaski Bridge, which becomes
McGuinness Boulevard in Greenpoint. Continue to
Greenpoint Avenue, turn right and go 1 block
to Manhattan Avenue.

At one time, more than fifty oil-refining plants were located in
Greenpoint. The most prominent was Astral Oil Works, a refinery
established by Charles Pratt in 1867. Astral became so important that
it was called "the fuel that lit the holy lamps of Tibet." It became part
of Standard Oil, providing the fortune that endowed Pratt Insitute and
built the Pratt family mansions. The refineries were consumed in a
spectacular blaze in 1930.

In 1916 the Schaefer Brewery opened on Kent Avenue, and
Kirsch Beverages opened a factory in 1927. Greenpoint jobs were

plentiful in that era, attracting immigrants from many nations to the neighborhood. Though there were periods of decline in this century as these industries waned and the Depression hit, waves of new immigration have kept Greenpoint vital.

The famous Iwo Jima flag-raising sculpture was cast in bronze in 1954 at the Bedi-Rassy Foundry. The foundry is still in operation at 227 India Street.

Between 1870 and 1920 many Poles immigrated to New York, seeking economic opportunity, and many gravitated to the jobs available in Greenpoint, eventually becoming the largest ethnic group in the neighborhood. St. Stanislaus Kostka Church was established in 1896, and a fine building was erected in 1903 that still serves as a social as well as a religious center. As a salute to these residents, a new bridge to Queens that opened in 1939 was named for Tadeusz Kosciuszko, a Polish volunteer who was a key tactician in the Revolutionary War.

The Polish population in New York grew dramatically during and after World War II, as Poles fled German domination and then Communist oppression. Newcomers to the United States gravitated to established Polish centers such as Greenpoint. Even today cafes cater to the men who come to America alone to earn money to help their families, hoping eventually either to return to their homeland or bring their loved ones to join them.

In recent years, arty residents spilling over from neighboring Williamsburg have added a hip element to Greenpoint, but it is the Polish flavor that predominates, especially along Nassau Street.

A Shopping / Walking Tour

When you emerge from the Nassau Street subway stop, you'll know you're in the right place if you see a newsstand stocked with Polish newspapers. Walk down Manhattan Avenue for 1 block and turn left onto Driggs Avenue to reach Humboldt Street, the site of **St. Stanislaus Kostka Church (1),** dominating the local skyline with its octagonal spires. The sign at the intersection, POPE JOHN PAUL II SQUARE, honors the pope, who visited the church in 1969, when he was still a cardinal. Lech Walesa Place is named for the Polish workers' Solidarity leader who eventually became Poland's president. Pictures of these Polish heroes can be found in many area shops.

If the doors are open, by all means go inside to see the beautiful interior of the church—pristine white with altar figures painted in glowing hues of rose and blue.

Walk 1 block farther on Driggs and turn left onto Russell to **Monsignor McGolrick Park (2),** a pleasant square of greenery surrounded by homes. The handsome shelter pavilion, a designated landmark, was built in 1910 in eighteenth-century French style. The park contains a monument to the ship *Monitor*.

The century-old **German Lutheran Church of the Messiah (3),** across from the park on Russell Street, is one of many local churches that show the diverse population of the neighborhood.

The homes of Greenpoint are modest two- and three-story, flat-roofed row houses of clapboard and shingle, with an occasional fake brick front. They are immaculate. Every house seems to be freshly painted; and the palette of soft shades of aqua, olive, brick red, tan, and beige makes for a pleasant backdrop as you stroll.

Follow Russell Street to Nassau Avenue and turn left. Manhattan Avenue is the busiest of the area's shopping streets, but Nassau is the

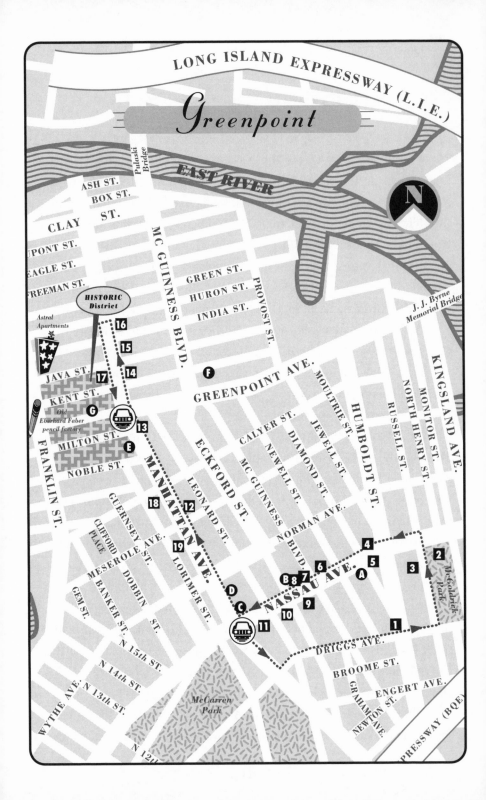

most pleasant and the most thoroughly Polish. Stop at the **Busy Bee Grocery (4)**, 185 Nassau Avenue, (718) 389–2188, which takes up the whole small block between Jewel and Humboldt Streets, to see some of the local bounty among the more usual groceries—kielbasa sausages hanging from the ceiling; barrels of pickles and herring; a wide selection of canned goods, including pickles and pickled tomatoes made locally; Polish jelly-filled cookies called szampanski and packages of wafer sheets and rolls to be filled with whipped cream, a traditional dessert. They make their own pirogi here, and you'll find it in the refrigerator case, ready to be cooked at home.

Across the street on the corner of Humboldt is **Young's (5)**, 192 Nassau Avenue, a particularly large and well-stocked greengrocer.

A couple of cafes down the block are good bets for lunch.

The tiny **Jaslowiczanka Polish Bakery (6)**, 163 Nassau Avenue, (718) 389–0263, is filled with treats made on the premises. Ask the proprietors, Bogdan and Nanina Jaslowski, for advice. They'll explain which cakes come with poppy seeds and which with walnuts, and which cookies are the "angel's wings"—the traditional fried pastry treats dusted with confectioner's sugar. The cakes with glazed fruit topping are favorites, and the babka (coffee cake) sold here is so good you'll wish you'd bought half a dozen more for the freezer.

You will see a sign of the times when you pass the Polish-Net Internet Cafe at 151A Nassau Avenue, (718) 339–0600, a good way for residents to reach friends and family back home.

You'll also pass several travel agencies, good bets for low rates if you are thinking of traveling to Warsaw.

Everything from statues of saints to wedding-cake ornaments to gifts can be found at **Arch Religious Articles (7)**, 127 Nassau Avenue, (718) 349–6294.

The Greenpoint Historic District

The Greenpoint Historic District, so designated in 1982, is bound roughly by Java, Leonard, Calyer, and Franklin Streets, beginning just off Manhattan Avenue. The buildings reflect differing income and status levels.

The Astral Apartments, 184 Franklin Street between Java and India Streets, may not look like much today, but when they were built by Charles Pratt in 1885, they were considered models of affordable housing. Each contained ample windows, hot and cold running water, a toilet, and many other amenities not usually available to working-class families of the day.

Still quite handsome are the homes of business owners and managers, Italianate brick town houses adorned with cast-iron window lintels and door hoods and ornate stair railings that might have been created in local foundries. Some of the most attractive examples are on Noble, Milton, and Kent Streets between Manhattan Avenue and Franklin Street.

The former factory of the Eberhard Faber Pencil Company, at the corner of Greenpoint Avenue and Franklin Street, is in disrepair, but it is fun to see because you can still discern the long yellow pencils that decorated the facade.

Several notable churches are within the Historic District, including two on Kent Street: the Church of the Ascension, 129 Kent, an Episcopal church built in 1865–1866 in English Gothic style; and the former Reformed Dutch Church of Greenpoint, now the Saint Elias Byzantine Catholic Church, 149 Kent, a Gothic Victorian building circa 1869–1870 that is notable for its alternating red-and-gray design, the octagonal Sunday School, and a cast-iron fence with Gothic crests.

The next food stop, **Podlaise Market (8),** 121 Nassau Avenue, (718) 383–3809, is a spotless, old-fashioned store with tile floors and a dozen kinds of sausage with varied seasonings and textures, all smoked right here. Ask for tastes to see which most pleases your palate. You can also pick up some Polish mustard and soup mixes for kapusniak, traditional cabbage and mushroom soup, or borscht.

At the corner of Eckford Street is Pod Wierchami, one of the small cafes catering to the stag workers in the neighborhood, with

good hearty food at really low prices. It's a good bet for visitors who don't mind a no-frills ambience. (See page 68.)

Across the street is **The Exlibris Polish Book Gallery (9),** 140 Nassau Avenue, (718) 349–0468, which has a large stock of Polish books along with crystal and gifts. This is a good place to learn about the Polish performers soon to appear in the area. You will pass another branch of this store later in your walk at 882 Manhattan Avenue.

On the next block, another well-respected butcher shop, **Steve's Meat Market (10),** 104 Nassau Avenue, (718) 383–1780, has an awning proclaiming BEST KIELBASY IN THE U.S.A. The Polish ham is not to be ignored, either.

Walk into the **Murawski Pharmacy (11),** 94–98 Nassau Avenue, (718) 389–7600, to see some of the imported creams, herbs, and scents that Polish ladies miss from the Old Country.

If you look ahead straight down Nassau Avenue, you can clearly see the buildings of Manhattan, just across the East River but a world away.

Turn right onto bustling Manhattan Avenue and another view of Manhattan. More Polish shops and restaurants are ahead, but now they are mixed with clothing stores, Chinese, Italian, and Thai restaurants, McDonald's, and all the other accoutrements of a busy neighborhood.

The sweet young girls behind the counter seem just right for **Stodyce Wedel (12),** 772 Manhattan Avenue, (718) 349–3933, a confection of a shop filled with Polish chocolates, loose and in fancy packages, along with imported cookies and hard candies.

The 240-foot spire of the impressive redbrick and white limestone **St. Anthony of Padua Church (13),** 862 Manhattan Avenue at Milton Street, (718) 383–3339, is a local landmark. The Roman Catholic church was built in 1874.

Ahead are more popular meat shops, such as **Starpolski Delicatessen (14),** 912 Manhattan Avenue, (718) 389–0294, selling tasty kielbasa and Polish black bread.

Here there are lots of tempting bakeries. Definitely worth a look is **Julabilatka (15),** 940 Manhattan Avenue, (718) 389–4730, a bake shop where the specialty is rurki, rolls filled with cream.

Stop into **Ksiegarnia Literacka (16),** 161 Java Street (Just off Manhattan), (718) 349–2738, another well-stocked bookstore where you'll find Polish music and greeting cards and the latest John Grisham novel in Polish.

Cross to the other side of Manhattan Avenue and turn right at Kent if you want to see the Greenpoint Historic District. If you stay on Manhattan, you'll come to one of the busiest markets in the neighborhood, **W. Nassau Meat Market (17),** 915 Manhattan Avenue, (718) 389–6149. Clerks in jaunty red hats stand behind a veritable curtain of sausages, trying to keep up with the lines of customers buying sausages, ham, liverwurst, and stuffed cabbage and bigos (stew) made on the premises.

As you walk back on the west side of the street toward the subway, you'll pass the **Greenpoint Savings Bank (18),** on the southwest corner of Calyer Street. The bank signed up its first customer in 1869 and built this fine domed and columned headquarters in 1908. Between Messerole and Norman Streets you'll see one of the last remaining cast-iron sidewalk clocks **(19),** typical of the clocks that were used to advertise jewelry stores and other businesses in the early 1900s. It is one of the reminders of the endurance of a neighborhood that proudly wears its Polish colors.

Polish Cuisine

Like the foods of its Eastern European neighbors, Polish cuisine is not about subtlety or sauces but about honest, hearty, and filling food, similar to the menus found in Ukrainian restaurants in Manhattan (see pages 198–99). But while Polish dining isn't fancy, it can be wonderfully satisfying—like Grandma's home cooking.

Among the most delicious dishes are the robust soups, which are almost enough for a meal. Mushroom barley is a popular example, along with borscht served with meat (Ukrainian-style) or without.

Expect generous cuts of pork (roast or chops), sauerkraut, mashed potatoes, lots of mushroom or onion gravy, Polish hams, and dense peasant breads. Kielbasa, a smoked sausage seasoned with garlic, is the signature Polish dish, and humbler meats such as pig knuckles and tripe are not disdained. Breaded cutlets, goulash, stuffed cabbage, and beef stroganoff are dishes that are also common among other ethnic groups. Dill and garlic are frequent seasonings in Polish cooking.

A POLISH SAMPLER

Here are some of the dishes on a typical Greenpoint menu:

Bigos: a traditional stew, a mix of sauerkraut with meats that may include ham, pork, kielbasa, and bacon.

Blintzes: crepes filled with fruits and/or cheese, served as an entree or dessert.

Borscht: may be clear beet soup or Ukrainian-style with meat, served hot or cold in summer.

Goulash: a rich beef stew, with onions, tomatoes, and potatoes, generously seasoned with paprika, and often served with kasha.

Kopytka: potato dumplings, fried or boiled.

Pirogi: packets of dough filled with cheese, potato, meat, or sauerkraut with mushrooms, or any combination of the above. May be fried or boiled. Often served with sautéed onions or with sour cream or apple-sauce as a side dish.

Rumsztyk: rump steak served with onions and mushrooms; sometimes topped with a fried egg, sunny side up.

Zurek: sour soup; a stock or broth based soup with a tinge of sour taste, served with slices of kielbasa on top and mashed potatoes on the side. The proper eating technique is to put a bite of potato on the spoon before you dip for soup. Filling and delicious.

R E C O M M E N D E D 🍽 R E S T A U R A N T S

Old Poland Bakery and Restaurant (A) ($), 192 Nassau Street, (718) 348–7775, is a casual spot where you order at the counter and take your food to a table, joining locals who are busy watching the Polish news on television. But there is nothing casual about the kitchen; the soups and traditional dishes are delicious and cheap. Order a Polish Plate for a full sampling: two potato pancakes, three pirogi, hunter's stew, fried kielbasa, and stuffed cabbage or ground cutlet. You can pick up a take-home treat at the bakery counter on the way out.

Pod Wierchami (B) ($), 119 Nassau Street, (718) 383–0670, where many Polish working men come for good inexpensive food. Order at the counter, help yourself to free sauerkraut and slaw at the sideboard, and have a seat at the wooden tables.

Lomzynianka (C) ($), 646 Manhattan Avenue, (718) 389–9439, is small, dim, and cozy, with all the usual Polish specialties on the menu. The Polish Platter includes stuffed cabbage; bigos, the traditional hunter's stew; and three pirogi. Veal meat balls in a creamy dill sauce served with mashed potatoes is a traditional favorite and blueberry blintzes make an excellent dessert.

Stylowa (D) ($), 694 Manhattan Avenue, (718) 383–8993, a favorite with artist types from neighboring Williamsburg, is a small restaurant that serves large portions. Choose from three kinds of borscht, including red borscht with meat dumplings and white borscht served with kielbasa and egg. The combination platter lets you sample potato, sauerkraut, and meat pirogi. Breaded pork chops and stuffed cabbage are popular choices. Whatever you order, you'll probably go home with leftovers.

Christina's (E) ($), 853 Manhattan Avenue, (718) 383–4382, is a cheerful, modern spot that looks like a luncheonette, but the food is fine and the soups are special. Look for the special soup of the day. Pork loin schnitzel topped with egg is a tasty choice.

Polish and Slavic Credit Union (F) ($), 175 Kent Street, (718) 349–1400, is the place if you are on a tight budget and you

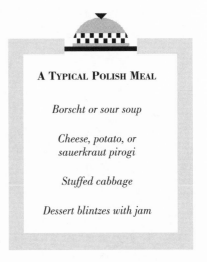

A Typical Polish Meal

Borscht or sour soup

Cheese, potato, or sauerkraut pirogi

Stuffed cabbage

Dessert blintzes with jam

want to see an authentic neighborhood scene. The cafeteria serves up decent food at ridiculously low prices. It is patronized by old-timers, newcomers, and everyone in between. Besides providing inexpensive food, the credit union helps finance much of the housing in Greenpoint.

Little Poland (Polska) (G) ($), 136 Greenpoint Avenue, (718) 389–8368, a pleasant cafe with a menu that covers just about every Polish classic. It is often recommended to visitors as the best in the neighborhood. White borscht, here called sour soup, is a house specialty. The combination platter offers stuffed cabbage, kielbasa, cheese and potato pirogis, bigos, beets, and bread for an amazingly small tab.

If you want to see some of the changes arty newcomers have wrought in Greenpoint, have an after-dinner drink at one of the trendy new bars on this block such as Splendid, 132 Greenpoint Avenue between Manhattan Avenue and Franklin Street, or The Pencil Factory, 142 Franklin Street at Greenpoint Avenue, near where the old Eberhard Faber factory once stood.

Bat Dai Do: Brooklyn's Chinatown

The burgeoning Chinese population of New York has staked out a new home in the Brooklyn neighborhood of Sunset Park along Eighth Avenue, the street known in Chinese as Bat Dai Do. Since a lone pioneer merchant opened a grocery store here in the 1980s, the shops and population have exploded. The 1990 census gave a figure of 12,000 Chinese in Sunset Park, but current estimates are closer to 60,000. This is New York's fastest growing Chinese enclave.

How to Get There

Take the N Train to the Eighth Avenue stop,
about forty-five minutes from Midtown.

THE HISTORY

Unlike Flushing, with its young population and ties to Taiwan, many of the Chinese drawn to Sunset Park were overflow from Manhattan's crowded Chinatown. Brooklyn represented a less-congested place where they could still have a direct connection to the old Chinatown via the N Train. While many Chinese still work in Manhattan, taking the "dollar vans" that roam the neighborhood, newly arrived immigrants who speak little English also find jobs available in Brooklyn in the garment factories that have opened to take advantage of the new labor supply.

... *A Shopping/Walking Tour* ...

For visitors, this is the calmest of New York's three Chinatowns. Unlike Manhattan's Chinatown or Flushing, where streets wander, the shops, restaurants, and markets here are clustered almost non-stop in a straight line on Eighth Avenue roughly between 50th and 60th Streets. A few special stops are noted, but you can easily make your own discoveries. Some shops are smaller branches of the same merchants found in Manhattan or Flushing.

Almost as soon as you leave the subway, you will see across the street the big **Hong Kong Market (1),** 6013 Eighth Avenue, (718) 438–2288, with every imaginable kind of Chinese produce and products.

On the next block, a big multethinic market and a mosque tell you that this neighborhood, like all of New York, is shared by several nationalities. But there is little doubt who dominates, as made obvious by the long line of Chinese shops extending now for many blocks, and emporiums such as the **W. J. Bookstore (2),** 6007 Eighth Avenue, (718) 871–5000, packed with books and periodicals in Chinese.

Two well-known tea emporiums are on the same block between 58th and 59th Streets: **Ten Ren Tea and Ginseng (3),** 5817 Eighth Avenue, (718) 853–0660, and **Tea and Tea (4),** 5801 Eighth Avenue, (718) 437–6622. In addition to selling teas, both serve delicious tall green-tea drinks whipped together with fruit flavors from litchi to mango, with the tapioca balls known as "pearls" in the bottom. Tea and Tea also offers tasty snacks.

On the next two blocks are more markets. **The Lien & Hong Market (5),** 5705 Eighth Avenue, (718) 436–8728, is a traditional Chinese market with stalls out front piled high with Chinese vegetables, dried fish, and mushrooms. The well-stocked **Fung Wong Supermarket (6),** 5615 Eighth Avenue (718) 633–0788, was a neighborhood pioneer when it opened for business in 1986 and remains a favorite, almost always bustling with customers.

Two shops ahead, with Chinese herbs and medicines to cure what ails you are **Chung Yuan Herb Corp (7),** 5411 Eighth Avenue, (718) 438–3515, and **Oriental Herbs (8),** 5315 Eighth Avenue, (718) 633–1020.

Cross the street and you'll spy **Everson Kitchen Supply Company (9),** 5316 Eighth Avenue, (718) 851–5888, a small shop

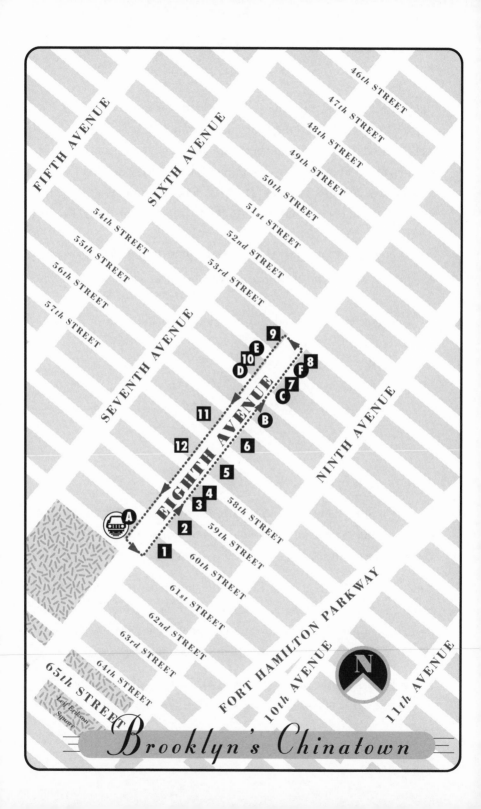

Brooklyn's Chinatown

stacked with almost anything you might need for Chinese cooking.

As you head back toward the subway, you will pass several small bake shops laden with delicious pork buns, almond cookies, black bean cakes, and sweet desserts. Among those recommended are two locations of **Kingly Bakery II (10),** 5410 Eighth Avenue, (718) 972–9833, and a second **Kingly (11)** location at 5722 Eighth Avenue, (718) 567–7018.

Sea Town Fish and Meats (12), 5802 Eighth Avenue, (718) 439–1818, has a typical Chinatown display of fresh fish at excellent prices.

And now you are faced with the delightful dilemma of deciding where to dine.

Chinese Cuisine

(See Chinatown page 175)

R E C O M M E N D E D 🍴 R E S T A U R A N T S

The main attraction in Brooklyn's Chinatown is bountiful dim sum at two restaurants that have attracted wide praise from food critics, Ocean Palace and Jade Plaza, but there are other choices, as well.

Jade Plaza (A) ($), 6022 Eighth Avenue between 60th and 61st Street, (718) 492–6888, is a spacious bustling Hong Kong–style dining room packed every day at lunch hour for it generous dim sum selection; it's also known for excellent seafood dishes.

Fung Sing Noodle Shop (B) ($–$$), 5603 Eighth Avenue, (718) 437–7562, with take-out on one side, and pleasant dining room on the other, offers lots of soups laden with a choice of three kinds of noodles, egg, rice, or flat, as well as a full Chinese menu.

Ocean Palace (C) ($–$$), 5423 Eighth Avenue near 55th Street, (718) 871–8080, an old-timer fresh from a stylish renovation, rivals Jade Plaza for the claim of best dim sum on the Avenue. Some say it's even better.

Ocean Empire (D) ($–$$), 5418 Eighth Avenue, (718) 851–8008, leaves little doubt of the house specialty. When you walk in, you face stacks of 50-gallon tanks of fish and crustaceans. All you have to decide is how you want your fish prepared. (Don't forget about the shrimp dishes; they are equally fresh and delicious.)

Other Asian choices:

Like Manhattan's Chinatown, Eighth Avenue has attracted cuisines from other Asian countries. These two eating places have earned good reviews.

Gia Lam (E) ($), 5402 Eighth Avenue, (718) 567–0800, is always crowded, a testament to the excellence of the Vietnamese fare. Crispy summer rolls make a great starter, and chicken in curry sauce or sizzling meat dishes will make your taste buds happy.

Nyonya (F) ($), 5323 54th Street at the corner of Eighth Avenue, (718) 633–0808, is a sibling of the Manhattan Malaysian restaurant that has won unanimous raves from food critics. Many of the dishes are similar to a Chinese menu, but the most interesting ones are the mix of the three cultures found in Malaysia: South Indian, Malaysian, and Chinese.

The Old World in Williamsburg

One writer called it *Anatevka*—the Eastern European village from the musical *Fiddler on the Roof*. No question that this is a world apart, home to 40,000 members of the Satmar sect, the most reclusive of Brooklyn's many Hasidic groups.

They occupy a small world some 15 blocks by 4 blocks in size, filled with hundreds of *shtieblachs* (small houses of worship) and dozens of yeshivas, religious schools where boys and girls study separately. On the streets baby carriages are pushed by pretty, modestly dressed young mothers wearing sheitels (wigs) and hats, young boys sport *yarmulkes* (skullcaps) and long front curls (earlocks, called *payehs*), and men in long black frock coats and black hats go to prayer. On holidays and the Sabbath, many of the men don their *shteimls*—broad, round fur hats. Some of them wear white knee-length

How to Get There

By subway: Take the J or M Subway Line across the Williamsburg Bridge to Marcy Avenue.

By car: Exit the Williamsburg Bridge at Division Avenue and drive west (right) to Lee Avenue.

stockings, like Polish noblemen wore two centuries ago. (To read more about the Hasidic ways, see page 28.)

Unlike busy, worldly 13th Street in Borough Park, Lee Avenue, the main commercial street in Williamsburg, is quiet and filled with shops concerned only with serving the neighborhood. Pharmacies stock kosher cough medicine, and the hardware store has a ritual bath for dishes.

While they stay apart from other Hasidic groups, the Satmars do not seem to mind nonreligious visitors to their little enclave. Come dressed appropriately and with a respectful attitude and discover one of New York's most unusual areas.

THE HISTORY

Williamsburgh was a separate entity until it consolidated with the City of Brooklyn in 1855 and lost the "h" at the end of its name. It grew thanks to a ferry that provided an outlet for farmers to sell their produce in New York and the establishment of the

Shaefer Brewery and a distillery in 1819. Some sections were favored as a resort by wealthy New Yorkers until the building of the Williamsburg Bridge in 1903 brought a flood of Jews from the Lower East Side into Williamsburg. The bridge was nicknamed "the Jewish highway."

The elegant families moved away and the neighborhood became overcrowded, with some of the highest population densities in the newly unified New York. A Reform temple was opened on Keap Street by German Jews before the turn of the century, but as they moved on and the number of poorer and more Orthodox Eastern Europeans increased, the temple became Orthodox in 1921.

When the urban-renewal movement began, Williamsburg was one of the first areas to be chosen. Many slums were cleared in the 1950s and 1960s, and high-rise housing projects took their place. The Brooklyn–Queens Expressway, completed in 1954, also changed the neighborhood, displacing some 5,000 people and destroying the retail center of the area.

The arrival of the Satmars helped to revitalize the neighborhood. The Satmars, a community of Hungarian origin, are the most zealous of all the Hasidic sects. In 1946 Rebbe Joel Teitelbaum and some 1,400 of his followers, having survived the Holocaust, came to this Orthodox neighborhood and established their own community. They built a fine home for their rebbe, indicating their intention to stay. Though many of their members are poor, they have managed to raise some $20 million to build what will be the largest synagogue in the world, accommodating 10,000 to 15,000 worshippers. The community continues to grow dramatically.

The Satmars are anti-Israel, believing that the "true Israel" can only be created by the Messiah, who has yet to come. It is an issue that sets them apart from the rest of the Hasidic groups. A feud broke out in the 1980s with the Lubovichers of Crown Heights, whom the Satmars accused of trying to lure away their young men.

They have also had differences with their Williamsburg neighbors, a large Latino community, over who will be favored for spaces in subsidized-housing projects in the neighborhood and other political matters. When the Independence Towers and Jonathan Williams complexes went up in the 1960s, for example, the builders installed "Shabbos elevators," which automatically stopped on every floor on the Sabbath so that no one would have to push a button, to make the buildings appealing to the Satmars. Though tensions remain, the two groups have existed side by side largely without incident.

· · · *A Walking Tour* · · ·

Walk west from the Williamsburg Bridge on Marcy Avenue to South llth Street and turn right; then turn left again onto Clymer to reach Bedford Avenue. Here you can see the transition from the grand homes that once marked the neighborhood—such as 563 Bedford, an 1875 mansion that was once the exclusive Hanover Club and is now Bais Yaakov of Adas Yereim, a Hasidic girls' school. The mansion in New Renaissance style at 505 Bedford, built in 1896 by the son of a wealthy sugar-refinery owner, is now a yeshiva for boys.

At the corner of Bedford and Wilson, you can see the giant new synagogue under construction. Between Wilson and Ross Streets is the columned home (1) built for Rebbe Joel Teitelbaum; it has two complete kitchens, one exclusively for Passover. Next door, at 541 Bedford Avenue, is a small house of study, with space for a *succoh*.

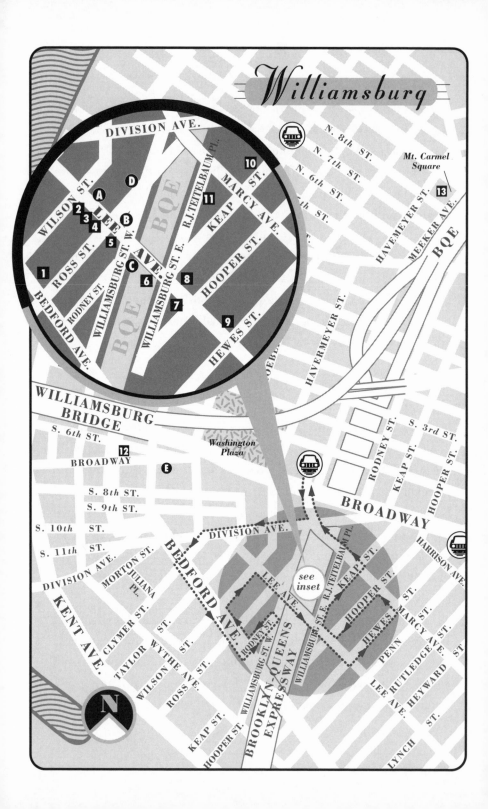

The home of the current rebbe is the red brick house on the corner across the street. The building at 554 Bedford is a synagogue as well as a house of prayer and a social center.

You'll see many other synagogues on Bedford and all through the neighborhood. The current main synagogue, built in the 1960s, is around the corner at 150 Rodney Street.

On the holiday of Simchas Torah, which usually occurs in October, this whole area is closed off for dancing and clapping in celebration of the completion of the cycle of reading the holy scrolls of the Torah, which will begin all over again the next day.

Come back to Wilson Street and turn right onto Lee Avenue for a stroll on the main shopping street of the Satmars. This is a modest street devoted to the needs of its neighborhood. You may not need a wig or a felt hat or a children's game in Yiddish, but it is interesting to see this world, and there are some food-shopping stops as well, especially for baked goods.

Flaum Appetizers (2), 40 Lee Avenue at the corner of Wilson, (718) 387–7934, is a longtime standby for smoked salmon, whitefish, pickles, and kosher candies from Israel, all at prices far below those at Manhattan appetizer shops. Look closely at the brands of potato chips—they won't be familiar. These are glatt kosher, inspected and rid of even the smallest impurities.

Next door is **Osso Hardware (3),** 42 Lee Avenue, (718) 387–0992. Come in and walk past the closet hooks and pots and pans to see the small, cement-clad pool that is a ritual bath where new dishes and utensils are dipped as a symbol of their purity. Another thing you won't find in your average corner hardware store is a *blech,* a metal sheet that is placed over the range on the Sabbath, when cooking is forbidden, though a small flame is allowed underneath the sheet.

The 4 blocks ahead to Hooper Street have interesting stops all the way. **Berger Gift Shop (4),** 48 Lee Avenue, (718) 387–2130, has windows full of beautiful, ornate silver candlesticks and goblets. The pharmacy at 70 Lee sells cough medicine called Adwaytussin, made by a small Orthodox company with a formula using a vegetable base instead of animal glycerin (which is not kosher). **Landau's Quilts and Pillows (5),** 72 Lee Avenue, (718) 782–2302, carries attractive linens and ceremonial items such as embroidered clothes for covering bread on the Sabbath.

Lee Avenue Sforim Center (6), 114 Lee Avenue, (718) 782–7782, is one of the best of the many shops selling books and religious items as well as tapes and records of Jewish music.

At the corner of Hooper, you'll see **Singer Men's Clothing (7),** 157 Hooper Street, (718) 384–6200, serving Hasidic men with fabrics that never mix wool and linen, another taboo.

Across the street is the **Traditional Kosher Bakery (8),** 123 Lee Avenue, (718) 387–4333, one of several excellent stops for baked goods such as challah and rugelach. Another recommended bakery is **S&S Bake Shop (9),** 159 Lee Avenue, (718) 387–7411.

Wind your way back to Marcy along streets like Hewes, Hooper, and Keap to see blocks of handsome brownstones that have survived the changes in the area. The Moorish-looking building **(10)** at 274

The Williamsburg Mix

The Hasidic and Latino cultures are only part of the Williamsburg story. On the other side of the bridge is a rapidly growing enclave of young artists, designers, and musicians occupying loft spaces in former factories and creating their own hip and happening district of tiny, very avant-garde galleries, cafes, pubs, clubs, and funky shops.

You can get a sampling of the new action by following Bedford Avenue as it curves north. A good place to catch up on the latest art shows and events is the **Williamsburg Art and Historical Center (12)**, 135 Broadway between Bedford and Driggs, (718) 486–7372, which is also the scene of experimental music, poetry, and dance performances. Nearby is **Peter Luger Steakhouse (E)**, 178 Broadway, (718) 387–0500, established in 1887, where the decor still looks like an old beer hall and the steaks have long been considered the finest in New York.

The shopping and dining heart of the hip new Williamsburg is on Bedford Avenue near the subway station on North Seventh Street.

Williamsburg is also home to a large Italian community, centered around Lorimer Street to the east. The Italians hold a uniquely colorful celebration each year for ten days in July, marking the Feast of St. Paulinus. The legend of the saint is re-created on Sundays during the festival, by parading enormous replicas of a boat and a 65-foot-high spire representing the southern Italian town of Nola. The festivities center around **Our Lady of Mount Carmel Church (13)**, 278 North Eighth Street, (718) 384–0223. Phone for current dates.

Keap Street is a synagogue built in 1876 by German Jews who wanted it to resemble a church.

If you detour to 212 Williamsburg Street East, paralleling the Expressway, you'll see a *mikvah* **(11),** a ritual bath used by Orthodox Jewish women once a month and before marriage.

When you climb the stairs and board the elevated train once again, you'll find it hard to believe that Manhattan is just one stop away.

RECOMMENDED ¶|◉| RESTAURANTS

This is a neighborhood better suited to take-out than dining in, but here are some modest stops along the way.

Itzu's Dairy Restaurant (A) ($), 45 Lee Avenue, (718) 384–8631, has no atmosphere but serves vegetable dishes and tasty blintzes.

Landau's Glatt Kosher Delicatessen (B) ($), 65 Lee Avenue, (718) 782–3700, is the place for corned beef or brisket, to eat here in a generous sandwich or to take home.

Lee Avenue Kosher Pizza Shop (C) ($), 108 Lee Avenue, (718) 384–2191, serves pizza made with kosher cheese. It may not win prizes, but it is filling.

Green & Ackerman's Kosher Dairy Restaurant & Pizza (D) ($), 216 Ross Street, (718) 384–2540, is a very busy cafeteria where you'll join the Satmars in line for vegetarian stuffed cabbage, blintzes, fish dishes, kosher pizza, and other nonmeat choices.

The Bronx

A great zoo, a great garden,
and the best Italian shopping
in New York City await you in
the Bronx.

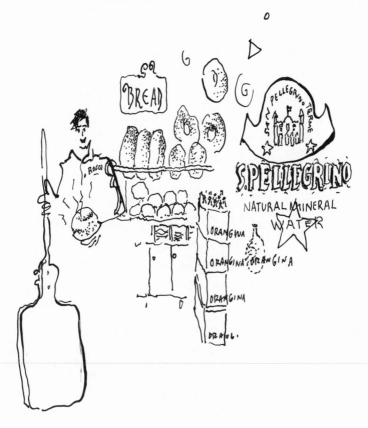

Italian Bounty on *Arthur Avenue*

If you love Italian food, make haste to Arthur Avenue. This may well be the ultimate food-shopping neighborhood in New York. It's lined with dozens of small stores, many in the same family for generations, selling everything from rare Italian wines to handmade pasta to rich imported cheese. The quality is tops, the prices are low, the welcome is warm and personal. As for the restaurants, they are authentic Old World Italian. The only problem with Arthur Avenue may be deciding where to go first.

THE HISTORY

Arthur Avenue is in the Belmont neighborhood of the Bronx, bordered by Fordham University and the Bronx Zoo. This was once part of the Jacob Lorillard estate called Belmont, hence the name.

It is not an Italian neighborhood by accident. Starting in the 1880s the City of New York cut streets through what was still farmland, and developers began to put up housing, spurred by the extension in 1890 of the elevated train line to Fordham Road. In 1895 the New York Zoological Park, better known as the Bronx Zoo, was founded and began developing the world's first zoological research center in Bronx Park. The New York Botanical Garden began landscaping nearby in 1899. There were many jobs available

How to Get There

*Arthur Avenue is south of Fordham
University and 7 blocks west of the Bronx Zoo.*

By subway: Take the D or #4 Train to Fordham Road, and transfer to the BX12 Bus to reach the East Fordham Road/Arthur Avenue stop. The D Train is closer, but it's still a 10-block walk. Metro North has a closer stop, at Fordham Plaza. In warm weather Metro North offers Belmont/Bronx Zoo packages, which include a train to Fordham Station and a bus ride into Belmont.

By car: Take the Fordham Road East exit from the Major Deegan Expressway (I–87) or Bronx River Parkway; proceed east on Fordham Road, past Fordham University, and turn right onto Arthur Avenue. From the New England Thruway (I–95) or the Hutchinson River Parkway, take Pelham Parkway West, which leads into Fordham Road, and turn left onto Arthur. Parking is on the street or at the metered Belmont Municipal Parking Field, just south of East 187th Street. Vehicles may enter directly off Arthur Avenue at East 186th Street or from the less congested Hoffman Avenue, 1 block west of Arthur Avenue.

in landscaping and construction, two fields in which Italian immigrants had proven their prowess, and developers appealed to Italians to settle in Belmont. In 1906 the parish of Our Lady of Mount Carmel Roman Catholic Church was established in a storefront; the current, imposing neo-Gothic church stands on East

187th Street between Hughes and Belmont Avenues. Masses are still said in Italian here.

The community also embraces its cultural heritage at the Enrico Fermi Cultural Center, which serves as a resource center for information about Italian Americans and maintains a large library of books in Italian. It was named for the Nobel Prize–winning physicist, who was an Italian immigrant. The Belmont Playhouse on Arthur Avenue is the only repertory theater in the United States dedicated to works by Italian writers.

Until 1940 Arthur Avenue, the main shopping street, was lined with pushcarts. In his citywide move to do away with sidewalk selling, Mayor Fiorello La Guardia had the food sellers relocated indoors to the Arthur Avenue Food Market, which still thrives today.

Arthur Avenue is an Italian enclave in a changing neighborhood. Many younger families have moved on to the suburbs. The homes they left behind have been occupied by blacks, Latinos, and in recent years by Albanians fleeing the unrest in their home country.

But the area still draws new immigrants from Italy, and even those Italians who have moved away return to worship and to shop in the old neighborhood. The stores on Arthur Avenue are always crowded. Columbus Day is observed in a big way in the neighborhood, with many shops offering special discounts for the occasion.

. . . *A Shopping Tour* . . .

The Italian colors painted on the street at the intersection of Arthur Avenue and 187th Street tell you that this is the heart of Little Italy in the Bronx. Shops await in either direction, with equal lures.

Here are some recommended stops, but there are several choices for every kind of food. This is an area where you'll no doubt find your own favorites by talking to the shopkeepers.

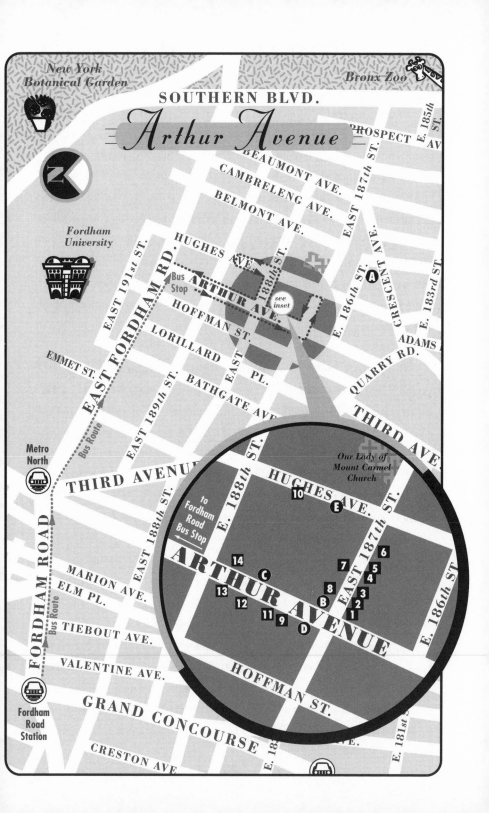

Beginning on 187th Street, the first stop is **DeLillo's Pastry Shop (1),** 606 East 187th Street, (718) 367–8198, where temptations include minipastries like chocolate cannoli, napoleons, and eclairs as well as individual servings of tiramisu.

There are few stores anywhere to compare with the selection of Italian wines at **Mt. Carmel Wines & Spirits (2),** 612 East 187th Street, (718) 367–7833, where they've been importing the best since 1935. Chianti to grappa, inexpensive to famous names like Barollo at $90 or $100 per bottle—they've got it all. The giant bottles of chianti are sure to be a hit the next time you serve an Italian company meal. The selection of marsala guarantees that your next veal marsala will be a triumph.

More sweet temptations await at **Egidio's Pasticceria (3),** 622 East 187th, (718) 295–6077, a neighborhood standby since 1912. More cannoli, strawberry tarts, and cookies of all kinds line the cases. You can sit down and enjoy your purchase with a cappuccino or a homemade Italian ice.

Religious items of all kinds can be found at the **Catholic Goods Center (4),** 630 East 187th Street, (718) 733–0250. Franciscan wood rosaries and scented votive candles from the Holy Land make lovely gifts.

The pastamaker is always rolling out fresh sheets of dough at **Borgatti's Ravioli & Egg Noodles (5),** 632 East 187th Street, (718) 367–3799. On the back wall is a photo of the grandfather who started this business more than sixty years ago.

You can have the pasta cut to your order, buy it dried, or take home packages of frozen, ready-to-cook stuffed manicotti and ravioli. They don't even need thawing; just pop them in the oven or into boiling water.

One store that personifies all that is great about this neighborhood is **D'Auria Brothers Pork Store (6),** 652 East 187th Street,

(718) 584–1040. The shop is tiny, and at least one of the brothers, Dominick or Michael, is usually in the back making sausages, as this family has been doing since 1938. They make it sweet or hot, with or without fennel seeds, and sometimes with paprika, which turns the sausage red. What makes their sausage different? "TLC," smiles Dominick. "Also, because we are small and make small batches, we can control the seasoning." A plate with samples is on the counter.

This shop also imports Italian cheeses such as Pecorino, provolone, and a Parmesan that will make you swear off the packaged stuff forever.

Cross the street at the corner and walk back toward Arthur Avenue for **Capri Gifts (7),** 615 East 187th Street, (718) 367–1843, where you'll find everything from Italian soccer jerseys to contemporary artist–designed espresso sets.

A few doors down, **Tino's Deli (8),** 609 East 187th Street, (718) 733–9879, is the place to buy a container of homemade tomato sauce to go for your pasta or homemade eggplant parmigiana. There's a big selection of dried pasta and Arborio rice for making risotto.

Cross the street and head down Arthur Avenue for a dizzying array of shops at the **Arthur Avenue Retail Market (9),** 2344 Arthur Avenue. The prices are a fraction of what you would pay for such quality in Manhattan. Mt. Carmel Gourmet Food, (718) 933–2295, has hand-rolled dry pasta, tubes of tomato paste, bags of dried oregano imported from Sicily, and a wide selection of balsamic vinegars from Modena. Mike's Deli, (718) 295–5033, makes its own fresh mozzarella, plain or in a layered appetizer loaf with prosciutto, basil, and peppercorns, along with delicious focaccia and great deli sandwiches. It's hard to choose between Peter's Meat Market, (718) 367–3136, and Mario's Meat Specialties, (718) 584–6969, right next door; both have choice cuts. Peter's also has a wide choice of sausages, your pick of chicken, veal, fennel or broccoli rabe.

The market stretches for a full block to Hughes Avenue. The Cafe al Mercato at the far end is a fine place for a sit-down lunch. (See page 98.)

Save room for dessert at **Addeo's Bakery (10),** 2372 Hughes Avenue, (718) 367–8316, known for its crusty breads baked in a brick oven. Addeo also sells cannoli shells, the popular Italian holiday cake called panettone, cheese breadsticks, and tasty fennel, raisin, and provolone breads.

But don't overbuy; ahead, back on Arthur Avenue, is **Madonia Brothers Bakery (11),** 2348 Arthur Avenue, (718) 295–5573, where the biscotti are delicious and the cannoli are filled when you order so that the pastry doesn't get soggy. The family here goes back three generations.

One of many markets with a beautiful selection of fresh fish is **Cosenza's Fish Market (12),** 2354 Arthur Avenue, (718) 364–8510. Imported Italian sardines, squid, dried cod, and good-looking cherrystone clams are among the choices displayed on beds of ice in front of the store. The business has been operating since 1918.

If you need an espresso or cappuccino machine, or fresh roasted coffee beans, you'll find them at **Marie's (13),** a coffee shop at 2378 Arthur Avenue, (718) 295–0514.

Across the street is the **Belmont Italian American Playhouse (14),** 2385 Arthur Avenue, (718) 364–4700, where you can see classical and contemporary Italian dramas as well as children's theater. The Playhouse also sponsors cultural and historical walking tours; phone for information.

You haven't begun to exhaust all the food-shopping possibilities on Arthur Avenue, but by now you may be ready for a good Italian meal. And you'll find many choices for that as well.

Bronx Beauties

Two of the best attractions in New York City, the Bronx Zoo and the New York Botanical Garden, are a short drive from Arthur Avenue. On foot it is a long but doable walk along Fordham Road from the Southern Boulevard side of either site.

The Bronx Zoo, *now officially known as The International Wildlife Conservation Park, is at Fordham Road and the Bronx River Parkway, (718) 367–1010, www.bronxzoo.com. It is the largest urban zoo in the United States, home to more than 4,000 animals representing some 764 species, living in realistic representations of their natural habitats, from wild Asia, to the Himalayan highlands, to the African plains. The zoo is open daily 10:00 A.M. to 5:00 P.M. Monday to Friday, to 5:30 P.M. Saturday and Sunday from April to October, and to 4:30 P.M. daily the rest of the year; admission is $11.00 for adults; $8.00 for children and seniors, April through October; reduced rates, November to March; Pay what you wish on Wednesday. Parking fee, $7.00.*

A day at this great zoo, ending with a dinner on Arthur Avenue, is as good as it gets. Unless, of course, your taste runs to plants rather than animals, in which case head for the New York Botanical Garden, *200th Street and Southern Boulevard, (718) 817–8700, www.nybg.org. One of the oldest and largest botanical gardens in the country, it includes formal plantings and a large tract of unspoiled woodland along a winding river, the last remnant of New York's primeval forest. The showpiece is the Enid A. Haupt Conservatory, a world tour of plants under glass. Grounds are open Tuesday to Sunday and Monday holidays 10:00 A.M. to 6:00 P.M. April to October, to 5:00 P.M. the rest of the year; admission $6.00 for the grounds, $10.00 also includes conservatory, children's garden, and tram tours.*

Italian Cuisine

(See page 237)

R E C O M M E N D E D 🍽 R E S T A U R A N T S

Roberto's (A) ($$–$$$), 632 East 186th Street, (718) 733–9503, gets Zagat readers' votes as "best in the Bronx," high praise given the competition. Let Roberto, the chef-owner, guide you and you can look forward to a memorable Italian dinner.

Ann and Tony's (B) ($$), 2407 Arthur Avenue, (718) 933–1469, has been on the block since 1927. Familiar favorites here include fried calamari and many choices of pastas, chicken, and veal dishes. Spumoni makes a good light dessert, since you'll probably be stuffed.

Dominick's (C) ($$), 2335 Arthur Avenue, (718) 733–2807, a standby for more than forty years, has no menu, no reservations, no credit cards—and lines almost every weekend. The waiter tells you what is best today, and you'd do well to heed his advice. Come early or late to avoid a wait.

Mario's (D) ($$–$$$), 2342 Arthur Avenue, (718) 584–1188, in the same family since 1919, serves pasta prepared ten ways, osso buco, scampi, clams oreganate, and lots of other good things. The prices are a little higher than the rest of the block. For dessert try the tartufo or the tortoni.

Cafe al Mercato (E) ($), 2331 Hughes Avenue, (718) 364–7681, is the cafeteria at the Hughes Avenue end of the Arthur Avenue Retail Market. If you want a good, cheap lunch, get in line for rice balls, stuffed shells, a frittata, or the pizza of the day.

Queens

Welcome to the "borough of neighborhoods," where a third of the population are foreign-born and every subway stop brings you to a different culture—to Indian sari shops, Greek tavernas, Colombian nightclubs, Mexican bakeries, or Korean barbecue joints.

Going Greek in Astoria

Older men in dark suits occupy sidewalk benches and mingle in the parks, exchanging the news of the day or playing cards. Cafes beckon with dark, strong Greek coffee and melt-in-your-mouth pastries. Tavernas serve up Greek salad and seafood perfectly broiled over charcoal—crisp on the outside, sweet and tender within. Later you can listen to Greek music. And you'll surely want to take home a supply of Greek olives or olive oil and some delicious Greek cheeses imported from their source.

This is Astoria, with the largest Greek community outside the motherland, estimated at some 60,000 to 70,000 people, many of them first- and second-generation with strong ties to their home culture. They add richness to a community with a varied ethnic population and a scenic location on the East River. Three bridges—the Queensboro, Triboro, and Hell's Gate—connect this colorful corner of Queens to Manhattan. Beneath the latter two bridges, Astoria Park has one of the loveliest sites in New York City, a green respite with views of upper Manhattan. It's about a fifteen-minute walk from Ditmars Boulevard, the beginning of the shops and cafes. Several important museums provide additional incentive for the trip.

THE HISTORY

Now a part of Long Island City, Astoria has been a rural village, a retreat for the well-to-do, and the early movie industry's East

How to Get There

By subway: Take the N Train to Broadway or Ditmars
Boulevard (ten to fifteen minutes from 59th Street and
Lexington Avenue).

By car: Take Queensborough Bridge to 31st Street and drive
left (north) toward Ditmars Boulevard. Parking is
possible on the side streets.

Coast production headquarters. It was the birthplace of the world's
grandest piano—the Steinway—and of Hellman's Mayonnaise and
the first Xerox copier.

It was the presence of fertile farmland that encouraged the
Dutch to settle the area in the 1640s, and for 200 years farms pre-
dominated. In 1839, Steven Halsey, a fur merchant, founded a village at Hallet's Cove and started the 92nd Street Ferry service to
Manhattan.

The community was named for John Jacob Astor, who lived just
across the ferry landing in Manhattan, with the hope that he would
be inspired to invest in the area, a wish that did not come true. Still
Astoria prospered, and the early development at Hallet's Cove
attracted many wealthy New Yorkers, who built fine homes on 12th
and 14th Streets and 27th Avenue. Many still stand, though greatly
altered over the years.

In 1870, the village of Astoria and several adjacent hamlets
including Steinway, Ravenswood, and Hunters Point—were

Sight-seeing in Astoria

Astoria and adjacent areas of Long Island City are home to an increasing number of museums and galleries that can easily be combined with a visit to the Greek restaurants and shops of the area.

The American Museum of the Moving Image *(35th Avenue at 36th Street, 718–784–0077; www.ammi.org),* the closest museum to the Greek community, will interest anyone who enjoys movies and television. Besides regular screenings of classic movies, the core exhibit, "Behind the Screen," explains what it takes to produce and market moving images. It includes more than one thousand film and television artifacts, computer-based interactive experiences, commissioned installations, audio-visual materials, demonstrations of professional equipment and techniques, and changing exhibits. One recent display, "Robert De Niro: Costume and Character," showed more than two dozen complete costumes from the actor's own collection. The hands-on Digital Media Gallery allows visitors to interact with the newest in digital moving images. Hours are Wednesday to Friday 11:00 A.M. to 5:00 P.M., Saturday and Sunday to 6:00 P.M. Admission is $10.00 for adults; $7.50 for students and seniors; $5.00 for ages 5 to 18. Movies are shown in the early evening on Friday, Saturday, and Sunday.

To reach the museum, take the R Train to Steinway Street and exit at the 34th Avenue end of the station. Walk along Steinway to 35th Avenue, turn right and proceed to 36th Avenue.

The museum is part of the 14-acre complex of Kaufman Astoria Studios *(34-12 36th Street, 718–392–5600; www.kaufmanastoria.com),* an important center for movie, television, and sound production from the days of silent films to today's digital era. Built in 1920 as Paramount's East Coast production facility, it is listed on the National Register of Historic Places. Everyone from Rudolph Valentino to Bill Cosby to Big Bird has worked here. The busy studios are used by many companies and are presently home to Lifetime TV, WFAN Radio, and a 24-screen United Artists movie theater.

Big news for art lovers in Queens was the arrival of the Museum of Modern Art—MoMA QNS—(33rd Street at Queens Boulevard, 212–708–9400; www.moma.org). It is ensconced in a former Swingline staple factory while the Manhattan building is under renovation until 2005. Some of MoMA's greatest masterpieces are on display, along with top-quality changing exhibits. The museum is adjacent to the 33rd Street Station of the #7 local Train. From Astoria, take the N or W Train back toward Manhattan and change to the #7 Train outbound at Queens Plaza. Hours are Thursday through Monday, 10:00 A.M. to 5:00 P.M., and until 7:45 P.M. Friday. Adults $12.00, students and seniors $8.50, under 16 free with adult. Pay what you wish after 4:00 P.M. Friday.

The Isamu Noguchi Museum, (9-01 43rd Avenue, 718–544–8842; www.noguchi.org), re-opens in April 2004 after nearly three years of extensive renovations to the space that was Noguchi's workshop. Renovations include a redesigned cafe and shop, new lighting, windows, and some new plantings in the serene Japansese garden he designed. The museum will continue to display a comprehensive selection of over one hundred examples of the sculptor's work and for the first time will offer changing exhibits by other artists who influenced Noguchi or were inspired by him. Allow plenty of time; this is a fabulous museum. Phone for directions, new hours, and to find out whether the museum will once again offer weekend mini-bus transportation from Manhattan.

At 36-02 43rd Avenue is the excellent Museum of African Art (718–784–7700, www.africanart.org), with outstanding exhibits of artworks from Africa. It will remain here until new quarters at 105th Street and 5th Avenue in Manhattan are completed, with a target date of 2006. Admission for adults is $6.00, children and seniors, $3.00. Hours: Thursday, Friday, Monday, 10:00 A.M. to 5:00 P.M., Saturday and Sunday, 11:00 A.M. to 6:00 P.M.

Other attractions in Long Island City include P.S.1 (22-25 Jackson Avenue, 718–784–2084; www.moma.org), an affiliate of the Museum of Modern Art, showing cutting-edge contemporary art in a converted landmark school-house. The Socrates Sculpture Park (Broadway at Vernon Boulevard, 718–956–1819; www.socratessculpture park.org), an outdoor riverside garden built on former landfill, shows enormous junk sculptures and other con-temporary works with the Manhattan skyline as a back-drop; it also features outdoor movies on Wednesday nights. Contact each attraction for directions.

consolidated to form Long Island City, which was, in turn, incorporated into the City of New York in the consolidation of 1898.

The first rapid-transit line, the N Train, known as the Astoria Elevated, or El, opened along 31st Street in 1917, leading to the construction of apartment buildings and projects in the years that followed. Subway service came to Steinway Street in 1933, and the Triboro Bridge was opened in 1936, further accelerating development.

The first Greeks arrived in the 1920s, establishing their place by building churches. St. Demetrios, one of eleven Greek Orthodox churches in the area, is said to have the largest congregation outside Greece.

American prosperity after World War II attracted many immigrants fleeing the Greek Civil War of 1944–1949. It was a time when Astoria was losing much of its large Italian population to the suburbs, and the Greeks opened businesses in empty storefronts, helping to revitalize the community.

When immigration laws were liberalized in 1965, a new influx arrived. A Greek-American Homeowners Association and many other organizations helped the newcomers, and numerous hometown and regional organizations grew up with ties to a particular Greek village or region.

... A Shopping/Walking Tour ...

Greek Astoria has four main shopping districts off 31st Street: Ditmars Boulevard, 23rd Avenue, 30th Avenue, and Broadway. You can cover them all easily in a twenty- to thirty-minute walk along 31st. The stroll beside the El tracks is not exactly scenic, but there's plenty to see along the way, and you'll no doubt make your own discoveries as you go along. The Arab, Czech, Colombian, and Italian establishments you pass will tell you that Greeks do not have a monopoly on dining in Astoria, but their impact on the community is plain to see. In case your energy flags, the N Train runs straight down 31st, with stops at every main intersection.

To take in everything ride to the end of the line, Ditmars Boulevard, and work your way back. When you come down from the El station to busy 31st Avenue, amidst banks, drug stores, and florists that could be anywhere, notice the newsstand, where three

Greek newspapers are displayed, and the fish store, with signs written in Greek, and you'll know you've come to the right place.

Walk down to Ditmars, the commercial hub of the area, cross to the far side of the street, and turn right. Stop when you spy **Angelo's Food Emporium (1),** 31-27 Ditmars Boulevard, (718) 278–0705. The shop seems small—but look a bit more closely. There are more than thirty kinds of Greek cheeses in the front case, and the gregarious shopkeeper, Evangelos Barous, will guide you in your selection. Taste a few varieties. The feta is great, but don't miss the Kaseri or the Cypriot sheep cheese. On the shelves are more kinds of olive oil than I knew existed (Angelo says that Horio is very popular, but Tricola is the very best), not to mention a dozen kinds of olives, nuts, bulgar, shelled wheat, whole wheat, lentils, canned specialties such as stuffed grape leaves, and just about anything else needed for a great Greek meal.

This is a good place for an education on the difference between Kalamata olives (dark purple, small, and almond-shaped) and Amfissa (black, round, and with a nutty-sweet taste).

If you've whetted your appetite, Kyclades, a pleasant restaurant, is just ahead (see page 115). Afterward, check out the fine array of produce at the end of the block at **Top Tomato (2),** 33-15 Ditmars Boulevard, (718) 721–1400, a giant fruit and grocery market that is open twenty-four hours a day.

As you stroll look down the side streets to see the rows of neat, redbrick dwellings, each with a well-tended garden in front. The five-story apartments on the blocks between 33rd and 36th Streets to the left of Ditmars were built by the Metropolitan Life Insurance Company in 1924. The two-family houses to the right on 37th Street are especially attractive, each with a bay window in front.

The Greek influence on the community is easy to see as you

stroll. The blue and white awning of the Astor Pharmacy includes Greek lettering and the Pizza Palace advertises Greek specialties.

If you're thinking of taking a trip to Greece, check the prices at the Stork Travel Club, 35-09 Ditmars, (718) 204–1024; it usually has the cheapest rates around.

When you get to Steinway Street, cross and make a left turn for a short detour to the **Victory Sweet Shop (3)**, 21-69 Steinway Street, (718) 274–2087, where the heavenly aroma of fresh baking is irresistible. Buy some baklava or a small tray of assorted sweets, or try the tsoureki, a sweet bread with almonds on top.

Turn back and head up Steinway past Ditmar Park, which is filled with men, both Greek and Italian, playing cards, rolling a bocce ball, or watching the action. Not a female in sight—at least not until you get to the other side of the park, where mothers are minding kids in the playground. Turn right again onto 23rd Avenue and stop to admire the small, whitewashed **St. Irene Chrysovalantou Greek Orthodox Church (4)**, 36-25 23rd Avenue. If the doors are open, by all means go inside to see the charming marble and painted vaulted interior, which one guide calls "a folk art religious experience." Many of the icons are encased in silver.

Another Greek Orthodox church, Saints Catherine and George, can be seen to the right on 33rd Street. You'll also see a Greek deli and the Greek and American Retired Men's Club to tell that you are in the heart of things.

As you walk back toward 31st Street, you'll see two murals adorning an overpass, one a commemoration of 9/11, the other a salute to the 2004 Olympic games in Athens.

The corner of 31st Street and 23rd Avenue is home to two popular dessert cafes, Lefkos Pirgos and the Paradise Cafe. (See page 119.)

You can also browse three gift shops around this corner, **Astron Gift Shop (5)**, 22-81 31st Street, (718) 932–7012; **George's Hellenic Gifts (6)**, 31-02 23rd Avenue, (718) 726–1996, and **Kentrikon Noufaro (7)**, 23-33 31st Street, (718) 721–9190. Among the offerings are Greek style vases and pottery, religious pieces, cookbooks, dolls and a large stock of the candles used to top the elaborate layers of white netting used at Greek weddings and christenings.

Cross the street and walk away from Ditmars to 24th Street and a surprising discovery, the **Bohemian Hall and Garden (8)**, 29-19 24th Avenue, (718) 274–4925. This is not Greek but a hall preserving the traditions of the Czech and Slovak communities of the area, and it includes the last of the original beer gardens in New York, which once numbered 800. Lights strung above the garden and picnic tables invite you to sit and enjoy the bratwursts and beer served when the garden isn't rented out to a group. The entrance is through the Bohemian Hall, a social center. The garden is open weekends Memorial Day to Labor Day and hosts many ethnic festivals that are open to the public—Irish to Cuban to Czech—and a gala Octoberfest. An indoor restaurant open Wednesday to Sunday serves a traditional menu including goulash, pirogis, chicken paprikash, schnitzel, and steak Bohemika topped with ham and cheese. You can order sides of dumpling and red cabbage, and enjoy a dessert of palacsintas, crepes with fruit filling topped with cream.

Back to things Greek, the largest Greek supermarket in Astoria is **Titan Supermarket (9),** 25-56 31st Street (between Astoria Boulevard and 28th Avenue), (718) 626–7771, with aisle after aisle of Greek olives, cheeses, olive oils, phyllo dough, and lots of foods to go, including delicious tzatziki and taramasalata spreads. The bakery will surely tempt you, and the lively Greek background music will put you in the proper shopping mood.

GMV, the Greek Music and Video Superstore (10), 25-50 31st Street, (718) 932–8400, is the place to pick up some Greek music guaranteed to liven up a party at home. Check out some of the choices at www.greekmusic.com

Just past 28th Street, next door to Opa Souvlaki, is **Opa O Fournos Bakery (11),** 28-46 31st Street, (718) 932–3113, packed with temptations. Take home some of the little cheese-filled dinner rolls; simply delicious!

The Zodiac Cafe and Restaurant at the corner of Newtown Avenue (see page 118) has a popular bar and live Greek music on weekends.

Across the street is Byzantio, where patrons sip coffee by day and ouzo by night; it is reputedly the hottest bar in the neighborhood.

Ahead is 30th Street, with its own share of nightlife. Symposio (see page 118) is known for its traditional Greek songstress as well as its dining room. If the weather is fine, you may want to join the crowd having a drink across the street at the outdoor tables at the Athens Cafe, a busy spot both day and night.

Another small shop ahead, crammed with wonderful Greek cheeses, olives, and other good foods, is **Greek House Foods (12),** 32-22 30th Avenue, (718) 545–5252.

Athens Square Park (13), off 30th Street, offers summer entertainment for all Astoria's ethnic groups. Tuesday is Greek Night.

Ahead is **St. Demetrios Church (14),** 30-11 30th Drive at 31st Street, (718) 728–1718. Built in 1927, the cathedral houses the largest Greek Orthodox congregation outside Athens. By all means go inside if you can to see the beautiful domed sanctuary, the elaborate altar screen, and the icon images to whom congregants pray in times of distress. The church sponsors the largest annual Greek festival each year in mid-May. The Acropol Bakery Cafe, just ahead, is popular with youngsters when the church school lets out. (See page 119.)

One more block is Broadway, the last major shopping street. Turn left, keep walking, and take your pick of the restaurants and coffee shops ahead. Great dining and great desserts are guaranteed.

Greek Cuisine

Greek cuisine is suddenly being discovered in New York, with restaurants popping up all over Manhattan. Of all the countries of the eastern Mediterranean, Greek food most clearly shows the influence of the Middle East. Greeks still bake flat, round pita breads and

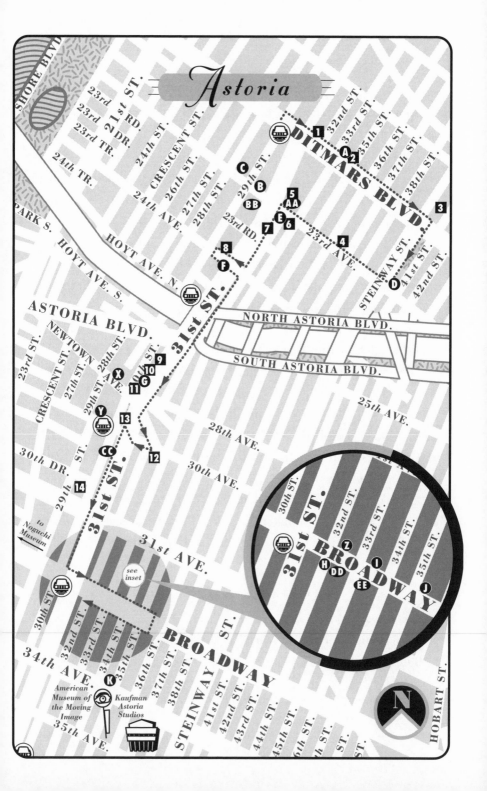

retain traditions of spit-roasted meat and cooking with yogurt.

But Greek cooking does have its own flavor—the combination of olive oil, lemon, and oregano, which seasons many delicious dishes.

The preparation is simple, with one-dish casseroles or grilling the main ways of preparing foods. Lamb is the meat used most frequently; kebabs and souvlaki, marinated then roasted on a spit, are popular offerings. Fish grilled over open coals is very popular, and it is done beautifully in many restaurants in Astoria.

Greek yogurts and cheeses are excellent. Feta is the best-known Greek cheese, commonly served with salad, but several other varieties are well worth sampling. Fried cheese makes a tasty appetizer.

Mezedes—hot and cold appetizers—are a delicious part of Greek meals. An array of appetizers, in fact, makes a tasty dinner.

Paper thin, flaky phyllo dough is a staple, used to make appetizer tarts filled with spinach or cheese as well as desserts. The best-known dessert is baklava, a phyllo pastry drenched in honey and nuts. It takes a skilled cook to use these rich ingredients and still produce desserts that are not overly sweet, but some of Astoria's bakers succeed admirably.

Greek coffee, served in a demitasse cup and covered with foam, is very strong. It can be taken with or without sugar, but no milk or cream is offered. Don't drink it to the last drop, as the grounds settle to the bottom of the cup.

A GREEK SAMPLER

Appetizers:

Avgolemono soup: chicken soup flavored with an egg and lemon mixture.

Bourekakia: phyllo puffs or triangles with various fillings—mushroom, shrimp, or meat.

Dolmadakia: grape leaves usually stuffed with a mix of rice and onions flavored with dill.

Horiatiki: Greek salad—lots of tomatoes, cucumbers, oregano, and olives, topped with an oil and vinegar dressing and feta cheese; sometimes served with small, stuffed grape leaves.

Kalamarakia: squid, usually served fried.

Keftedes: meatballs seasoned with oregano, onion, dried mint, and deep fried.

Melitzanosalata: a roasted-eggplant spread, made with onions, parsley, olive oil, and fresh herbs.

Saganaki: fried cheese.

Spanakokeftedes: spinach and cheese balls coated with bread crumbs and deep fried.

Spanakopites: phyllo triangles filled with feta cheese and spinach

Tahini: a sesame-seed paste.

Taramosalata: a spread made with fish roe, olive oil, lemon juice, and seasonings; slightly salty.

Tzatziki: a yogurt and cucumber spread seasoned with garlic, vinegar, and oil.

Greek Cheeses:

Feta: the classic, crumbly white cheese of Greece, often made with a combination of sheep and goat milk.

Haloumi: a semisoft cheese, similar to mozzarella, made from sheep milk.

Kasseri: a creamy yellow farm cheese made from sheep or goat milk; mild with the slightest salty taste. Excellent with fruit.

Kefalotiri: a hard, salty cheese, excellent for grating.

Manouri: a soft, unsalted cheese made from sheep or goat milk whey, often served with fruit.

Greek Casseroles:

Moussaka: a hearty layered casserole, usually with chopped meat, eggplant, and sometimes tomatoes, topped with a creamy béchamel sauce.

Pastitsio: a layered casserole made with macaroni and ground beef or lamb, white sauce, tomatoes, onions, oregano, and a sprinkling of cinnamon.

Grilled Dishes:

Garides: shrimp.

Gyro: various cuts of meat, usually lamb, chopped, minced, or ground, then compressed into a large cylindrical shape, put on a vertical skewer and broiled. Served on pita bread with lettuce, tomato, and tzatziki.

Lavraki: striped bass.

Paidakia: baby lamb chops with Greek seasoning.

Solomos: salmon.

Souvla: a skewer used for grilling.

Souvlaki: lamb, chicken, or another meat grilled on a skewer; marinated with oregano and other herbs, oil, and lemon juice.

Synagrida: red snapper.

Tonos: tuna.

Tsipoura: porgy.

Xyfias: swordfish.

(You probably won't need to know names of fish. In most restaurants the waiter will tell you what's fresh, or you can check the refrigerated case when you come in and decide what appeals to you.)

Greek Drinks:

Ouzo: a colorless alcoholic drink flavored with anise.

Retsina: a white or rosé wine flavored with pine resin.

Greek Desserts:

Baklava: layers of phyllo pastry interspersed with chopped nuts and topped with a honey-flavored syrup.

Esmek: shredded wheat topped with custard and whipped cream.

Galacktoboureko: phyllo stuffed with semolina custard.

Kadaifi: layers of shredded wheat with honey, cinnamon, and chopped almonds.

Koulourakia: sweet, golden butter cookies shaped by hand.

Kourabiedes: butter cookies shaped by hand and covered with powdered sugar.

Ravani: a flour cake.

R E C O M M E N D E D ¶|◉| R E S T A U R A N T S

Taverna Kyclades (A) ($–$$), 33-07 Ditmars Boulevard, (718) 545–8666, is small and cheerful, with brick walls and maps of Greece decorating the lacquered tables. You pick the fish, they cook it, and you can see the chefs at work in the small kitchen. Grilled seafood with lemon-roasted potatoes and grilled chicken breast are recommended. Spinach pie or fried cheese with salad makes a great light lunch. Some outdoor seating in summer.

Stamatis Restaurant (B) ($$), 29-12 23rd Avenue, (718) 278–9795, is just the kind of place you want to find in Astoria. The walls are adorned with textured murals of the Greek isles and sculpted gulls fly in the skylight well, setting the scene for a cheerful, unpretentious restaurant with terrific homemade food and a pleasant terrace for outdoor dining. The buzz of the many patrons speaking Greek assures you that everything is authentic.

Telly's Taverna (C) ($–$$), 28-13 23rd Avenue, (718) 728–9056. Pick your seafood from the glass case at the entrance or choose the lamb chops; you can be sure they'll be done to a turn at this long-time, no-frills favorite. Outdoor seating in summer.

Christos Hasapo-Taverna (D) ($$), 41-08 23rd Avenue, (718) 726–5195. Meat lovers won't mind the extra walk to reach this combination steak house/meat market with a Greek accent. Lamb and veal chops are tasty, and the sirloin and filet mignon are fine. Sometimes there's a young pig on the rotisserie.

Taverna Vraka (E) ($$–$$$), 23-15 31st Street (between 23rd and 24th Avenues), (718) 721–3007, a small, second-floor restaurant with

A TYPICAL GREEK MEAL

Appetizers:
Spinach pies, fried squid, or
tzatziki

Greek Salad

Grilled fish, souvlaki, or a casse-
role dish such as moussaka

Kadaifi for dessert

a folksy, country feel, good food, and authentic Greek music Wednesday through Sunday from 8:30 P.M. The grilled whole red snapper is a winner, and the moussaka is excellent.

Elias Corner (F) ($$), 24-02 31st Street at 24th Avenue, (718) 932–1510 (cash only; no credit cards). Behind the sea murals on the outside wall awaits one of the best-known restaurants in Astoria, and with good reason. The decor is nil, but the grilled fish is perfection and the fried squid is baby tender. Let the waiter guide your fish choice; he'll tell you what's freshest. Come on a warm night when the back garden is open and guests are calling to one another in Greek; New York will seem far away.

Opa! Souvlaki (G) ($), 28-44 31st Street, (718) 728–3638. The ultimate souvlaki sandwich is right here. The owner has changed but the store has been a neighborhood standby since 1969.

Stamatis Broadway Restaurant (H) ($$), 31-14 Broadway, (718) 204–8968 is less attractive than its sibling, but by some accounts, the food is even better. Both addresses have all the favorite Greek dishes, including those delicious appetizers.

Uncle George's (I) ($–$$), 33-19 Broadway, (718) 626–0593. The spit never stops spinning at this favorite for basic Greek home cooking at reasonable prices. The tzatziki, grilled meats and

— WEDDING CAKE

ACROPOL

seafood, and lemon potatoes are sure to please. Diner decor with glass walls all around.

Karyatis (J) ($$), 35-03 Broadway, (718) 204–0666. Peach-colored walls and Greek statuary set the scene for the most elegant dining in Astoria. The menu still features the basic favorites, and the prices are still a bargain as compared with Manhattan. Roast leg of lamb, baked cod, and broiled porgy are good choices, and there's a fine selection of Greek cheeses.

S'Agapo (K) ($$), 34-21 34th Avenue, (718) 626–0303, is a long block from Broadway, but fans say it's well worth the walk. From souvlaki to grilled shrimp with lemon and herbs, the dishes are divine and the terrace is pleasant on a summer evening. Try the cold dip appetizer, with six choices. There's often a singer and accordionist on weekends. The location is ideal if you want to visit the nearby American Museum of the Moving Image.

Dining and Music:

Zodiac Cafe and Restaurant (X) ($$), 30-15 Newtown Avenue, (718) 726–3995, spacious and attractive, this is a popular spot. The bar is usually crowded, the dining room gets high marks for dishes such as stuffed clams and grilled shrimp in garlic, and there is live Greek music Thursday through Sunday nights.

Symposio (Y) ($$), 30-19 30th Avenue, (718) 777–8536. The name comes from Plato, and literally means drinking together, but food and song go with the wine at Symposio. Every Wednesday, Friday, and Saturday, starting at 9:00 P.M., a singer and pianist offer contemporary and traditional Greek songs. Nicely decorated with original painted murals and photos of Astoria, the restaurant serves excellent lamb dishes, as well as the usual seafood and a fine platter of assorted mezedes.

Demetris Seafood Restaurant (Z) ($$), 32-11 Broadway, (718) 278–1877. On weekdays the live background music is nice, but on weekends the place comes alive with a bouzouki band playing in the vine-covered, glass-enclosed patio. Dinner will not disappoint; the freshest fish awaits on ice and the charcoal grill is ready. Just be careful not to fill up on the appetizers—the tzatziki, taramosalata, spanakopites, and the like are delicious.

Coffee and Desserts:

All of these restaurants are bright and modern, with a wide selection of pastries and great people-watching.

Lefkos Pirgos (AA), 22-85 31st Street (corner of 23rd Avenue), (718) 932–4423.

Paradise Cafe (BB) ($), 23-02 31st Street, (718) 545–1784.

Acropol Bakery Cafe (CC) ($), 30-76 31st Street, (718) 728–6308.

Omonia Cafe (DD) ($), 32-20 Broadway, (718) 274–6650.

Kolonaki Cafe (EE) ($), 33-02 Broadway, (718) 721–6911.

A Trip to Asia in Flushing

Markets spilling over with goods at bargain prices . . . herb shops filled with mysterious potions . . . bustling bakeries laden with temptations . . . and serene tea shops where you can taste and learn about the brews—all of this and more awaits in Flushing's mushrooming Chinese neighborhood. In many ways this is an easier place to visit than Manhattan's Chinatown. While there is plenty of bustle, this is a "suburban" Chinatown with modern shops, more clerks who speak

English, and more chance for leisurely browsing and buying. And some of New York City's best Chinese restaurants are found here.

Right next door is a rapidly growing Little Korea, with more to explore and a different cuisine to be savored. Add a few notable historic sights and a garden and there's very good reason to board the #7 Train bound for Flushing.

THE HISTORY

One of the original four towns of Queens, Flushing was settled in 1639 by the Dutch, who named their settlement Vlissengen, for the city that many of them had called home back in Holland. The English later altered this to Flushing. Several of the oldest structures in Flushing remain standing, including the original 1694 Quaker meeting house; the Bowne House, circa 1661; and the eighteenth-century Kingsland House, currently home to the Queens Historical Society.

Flushing calls itself "the birthplace of religious freedom in America." Quakers who had fled religious persecution in their European homelands took refuge here in 1657. They balked at Gov. Peter Stuyvesant's ban of anything except the Dutch Reformed Church in the area. The Quakers signed the Flushing Remonstrance, a document promising religious tolerance, and won support from the Dutch government.

One of the first nurseries in the United States, the Linneaean Gardens, opened in Flushing in 1737. This legacy continues in the Queens Botanical Garden.

Fast and direct rail service into Manhattan arrived in 1854. After the Civil War Flushing attracted many wealthy New Yorkers, who built elegant houses. Its citizens reportedly were not happy to have the subway arrive in 1928, fearing that easier transit might bring unwanted newcomers. They finally relented but drew the line at

How to Get There

By subway: Take the #7 Train to the last stop, Main Street, Flushing. About forty-five minutes from 42nd Street.

By car: Take Long Island Expressway to Kissena Boulevard. Exit north on Kissena, which runs into Main Street. Continue on Main past Roosevelt Avenue, hoping for a parking space in the lot on 39th Avenue. There may be parking spaces on the street on Northern Boulevard.

overhead tracks; the #7 Train station was placed underground, one of the few such stations on the route.

Flushing has been the site of two world's fairs, in 1939–1940 and 1964–1965. The one-time fairgrounds, Flushing Meadows, is currently home to Shea Stadium and the New York Mets; the U.S. Tennis Association headquarters, home of the U.S. Open; and several cultural attractions, including the Queens Museum of Art, the New York Hall of Science, and the Queens Wildlife Center.

After World War II many of Flushing's fine homes were replaced by apartment houses and the neighborhood began to deteriorate. It was saved by an influx of Chinese and Koreans, who moved in and filled vacant storefronts with their businesses. Indians, Arabs, and other ethnic groups have followed, but the Chinese and Koreans are still the predominant nationalities. Flushing is now densely populated, with well over 60,000 Chinese residents and one of the largest Korean settlements in America.

There are three distinct sides of central Flushing: Chinese, Korean, and historic. You can see any or all in a short visit and find fine restaurants wherever you wander.

CHINESE FLUSHING

When you emerge from the subway for the first time and see little but traffic and the Stern's department store and other everyday clothing shops down the block, you may wonder why you made the trip.

But head the other way toward the tall Sheraton hotel and the Asia Bank (walking on the opposite side of the street) and you'll quickly see a dramatic change: wall-to-wall Chinese emporiums. The majority of the Chinese who have settled in Flushing are from Taiwan. They constitute an upwardly mobile group with their own associations and few ties to the Cantonese of Manhattan's Chinatown. They give a more contemporary feel to the neighborhood.

Yi Mei Bakery (1), 135-38 Roosevelt, (718) 886–6820, is a choice first stop, whether for a snack or just to admire the display. It is large and bright, with dozens of selections shown along one wall, making it easy to choose what you want. Soft buns with varied fillings—from raisin, red bean, and taro to roast pork in sauce—cost less than $1.00. Chinese cookies and pastries come in all shapes and colors.

Now visit **Shun An Tong (2),** 135-24 Roosevelt, (718) 445–9358, a shop filled with Chinese herbs and medicines, potions said to cure everything from the common cold to impotence. Ginseng, the Chinese cure-all, can be found in teas, cosmetics, and supplements to be sprinkled on food. And if you're interested in acupuncture, Shun An Tong can oblige.

Next comes the attractive **Ten Ren Tea and Ginseng Co. (3),** 135-18 Roosevelt, (718) 461–9305, where dozens of tea varieties are kept in large, gold-colored canisters. The clerks speak good English and will happily explain the properties of different teas as well as give instructions on how to brew them properly. They often serve samples of some of the brews. A case in the rear of the store displays a variety of proper teapots. This is also a place for an explanation of the benefits of ginseng. Try one of the house specialties here, the "tea shake," a fad imported from Taiwan. Mint green tea, apple green tea, and lichee green tea are among the flavors served with chewy tapioca balls in the bottom of the glass to be sucked up through special wide straws. Milkshakes are also available in flavors such as chocolate, papaya, and red bean.

At the end of the block is the **Good Luck Market (4),** 135-08 Roosevelt, (718) 888–6618, one of many markets where you will find long rows of sauces, from oyster and yellow bean to banana. Shelves are laden with all sorts of Oriental goodies: rice wine for cooking, containers of shredded pork, tins of radishes in soy sauce, pickled cucumbers, and sesame paste.

Cross the street and go back down the block to check out the **Chung Hwa Book Shop (5),** 135-29 Roosevelt Avenue, (718) 353–3580, with hundreds of books, magazines, and greeting cards in Chinese. Books in English on how to pass graduate school entrance exams tell you that the Chinese value education. Come back to step

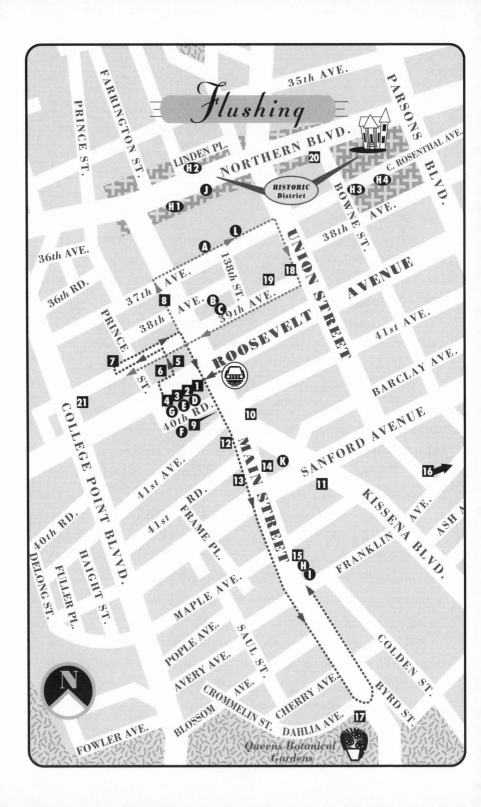

into the **Flushing Center Mall (6),** 135-15 Roosevelt Avenue, an arcade leading to the Sheraton hotel, lined with the area's most elegant shops. Perfume, jewelry, shoes, candies, and wedding gowns are among the wares to be browsed through while a cheerful player piano puts you in the shopping mood.

Come downstairs and out through the hotel lobby on 39th Avenue, and turn left to Prince Street. Cross the street, and just past the corner you'll find an interesting little **Oriental Card and Gift Shop (7),** 133-57A 39th Avenue, (718) 888–9212, with vases, china, carvings, Buddhas, and a nice selection of handsome and reasonably priced Oriental jewelry boxes.

Go back down 39th Avenue and turn left onto Main Street to find the big **Hong Kong Supermarket (8),** 37-11 Main Street, (718) 539–6868, in the small, shiny Hong Kong Mall, which is reminiscent of the glitzy look of its namesake. This is a store with everything from pastry wrappers for egg rolls to tanks of live bass, flounder, and lobster, guaranteed to be fresh. One long section is filled with Chinese dishes and utensils. A big attraction is the long counter filled with frozen dumplings, a great take-home treat.

Now you have a choice of more Chinatown shopping, a look at historic Flushing, or a brief stroll to Korean Flushing.

To complete your Chinese tour, turn and head back across Roosevelt Avenue. You'll be in the most congested part of the area. At the corner of 40th Road is one of the area's busiest food markets, the **Main Street 28 Food, Inc. (9),** 40-28 Main Street, (718) 359–3388. This short road is packed with Chinese establishments, including some top restaurants.

Ahead, at the intersection of Main Street and Kissena Boulevard, is the attractive new $35 million headquarters of the Flushing Branch of the **Queens Borough Public Library (10),** 41-17 Main Street, (718) 661–1200, the busiest branch in the entire New York City library system. Step inside; it's worth a look. The Queens library system accommodates its immigrant population with materials in more than forty languages. Hindi-language newspapers and Chinese mystery novels are well patronized by the older generation, *Sesame Street* books and story hours are an educational start for the children, and English classes and workshops on becoming a citizen or buying a house serve as how-to guides for newcomers. The library has eighty computer stations, an international resource center, and an auditorium with infrared earphones for United Nations–style simultaneous translations.

If you detour up Kissena Boulevard, you will find the **Chinese Cultural Arts Center (11),** 41-61 Kissena Boulevard, (718) 886–7770, sponsored by the government of Taiwan. Traditional Chinese musical instruments and masks are on display, and the auditorium is used by local cultural groups. The bilingual Hsiang-Yin chorus rehearses here on Sunday afternoons.

Farther along Main, numbers give way to street names, many of them names of trees, but the numbering continues in order. On the west side of the street are more herb shops, including a sidewalk stand with a sign promising HERBS FOR SKIN DISEASES, ALLERGY, ACNE, MIGRAINE, COUGH, BACK & LEG PAIN, CONSTIPATION, HEPATITIS AND FATIGUE. The **Fay Da Bakery (12),** 41-60 Main Street, (718) 886–4568, has the most delectable arrays of fancy cakes in the window, and **Seho Plaza Trading Company (13),** 42-22 Main Street, (718) 359–0430, carries a wide array of Oriental gifts, both Chinese and Korean.

On the east side of Main Street is the big, modern **Kam Sen Food Products (14),** 41-79 Main Street, (718) 939–2560, a supermarket with a little of everything, including a big take-out section with prepared foods and a bakery; you can even have your watch repaired here. **Sunrise Kitchen and Hardware Supplies (15),** 42-05 Main Street, (718) 886–5663, has stacks of utensils for Oriental and every other type of cooking.

On the far corner is East Lake, a big, lavish restaurant known as the "Queen of Dim Sum." (See page 133.)

A strip of Indian sari shops, a couple of restaurants, and small branches of large Indian grocery stores begins beyond Franklin Street, but the shopping in this mainly residential community seems drab compared to the vibrant Indian commerce in Jackson Heights.

However, another detour will bring you to one of the most authentic Indian sights in New York, the **Hindu Temple Society of North America (16),** 45-57 Bowne Street, (718) 460–8484. The temple, known as Sri Mha Vallabha Ganapti Devasthanam, is dedicated to the elephant-headed deity Ganesh, who is worshipped as the remover of obstacles. The stunning gray stone building with a pagoda, adorned with ornamental carvings, was mainly created in India and reassembled here in the 1970s. Carved elephants guard the stairway leading to the main entrance, and many deity figures wearing flower garlands adorn the incense-scented temple. Worshipers make offerings to the gods all during the day. Respectful visitors are welcome (be prepared to leave your shoes at the door when you enter), and the adjacent community center offers cultural programs and classes, including meditation and yoga. A canteen sells snacks and religious articles, and other shops are found near the temple.

Each year in August or September, depending on the lunar calendar, the temple is the scene of the Festival of Ganesh, a major event in India. The floor of the altar is covered with flower petals and offerings of fruit are placed before the statue of the god, who is lavishly adorned with flowers. At the end of the ceremonies, the worshipers parade a replica of Ganesh through Flushing on their way to the Flushing Meadow lake, where the traditional custom of immersing the god in the sea is carried out.

If the day is fine, better to save your Indian shopping for a visit to Jackson Heights and continue walking a few blocks farther to visit the **Queens Botanical Gardens (17),** 43-50 Main Street, (718) 886–3800; open Tuesday through Sunday 9:00 A.M. to 5:00 P.M.; donation requested. Trails wander through thirty-nine acres of seasonal displays, including gardens and a twenty-one-acre arboretum that was developed as a horticultural exhibit for the 1964 New York World's Fair. The garden is a green oasis in the middle of Flushing that attracts more than 300,000 visitors each year.

A footbridge in the arboretum provides access to Flushing Meadows Corona Park and its many attractions.

Historic Flushing

To find Historic Flushing, follow Main Street south about 4 blocks from Roosevelt Avenue to Northern Boulevard and turn right. In less than a block, you'll be in front of the Flushing **Quaker Meeting House (H1)**, 137-16 Northern Boulevard, (718) 358–9636, a simple wooden building begun in 1694, with additions made from 1716 to 1719. It is New York City's oldest structure in continuous use for religious services. A sign in several languages invites everyone to Sunday silent prayer.

Across the road on the corner of Linden Place you'll see the **Flushing Town Hall (H2)**, 137-35 Northern Boulevard, (718) 463–7700; open Monday to Friday 10:00 A.M. to 4:30 P.M., Saturday and Sunday noon to 5:00 P.M.; no admission charge. The masonry building in German-inspired Romanesque Revival style was built in 1862. Before the consolidation of New York City in 1898, every town had such a building; this is one of the oldest remaining. It is now headquarters for the Flushing Council on Culture and the Arts. It is enjoying a major restoration as a cultural center, with exhibits and many other events scheduled, including an opera series with the New York Grand Opera. A Grand Hall upstairs has been reno-vated as space for the performing arts.

Continue walking to Bowne Street and turn right for more history. The **John Bowne House (H3)**, 3701 Bowne Street, (718) 539–0528; open Tuesday, Saturday, and Sunday 2:30 to 4:30 P.M.; admission is $2.00 for adults and $1.00 for children (includes the Kingsland Homestead).

This is the oldest-surviving structure in Queens and one of the oldest in New York City. Bowne was arrested in 1662 for permitting Quakers to hold meetings in his home, but he was acquitted after appealing to the Dutch government in Holland, thus establishing the right of freedom of worship.

The **Kingsland Homestead (H4)**, 143-35 37th Avenue, (718) 939–0647, is the headquarters of the Queens Historical Society; open Tuesday, Saturday, and Sunday 2:30 to 4:30 P.M. The two-story home with a gambrel roof is the second-oldest home in Flushing; it was moved to this site from its original location when it was threatened by development. The original

shingles laid over the exterior in 1805 remain on three sides of the house. Restored in 1996, it features exhibitions from the collection of the Historical Society on the main floor. A second-floor parlor is decorated as if it belonged to a middle-class Victorian home. The Society presents frequent programs and walking tours.

Chinese Cuisine

(See Chinatown, page 175)

R E C O M M E N D E D ||◉|| R E S T A U R A N T S

Be forewarned—many restaurants in Chinese Flushing are big and noisy, Hong Kong–style. Many smaller restaurants accept cash only, so come prepared.

Joe's Shanghai (A) ($–$$), 136-21 37th Avenue, (718) 539–3838. This is the original that has inspired two clones in Manhattan. It is always packed with diners craving the delicious pork or crab soup dumplings (listed on the menu as "steamed buns"). There's a full menu of Shanghai specialties as well.

Sweet 'n' Tart Cafe (B) ($), 136-13 38th Avenue, (718) 661–3380, a fast-service cafe with noodle soups, dim sum, and specializing in Chinese dessert soups known as tong shui.

Jade Palace (C) ($–$$), 136-14 38th Avenue, (718) 353–3366, is big, bustling, and filled with Asians as well as visitors who appreciate the large and authentic variety of Chinese dim sum.

Sichuan Dynasty (D) ($–$$), 135-32 40th Road, (718) 961–7500, one of a slew of choices on 40th Road's "restaurant row," is one of the most authentic opportunities to sample spicy Sichuan fare, sure to please those who like it hot. It offers a nice feature for couples, "family dinners" that allow a choice of three dishes ($16.95 at press time), more than enough food for two, so you can taste a trio of specialties without having to order whole platters.

Gou-Bu-Li (E) ($), 135-28 40th Road, (718) 886–2121, is the only

U.S. branch of a very popular chain of cafes in China specializing in bo zu, stuffed steamed buns, sealed with the pleat that shows the maker is a master of the dish. The soft chewy buns come with half a dozen fillings including minced vegetables, pork, lamb, red bean, beef, cabbage, and pork. A cup of broth comes along with a bamboo steamer bearing eight to a dozen of these tasty morsels. A regular Chinese menu is also available, including a selection of dumplings and many kinds of soup with noodles.

Yang Tze River (F) ($–$$), 135-21 40th Road, (718) 353–8500, has a wide menu of specialties, from chicken with sizzling rice to jumbo shrimp with chili sauce to sautéed fresh eel Shanghai style, plus a long list of noodle soups and rice-based dishes. This is another place offering "family dinners," a choice of three dishes from a list of about sixty, for $16.95.

Shanghai Tide (G) ($–$$), 135-20 40th Road, (718) 661–0900, is an attractive spot with fish tanks, Chinese flute music, and photos of old Shanghai. The interesting Shanghai-style menu features dishes such as wined crabs, fried yellow fish with seaweed, and pork shoulder in a soy and ginger sauce on a bed of greens.

East Buffet (H) ($$$; full buffet), 42-07 Main Street, (718) 353–6333 offers an all-you-can-eat buffet that will satisfy every taste, with separate stations for sushi, dim sum, soups, noodles, Peking duck, Asian barbecue, all kinds of Chinese dishes, and satay, plus desserts and fruits. The prix-fixe dinner gives the chance to sample dishes like shark's fin soup and Peking duck that go for premium prices in most restaurants.

East Lake (I) ($–$$), 42-33 Main Street, (718) 539–8532, big and busy, a highly rated favorite in the quarters of a former diner. This restaurant is known for dim sum as well as excellent dinners including minced lobster, shrimp with asparagus, and braised abalone in oyster sauce.

KOREAN FLUSHING

Though they are fairly new arrivals in the overall scheme of things, industrious Koreans have become one of the most visible groups in New York. Their produce shops brighten the streetscape, and their dry-cleaning establishments and manicure parlors are found everywhere in the city.

The earliest arrivals from Asia (before the Act of 1924 barred the entry of Asians) were Protestants, students, and political refugees who opposed the Japanese takeover of Korea. A second influx of students came after the Korean War, many staying after their studies to become influential leaders in the Flushing community. Even larger numbers arrived after the new Immigration Act of 1965, including many who were well educated and well able to make their way in a new country.

The Korean population in New York City grew 24 percent from 1990 to 2000, rising from 67,718 to 86,473. According to census figures, more than three quarters of that increase was in Queens. The Korean community has its own newspaper plus English editions of three Korean-language newspapers and three radio stations and three television stations that broadcast news and South Korean entertainment programs. Nearly 400 Korean Protestant churches have been established as well as a few Korean Catholic churches and a dozen or so Buddhist temples.

The well-organized Koreans have also formed many associations, the most importing being the revolving-credit associations known as *kye*, which provide business capital and assistance for those starting businesses. The Korean Produce Retailers Association maintains its headquarters in Flushing, providing group insurance, tax guides, legal services, and seminars to members. The Association was also responsible for the first Chusok, a festival of thanksgiving now held annually at Flushing Meadow Park on the fifteenth day of the eighth lunar month in Korea, corresponding to a New York Sunday in October.

As the largest Korean settlement in New York, Flushing is perhaps the most important Korean center in the country, a business, shopping, and social hub. Korean brides come here to shop for their gowns, newcomers take English lessons, and shopkeepers open businesses geared to the community.

● ● ●   𝒜 𝒮𝒽𝑜𝓅𝓅𝒾𝓃𝑔 𝒯𝑜𝓊𝓇   ● ● ●

One long block past Main Street is Union Street, Flushing's Korean "main street," unmistakable since it is bedecked with dozens of signs in Korean. Compared to Flushing's sprawling Chinatown, Union Street shopping seems a tight little world. Tiny shops fill the blocks between Northern Boulevard and 39th Street and spill onto the side streets. A three-story complex at 37th Avenue is jam-packed with businesses and dozens of signs in Korean. The wares range from wedding gowns to cosmetics, stylish women's clothing to Italian fashions for men. Emporiums such as Wedding Dress—Tuxedo, 36-14

Union, (718) 359–1187, make for interesting browsing, since they feature both American and traditional Korean bridal costumes. A shop at 37-13 Union Street also features traditional costumes in the window. The best bet here is to window-shop and enter the shops that interest you. There are small bakeries and cafes here as well.

If you want a break, stop into the big, bright **Koryodang Bakery (18),** 39-02 Union Street (at the corner of 39th Avenue), (718) 762–6557, where you can see all the tempting sweets displayed. Another interesting stop is **Magicastle (19),** 136-80 39th Avenue, (718) 888–9843, stocking many Korean gifts, including a host of charming miniature figures in traditional dress.

There are two big Korean food markets within easy reach. **Han Ah Reum (20),** 141-40 Northern Boulevard (1 block past Union Street), (718) 358–0700, is the same chain as the big store on 32nd Street in Manhattan; it has all the offerings described on page 223. **Korea Town Plaza (21),** (also known as Assi Plaza) 131-01 39th Avenue, (718) 321–8000, west of Prince Street, is located in a former manufacturing neighborhood that is now beginning to develop commercially. This is a vast supermarket where you will find every conceivable type of Korean food, another good place to stock up before you head home.

Korean Cuisine

Korean foods are less well known than those of many other Asian countries, so dining here can be a happy adventure, particularly if the menu is Korean and the waiter does not speak much English!

Maybe because they come from a country with cold winters, Koreans like hot and spicy food, using lavish amounts of garlic as well as soy, chilis, pepper, and ginger. But those who don't like it hot need not worry—the most distinctive Korean dish is barbecue, thinly sliced and delicately marinated steak or short ribs, usually cooked by the diner on a grill brought to the table. It's likely to please every palate. Some restaurants today use portable propane grills instead of charcoal braziers, but the real thing tastes better, and it all seems better when you cook it yourself right at your table.

Besides barbecue, typical dishes include hot casseroles—all-in-one-meals sometimes served in a stoneware pot—and dishes made with neng myun, traditional Korean noodles.

A universal Korean custom is the serving of panchan, six to eight small dishes that come with every meal, a mixture of hot and cold, sweet and sour. These may include sprouts, squash, or spinach in sesame oil, dried squid or shrimp sometimes served on a bed of spinach, bean sprouts, grated turnip or radish, or something as familiar as potato salad. There is always kimchi, a pickled cabbage that is a Korean staple, important enough to have its own museum in Seoul devoted to the history and preparation of the dish. There is no single kimchi recipe—each cook has his or her own. Korean markets may have a dozen kinds of kimchi, from lightly spiced to burning hot.

A Typical Korean Meal

Panchan (a selection of appetizers served automatically with every Korean meal)

Mandoo (dumplings)

Korean barbecue (bulgogi) or a dish with rice and meat like bibambap

Fresh fruit

Though the Japanese are traditional rivals, Koreans have adapted some of their dishes, notably sushi. Most New York Korean restaurants have a sushi bar, perhaps as a way to attract diners who are not as familiar with Korean foods.

A KOREAN SAMPLER

Here are some of the dishes you'll likely see on a Korean menu, though spelling may vary slightly from place to place:

Bibambap: a rice dish topped with chopped or slivered beef, vegetables, egg, and hoisin or chili sauce. Served separately, but meant to be mixed together by the diner.

Bindaeduk: pancakes.

Bulgogi: the best-known Korean dish, thinly sliced steak marinated in soy sauce, sesame oil, garlic, and a little sugar, and grilled. It is served in many restaurants with crisp lettuce leaves. Meat slices are wrapped in the leaf, along with a dab of rice and sauce to form a tasty sandwich eaten with your hands.

Table barbecue dishes may also include Bulgalbi, short ribs cut into 2- or 3-inch lengths; sae-woo gui, jumbo shrimp; yum-eah gui, salmon; daeh-ju bulgogi, pork loin, and many other variations.

Kalbi: short ribs marinated and served in beef broth.

Kom t'ang: a long-simmered beef soup.

Man-Du or **Mandoo:** dumplings, may be steamed or fried.

Neng myun: cold, very thin noodles, a Korean favorite, sometimes served with sliced beef or fish and vegetables or kimchee, often in a broth.

Pajon: a good dish to be shared, a scallion and seafood pancake the size of a small pizza.

R ECOMMENDED 🍽 R ESTAURANTS

All of these establishments are open twenty-four hours a day!

Kum Gang San (J) ($$), 138-28 Northern Boulevard, (718) 461–0909. You'll find a waterfall and wooden bridge a la Seoul and a piano to provide background music while you cook your own dinner at this large, popular, and reliable restaurant.

Woo Chon (K) ($$), 41-19 Kissena Boulevard, (718) 463–0803, more great do-it-yourself barbecue and a photo menu that makes ordering easier.

Shin Jung (L) ($–$$), 136-33 37th Avenue, (718) 460–5026, a long-established neighborhood favorite, offers a serene setting with classical music in the background to accompany a full Korean menu, including table BBQ, noodles, casseroles, bibambap, mandoo, and pancakes. The proprietor is from North Korea and offers specialties from her home region.

Bombay to Buenos Aires in Jackson Heights

Jackson Heights is New York's melting pot at its most vibrant. Step off the subway at 74th Street and you'll almost feel like you are in India. The street is filled with shops selling brilliantly hued saris and lavish gold jewelry, and the markets are jammed with exotic grains and spices.

Keep walking, and the scene shifts to Latin America. Pulsating rhythms pour out of the record stores, and cafes promise (and deliver) authentic foods from Peru, Colombia, Ecuador, Uruguay, and Mexico.

To add to the pleasures of a visit, this is one of the city's most interesting neighborhoods, with an attractive 30-block Historic District just down the block from the ethnic shops.

THE HISTORY

The unique development of Jackson Heights began in 1909 with the completion of the Queensborough Bridge and intensified after the arrival of the IRT #7 Train in 1917. It was initiated by one man, Edward McDougall, a developer. In 1909, inspired by the Garden City movement that he had seen in England and other European

How to Get There

By subway: Roosevelt Avenue and 74th Street, the heart of
Little India, is the start of a shopping tour. Take the E, F, G, or
R Train to Roosevelt Avenue or the #7 Train to 74th Street and
Broadway, less than a block away. It is about fifteen minutes from
Midtown Manhattan.

By car: Take the Brooklyn–Queens Expressway to Roosevelt
Avenue. From the Triboro or Bronx–Whitestone Bridge,
get off at Broadway and turn right onto
Roosevelt Avenue.

countries, McDougall bought up six farms totaling about 350 acres
and formed the Queensboro Corporation. With architects George
Wells and Andrew Thomas, MacDougall helped adapt "Garden City"
principles to the practicalities of New York, erecting buildings set
back from the street and built around the perimeter of the block, with
landscaped gardens and courtyards in front and in the rear. They
were the first "garden apartments" in the United States, a pattern
that would be emulated throughout the country.

These also were the first apartment buildings with automatic elevators, allowing them to be six stories rather than the usual four of
that era. Many of the apartments were sold as cooperatives, the first
such buildings for the middle class, setting a precedent for the city.

The Depression years of the 1930s led the Queensboro
Corporation to build more traditional buildings on its vacant lots. By
the 1950s almost all the undeveloped land was gone.

After World War II the building boom throughout Queens took away the playgrounds, tennis courts, and golf courses that had been part of the gracious lifestyle in Jackson Heights. Old residents began moving to the suburbs, to be replaced in the 1970s and '80s by immigrants from other lands, particularly from India and Latin America, but with a growing number of Koreans as well.

Though Jackson Heights has felt its share of modern problems, particularly from the drug trade, it remains a desirable community with good shopping, attractive housing, and quick and easy access to Manhattan via several subway lines.

• • • *An Indian Shopping Tour* • • •

"Is this like Bombay?" someone asked our group leader. No, 74th Street is not really like India. There are no rickety "tuk-tuk" taxis, no temples, no beggars, no cows. But for a neighborhood fifteen minutes from Midtown Manhattan, it will surely do. Allow plenty of time for exploring this most intriguing enclave, mostly packed into a single long block and its environs. And plan on having a delicious lunch.

This is a street that dazzles, with wall-to-wall exotic shopping. Store windows are an Indian fashion parade. Some mannequins are wearing wraparound saris in the Hindu mode; others display caftans worn over pants, in the Muslim manner. Some garments are of cheap wash-and-wear synthetics in garish colors with too many spangles, while others are of fine silk fabrics, exquisitely embroidered—something for every taste and budget.

The jewelry must be seen to be believed. Whatever their economic status, Indian women believe in jewelry as the ultimate asset, and they want the best—only shiny twenty-two-carat gold will do. There are many shops showing lavish handmade, multistrand filigreed gold chains and dangle earrings. Some of the earrings are so heavy that they must be anchored over the back of the ear and pinned into the hair. All the jewelry shop windows are so tempting that it is impossible to recommend one store; just pick the ones whose displays please you most. Inside, you may find a family with the matriarch and a shy young bride examining the gold necklaces and bracelets that will be part of the traditional dowry for the bride, as much gold as her family can afford. A few shops feature necklaces inlaid with rubies or diamonds.

Several shops on the block display popular gifts to take home to the family in India or Pakistan, including blankets and electronics that work on 220 current.

When it comes to food, you'll notice that some markets and restaurants advertise BANGLA-INDO-PAK. These nationalities don't get along very well at home, but they coexist well here, happy to emphasize their similarities instead of differences.

Look down the block as you pass 37th Road to see the marquee of the **Eagle Cinema (1),** 73-07 37th Road, (718) 105–2800. This Art Deco–style survivor is now a showcase for popular Indian films

from the movie studios of Bombay, affectionately known as Bollywood. A typical Bollywood film involves comedy, music, lots of action, and madcap production numbers. There are no subtitles, but the plots are easy to follow. Samosas are sold alongside popcorn at the Eagle's refreshment stand.

Check out **INDO-US Books & Journals, Inc. (2),** 37-46 74th Street, (718) 899–5590, to see books and magazines in a dozen South Asian subcontinent languages plus English, as well as Indian videos, Buddhas and sitars, miniature elephants and incense burners, carved wooden screens and silver temple tables, ayurvedic herbs, and cooking utensils. This fascinating store makes good on its slogan, "Bringing India a step closer."

Across the road is **Patel Brothers Market (3),** 37-27 74th Street, (718) 898–3445, a giant Indian supermarket chain with U.S. branches in Chicago, Los Angeles, Atlanta, Detroit, and Houston. You can find just about everything here for Indian cookery. Farther down the block is the **India Sari Palace (4),** 37-07 74th Street, (718) 426–2700, the cream of 74th Street sari couture, with the finest stock of saris and prices up to $350. There is a bargain section where solid-color, low-quality silks from China sell for $10 or less. One counter sells the traditional loose men's shirts. The beautiful silk fabrics used to form a sari can also be lovely material for a Western-style dress. Also of special interest to Western shoppers are the Kashmiri shawls, made of the most exquisitely soft cashmere from Kashmir and costing around $200.

For some serious Indian food shopping, cross at 37th Avenue and proceed 1 block to **Subzi Mandi Market (5),** 72-30 37th Avenue, (718) 457–1848. This busy market feels more authentic than Patel Brothers. Outside, Indian ladies carefully inspect the heaping stands of seasonal vegetables—the duhdi squash; the daikon, which are long white radishes; and the eddo, a winter vegetable like potato or taro. In the summertime cartons of mangos await chutney-makers. Inside are shelf after shelf of legumes—lentils, black-eyed peas, kidney beans, lima beans, whole and split—all used to make the dal that is part of every Indian meal. There are endless shelves of spices as well, with turmeric, cardamom, fennel, cumin, cloves, and pepper, to name a few. You'll also find bins stocked with raisins and nuts and seeds, and with jars of ghee, the clarified butter that is commonly used in India. The store stocks a papadum bread made by a wives' cooperative in India, with a label that says SYMBOL OF WOMEN'S STRENGTH. It's the rare browser who leaves this store without a purchase.

Across the street is the unpromising facade of **Rajbhog Sweets (6)**, 72-27 37th Avenue, (718) 458–8512, hiding one of the area's best vegetarian shops and one of the most popular Indian catering firms. "Sweets" here also means snacks, and they make an unbeliev-able number of tasty ones, using chickpea flour and vegetables, sweet or bland or spicy. There are steamed, stuffed doughs that reminded me of Jewish knishes, little fried balls nicely seasoned with spices, even something made of a squash called duhdi that tastes like a candy. This is mostly a take-out shop, so you can buy an assortment of snacks to try at home. But there are a few tables in the back if you want to have a unique lunch—just point and ask for a selection.

Indian Cuisine

It would take at least an entire book to describe the range of cui-sine of a vast country with so many different food traditions in each region. One thing all regions have in common is the skilled blending of spices. Here's one example of the Indian approach from the excel-lent book *Indian Cooking* by Madhur Jaffrey: "We can give a great variety to, say, a vegetable like a potato, not only by methods such as boiling, baking and roasting but by cooking it with whole cumin one time, a combination of ground cumin and roasted fennel seeds another time and black pepper a third time. The permutations become endless, as does the possibility of variety in tastes."

The spices most commonly used in Indian cooking are ginger root, garlic, cumin, cardamom, turmeric, cloves, cinnamon, mustard seed, and fresh coriander. Because spices are so important, good cooks prefer to buy them whole and do their own grinding.

Curry does not mean one spice as we buy it in a little tin, but simply a dish made with sauce. In India each cook has his or her own special blend. Curries can be green or red and may or may not be highly spiced.

Lamb, goat, chicken, and seafood are the most common meats used in Indian cuisine, and Indian restaurants also serve many vegetarian dishes, since Hindus do not eat beef and Muslims do not eat pork.

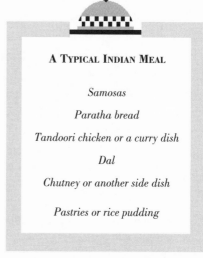

A Typical Indian Meal

Samosas

Paratha bread

Tandoori chicken or a curry dish

Dal

Chutney or another side dish

Pastries or rice pudding

AN INDIAN SAMPLER

The names of many dishes refer to the spices used. Here are some popular Indian dishes found in many restaurants:

Basmati rice: an Indian long-grain rice with a rich, nutty flavor and distinctive fragrance.

Biryani: a slightly sweet rice dish, usually flavored with saffron and cooked with raisins and nuts; may be made with meat or fish.

Chat papri: a tasty appetizer mix of crisps, potatoes, and chickpeas in a yogurt and tamarind sauce.

Dal or dhal: a legume such as lentils, beans, or split peas cooked with spices.

Dosa or dosai: crepes of rice flour served plain with chutney or filled with potatoes, peas, and nuts.

Kebabs: meat, chicken, seafood, or vegetables cooked and served on skewers.

Kheer or khir: a creamy rice pudding with raisins and dried fruits.

Korma: braised meat, chicken, or vegetables in a mild cream sauce made with yogurt.

Masala: a slightly sweet seasoning for many dishes. Garam masala, a popular version, is made from a mix of spices that includes cardamom, cinnamon, cumin seeds, cloves, peppercorns, and nutmeg. Some are made with coriander and turmeric.

Lassi: a refreshing drink made with yogurt; may be plain, sweet, salted or flavored with fruit.

Pakora: savory deep-fried appetizers.

Paneer: cheese.

Sag paneer: a tasty blend of spinach with small cubes of cheese.

Samosas: crisp fried turnovers filled with peas, potatoes, and sometimes meat; a popular snack or appetizer.

Tandoori: tandoori dishes are marinated in yogurt and mild spices and cooked in a deep clay oven, traditionally heated by charcoal or wood. The oven holds in heat, which builds up to high intensity, allowing a whole chicken to be cooked in a short time, with juices and flavors sealed in. The typical red color of these dishes is not from the oven but from food coloring.

Tikka: means that the chicken or fish in the dish is cut into small pieces.

Vindaloo: A hot, spicy, vinegar-based curry.

Indian Breads:

All the following except for crisp breads are baked in a tandoori oven:

Nan: a soft, pancake-shaped bread cooked on the inside wall of a tandoori oven, served puffy and delicious.

Papadum: a crisp, highly seasoned flatbread made from lentil flour.

Paratha: a chewy bread usually made from whole wheat; may be stuffed with vegetables or minced lamb.

Roti: a flat, soft bread made from whole wheat.

Indian Side Dishes:

Many kinds of relishes and small side dishes are served with an Indian meal. Here are a few:

Bhurtas: savory vegetables, typically potato or eggplant, mixed with other vegetables and spices.

Chutney: Sweet-and-sour fruit chutneys may be made from peach, mango, apricot, or apple; they have the consistency of preserves. Mint chutney is served with roasted meats.

Raitas: yogurt-based side dishes. Yogurt flavored with cucumber and cumin is a popular version.

R E C O M M E N D E D 🍴 R E S T A U R A N T S

Jackson Diner (A) ($), 37-47 74th Street, (718) 672–1232. It has moved to larger, more attractive quarters than the original plain diner, but it's still the food that brings the crowds to this unpretentious place. Many consider it the best Indian restaurant in New York. The $7.50 all-you-can-eat lunch buffet is a fabulous way to sample the riches.

Delhi Palace (B) ($–$$), 37-33 74th Street, (718) 507–0666. The setting here is more inviting, with colorful murals of village life, high-back chairs, and lucite tabletops decorated with fresh flowers. The recommended dishes are the curries, which come in many varieties.

Rajbhog Sweets (C) ($–$$), 72-27 37th Avenue. See **(6)** on page 146.

Shaheen (D) ($–$$), 72-09 Broadway, (718) 639–4791. This large dining room was the first Indian restaurant in the neighborhood, opened in 1972. Sweets from the bakery supply many restaurants and stores in the metropolitan area and are shipped throughout the United States. You can order pastries with coffee or tea to eat here, or buy them by the pound to go.

. . . *A Latin American Shopping Tour* . . .

At the end of the Indian block of 74th Street, turn right onto 37th Avenue. This peaceful shopping street has a mix of restaurants and lots of everyday shopping, but you'll soon see the Latin American influence. The largest Latino presence in Jackson Heights is Colombian. Government violence, unemployment, and overcrowding combined to created a huge middle-class exodus from Colombia in the 1950s to 1970s; the Colombian population of Jackson Heights alone has been estimated at more than 300,000. Colombians have established their own newspapers, soccer leagues, and social clubs.

But Colombians share the neighborhood with many other nationalities. One of the first restaurants you'll come to is the Argentinian La Porteña (see page 158).

On the next block is Las Brasas, the only restaurant on the avenue featuring the foods and music of Spain. Detour left onto 80th Street and come back on 81st Street and on 85th to 86th Streets to see some of the most interesting buildings in the Historic District.

Stop when you see the shop **El Dorado (7),** 81-07 37th Avenue, (718) 458–8820. For while the sign says Perfumeria, the shop also has a whole wall of delightful crafts from Latin America, including miniature houses and cantinas, delightful in their detail.

Ahead on 37th Avenue are several restaurants specializing in the grilled meats and poultry of Argentina and the distinctive dishes of Colombia, Ecuador, and Peru. Stop at **La Nueva Bakery (8),** 86-10 37th Avenue, (718) 507–2339, for a tempting array of foods to take home—empanadas, corn sticks, cheese bread, and desserts such as flan, churros, and rice pudding.

Now turn right onto 89th Street and then right again onto Roosevelt Avenue. The scene under the #7 El tracks is far different from tranquil 37th Avenue. Vying with the periodic rumbling of the train, loudspeakers blare Latin music. Shops offer the frilly dresses that many Latin mothers like for their little girls, and cowboy boots for big and little gauchos. Venders sell hot churros—sugared fried dough—four for a dollar, to be eaten on the spot.

The upper 80s on Roosevelt Avenue is mainly Mexican, with shops such as **Zapateria Mexico, (9),** 88-07 Roosevelt Avenue, (718) 899–1742, selling Mexican boots, belts and buckles, saddles, fancy shirts, and sombreros.

The **Mexicana Bakery (10),** 88-04 Roosevelt Avenue, (718) 507–6381, is not only a bakery but also a well-stocked grocery, with beans, salsas, spices, hot sauce, and a dozen kinds of peppers, plus glittery mariachi outfits, piñatas, and other gifts all packed into a tiny space.

At 84th Street, stop into the Roosevelt Shopping Center and visit the little shop of **Rudy Volcano (11),** 84-02 Roosevelt Avenue, (718) 651–7100, filled with colorful work of the artisans of Guatemala, from clothing to crafts.

If you want to see how well everyone gets along, notice the awning of **Los Paisanos (12),** 79-16 Roosevelt Avenue, (718) 898–4141. It

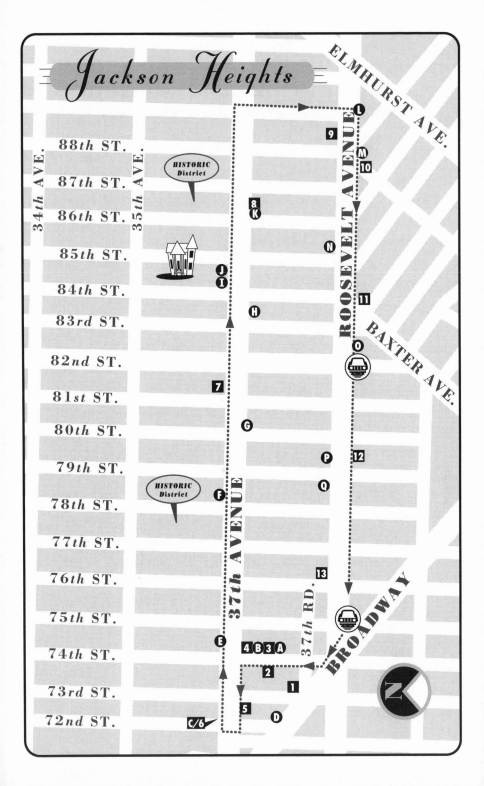

promises imported *productos típicos* from Ecuador, Peru, Colombia, Mexico, and Central America, with flags for each nation to prove the point.

You'll make your own discoveries as you stroll. If the beat on the loudspeakers puts you in the mood for music, **Rincon Musical (13),** 76-11 Roosevelt Avenue, (718) 651–8460, offers an enormous selection of favorites from every Latin country.

Back at the #7 Station on 74th Street, you've completed a two-continent tour in less than 20 blocks—and you haven't even begun to explore the Asian neighborhoods of Jackson Heights!

Latin American Cuisine

The cuisine of Latin American countries has been influenced both by the heritage of indigenous peoples and by the Spanish and other Europeans who ruled there for many years. There are many dishes in common, though each country retains its own specialties.

Mexican and Peruvian menus have the most Indian influence and have in common a variety of chilis used as flavoring. Grilled meats and rotisserie chicken are favorites in many South American lands and are specialties in Argentinean and Colombian restaurants. Many restaurants have rows of chickens cooking on spits in the window.

Since ovens were once a relative luxury, traditional one-pot dishes

The Jackson Heights Historic District

Much of the area from 76th Street to 88th Street between Roosevelt Avenue and Northern Boulevard was declared a Historic District in 1993. These were the first garden apartments in the United States, setting a pattern that was the standard for residential building for years to come. This planned community also established the principle that urban planning is about the full city block rather than the individual building or lot. The concept of a block of apartments with shared undivided rear gardens was initiated in 1921 on 84th and 85th Streets between 37th and Roosevelt Avenues. It reached its peak with the Cambridge Court on 85th and 86th Streets and the Chateau and Towers, a particularly attractive slate-roofed complex on 80th and 81st Streets.

"English-garden homes" for one or two families were added between 1924 and 1928 for those who wished private homes, with combined backyards leading to garages designed in the same style of the houses. The result is what architecture critic Robert A. M. Stern called a "mix of urbane apartment and rowhouses . . . a modern urban suburbia that demonstrates as none have since, what high density housing in the city should be."

The architecture is a mix of European influences—brick buildings with stucco, half timber, slate, ironwork, and terracotta embellishments. Rather than attempting to maintain a specific style, the developers were creating a promise of "the good and gracious life." This included exclusion of what the majority of buyers would define as "undesirable" neighbors—this part of Jackson Heights did not welcome Jews, Catholics, or people of color for many years.

The last garden apartments went up in 1939 on the blocks between 78th and 79th Streets and 34th and 35th Avenues, with more modern architecture.

cooked on top of the stove like stews are also popular, and soups are hearty. Organ meats are common, especially tripe.

Peruvian dishes are distinctive in the use of coriander, which is not typical in neighboring countries. Peruvian seafood dishes are excellent, as are potato dishes, such as Papa a la Huancaina—

A TYPICAL LATIN-AMERICAN MEAL

Empanadas or seviche

Arepas

Grilled meat or chicken

Cassava

Flan

potatoes in slightly spicy cheese sauce, usually served as an appetizer.

Most restaurants offer platters with a variety of typical dishes, one of the best ways to sample the cuisine. In Colombian restaurants, these are sometimes called mountain platters, because the portions are so enormous. Most Jackson Heights restaurants have translations on the menu to make it easier to order.

A LATIN AMERICAN SAMPLER

Here are some dishes found on many Latin American menus:

Arepas: grilled corn cakes, crisp on the outside, doughy inside.

Arroz: rice.

Arroz con pollo: chicken and rice.

Bacalao: dried, salted codfish, used in many dishes.

Bistek: beefsteak, usually flank steak.

Calabaza: green pumpkin, a winter squash.

Camarones: shrimp.

Carne asada: grilled or roasted marinated steak.

Cassava: a starchy root boiled as a potato substitute or ground as flour; the plant is also the source of tapioca.

Ceviche or **seviche:** raw seafood that has been marinated in citrus juice until firm, then tossed with chilis, onions, tomatoes, and cilantro.

Chicha: a slightly alcoholic, beerlike drink made from dried corn.

Chicharron: pork bellies or pork skins, deep-fried.

Chorizo: Spanish-style hot, spicy pork sausages.

Churrasco: skirt steak.

Churros: long, slim cakes similar to doughnuts in taste; dough fried and dusted with sugar.

Corvina: striped bass.

Empanadas: turnovers, usually pastry dough stuffed with ground beef, vegetables, and spices, but may have other fillings as well. Small sizes are used for cocktails; larger ones for first courses and snacks.

Flan: caramel-flavored custard.

Frijoles: beans.

Morcilla: black sausage.

Pargo: red snapper.

Pescado: fish.

Plantain: a fruit similar to bananas, but not as sweet.

Pollo: chicken.

Queso: cheese.

Sierra: mackerel.

Sopa: soup.

Sopa de garbanzo: chickpea soup.

Taro: an edible root vegetable.

Yuca: a cactus-family starchy vegetable.

A MEXICAN SAMPLER

Burritos: large, soft tortillas amply stuffed with meats and a variety of ingredients.

Chimichangas: similar to burritos, but rolled and deep fried, usually served with sour cream.

Enchiladas: fried corn tortillas wrapped around fillings of meat and cheese, covered with a chili sauce.

Fajitas: grilled strips of beef or chicken served with onions, peppers and chilies, often served on a sizzling platter with sour cream and guacamole on the side, and accompanied by tortillas to wrap around the fillings.

Guacamole: avocado, tomatoes, chilis, and seasonings mashed into a cold spread, often served with tortilla or corn chips.

Mole: a sauce made of hot peppers and bitter chocolate.

Quesadilla: a tortilla filled with cheese, beans, meat, or vegetables, folded and heated on a griddle.

Taco: a tortilla stuffed and rolled; the tortilla may be soft or fried until crisp.

Tamales: chopped meat wrapped in corn-flour dough, put into maize husks and steamed.

Tortillas: small, flat pancakes made with corn flour.

Tostadas: flat tortillas fried until crisp and topped with poultry, meat, or fish, lettuce, chili sauce, etc.

RECOMMENDED 🍴 RESTAURANTS

La Porteña (E) ($–$$), 74-25 37th Avenue, (718) 458–8111. The name means an inhabitant of Buenos Aires and the menu features Argentinean grilled meats. You can watch the chef at work in the window. The mixed-grill platter (parrillada) is enormous. For dessert try a flaming crepe.

Las Brasas (F) ($–$$), 78-23 37th Avenue, (718) 426–7272, is a bit of authentic Spain, with a tapas bar, dishes like paella, and flamenco guitar music on weekends.

La Boina Roja (G) ($–$$), 80-22 37th Avenue, (718) 424–6711, is a big, attractive Colombian steak house that specializes in charcoaled meats, though many other typical dishes are also on the menu. The name means "red beret," and the waitstaff is appropriately attired.

Pollos a la Brasa Mario (H) ($–$$), 83-02 37th Avenue, (718) 457–8800, also at 81-01 Roosevelt Avenue, (718) 639–5555, has colorful Latin American architecture and decor, making these two Colombian rotisserie restaurants particularly pleasant. In the window you can see the specialty, rows of succulent poultry roasting on spits. Tasty side dishes include beans, corn cakes, and plantains, and there are combination platters if chicken doesn't appeal.

La Picada Azuaya Restaurant (I) ($–$$), 84-19 37th Avenue, (718) 424–9797, offering dishes of Ecuador, has combination plates (such as Picada Azuaya, a platter of chicken, beef, shrimp, and plantains with salad) that let you sample several typical dishes. Appetizing house specials include hornado, roasted pork served with white hominy and potatoes.

Chifa (J) ($), 84-10 37th Avenue, (718) 396–0835, boasts that it serves New York's best

A TYPICAL MEXICAN MEAL

Guacamole

Chicken mole or a tortilla-based dish such as a quesadilla

Deep-fried, sugar-dusted pastries

Peruvian chicken, and no one has come forth to argue the claim. The menu also offers nearly twenty kinds of "typical plates" to let you sample the local cuisine.

Inti Raymi (K) ($–$$), 86-14 37th Avenue, (718) 424–1938, a Peruvian restaurant in business for more than twenty years, is one of the area's best. It has authentic atmosphere, with a pre-Columbian gold figure in the window, stucco walls hung with paintings of village scenes, and Incan tile designs in the ceiling. The menu features many unique native dishes, particularly seco de carne, a Peruvian beef stew in a cilantro-flavored sauce. Order it over tacu tacu, a delicious combination of rice and beans. And don't miss the chupe de pescado, a Peruvian fish chowder, thick with chunks of grilled fish. It's almost a meal in itself.

Plaza Garibaldi (L) ($–$$), 89-12 Roosevelt Avenue, (718) 651–9722, is a lively Mexican restaurant with music on weekends.

Tacos Mexico (M) ($–$$), 88-12 Roosevelt Avenue, (718) 899–5800, as the name suggests, is Mexican fast food, for natives who know how it should be done.

Guadalajara de la Noche (N) ($–$$), 85-09 Roosevelt Avenue, (718) 898–4967, promises *comida típica*, authentic food and music of Mexico.

Tierras Colombianas (O) ($–$$), 82-18 Roosevelt Avenue, (718) 426–8868, gets good reviews for generous portions of Colombian-style meats and seafood. Recommended dishes include lentil and oxtail soups, broiled porgy or snapper, grilled rib-eye steak, and the "mountain plate" of chopped beef, fried pork, beans, plantains, and arepas. Guaranteed, you won't go away hungry.

The #7 Train:
The International Express

When the White House Millennium Council was selecting routes representing the best of America, they chose only one train route as a National Millennium Trail, the #7 Subway between Manhattan and Queens, which has been dubbed "The International Express."

Along this train route is the most vibrant and varied collection of ethnic communities in New York and perhaps in the nation. When the tracks were laid in the early 1900s, Queens was a rural borough, but it developed rapidly as the train line gave the many immigrants crowded into Manhattan an opportunity for a better life while still having easy access to jobs in the city. The first pioneers settled near the train and opened familiar bakeries, groceries, clothing stores, and restaurants representative of their cultures. As the numbers of people grew, so did the shops. Even those who have prospered and moved on to the suburbs frequently return to shop and dine in these authentic neighborhoods.

The Queens chapters in this book offer walking tours of the largest of the communities along the #7 route, Jackson Heights and Flushing. But a wealth of riches await at every stop of the train, in ethnic enclaves so compact they do not require a map or a walking tour. All you need is a $4.00 Fun Pass, allowing unlimited subway rides for a one-day tour around the world. Hop off at 40th Street in Sunnyside or 61st Street in Woodside and explore the Irish bakeries, diners, and pubs nearby. Take the 46th Street exit for a taste of the Middle East, or the 69th Street stop to sample the pastries, foods, and music of the Philippines. At the 111th Street Station, watch the bocce games in William E. Moore Park on 108th Street, fondly known locally as "Spaghetti Park," stock up on cheeses and sausages, and have an authentic Italian ice at the Lemon Ice King of Corona.

To lead the way, the Queens Council on the Arts has published a booklet, The International Express, with descriptions and addresses of some of the most interesting ethnic stops at each station on the #7 Line. It can be ordered by mail for $1.00 from Queens Council on the Arts, 79-01 Park Lane South, Woodhaven, NY 11421.

Cositas Ricas (P) ($–$$), 79-19 Roosevelt Avenue, (718) 478–1500, is a bit of everything—counter coffee shop, soda fountain, bakery, restaurant, and steakhouse. Whether you order a mango milkshake or a skirt steak, it will please, and the pastries for sale under the sign PANADERIA (bakery) will provide a treat when you get home.

Chibcha (Q) ($–$$), 79-05 Roosevelt Avenue, (718) 429–9033, a nightclub named after a Colombian Indian tribe, has a menu mixing Colombian and Continental cuisines and a live show after dinner at 11:00 P.M. on Friday and Saturday.

Two restaurants beyond the bounds of this tour but well recommended are La Cabaña Argentina, 95-51 Roosevelt Avenue, (718) 429–4388, featuring grilled meats and other Argentinean cuisine, and La Espiga Bakery, 42-13 102nd Street, Corona, (718) 779–7898, a Mexican market/cafe.

Manhattan

Many of Manhattan's ethnic neighborhoods are
dwindling, as immigrants move up and out and gentrification does away with old landmarks. But if you
take the time to explore, you can still travel from
Kiev to Seoul, from Budapest to America's largest
Chinatown—all on the streets of Manhattan.

Chinatown . . .
and More Chinatown

Crowded with tourists, packed with shoppers haggling in Chinese, overflowing with exotic foods at bargain prices, Chinatown remains authentic even though it is a mecca for visitors. While other immigrant neighborhoods are shrinking in Manhattan, this one is growing by leaps and bounds. Most of the people crowding the streets really live here, often in apartments so small that they have little storage, requiring that they shop for food every day. They insist on absolutely fresh goods and good prices from vendors. Visitors can share the bounty.

It has been estimated that Chinatown holds an astounding 200 restaurants, from hole-in-the-wall to giant, glittery palaces, and there are dozens of gift shops with everything from back scratchers to fine antiques. It's a trip that you can make again and again, with new discoveries every time.

How to Get There

By subway/bus: Take the N, R, #6, J, M, or Z Train to Canal Street. The M101-102 Bus also runs through Chinatown.

THE HISTORY

Chinese were late to arrive in New York City in large numbers. They numbered only slightly more than 2,000 when the Chinese Exclusion Act of 1882 prohibited new immigration and citizenship and prevented most men from bringing their families. Manhattan's Chinatown remained a tiny community, almost entirely male. They worked at menial jobs, such as in laundries, and began opening small restaurants with Americanized versions of their native foods.

The original settlement, bounded by Pell, Doyers, and lower Mott Streets, was an isolated, protective enclave where men socialized at teahouses or by gambling at mahjong. It was controlled by its own secret organizations, known as tongs. Some of these were simply family associations that provided loans and other assistance. Others were criminal fraternities, frequently at war with one another. Tiny crooked Doyers Street was called the "bloody angle," because enemies were lured there and set upon by gang members waiting around the bend.

In 1943, after China became a U.S. ally in World War II, the Exclusion Act was repealed; but there was still a quota of just 105 persons per year. It was not until the quota system was abolished in the 1960s that the numbers of Chinese immigrants grew substantially and the boundaries of Manhattan's Chinatown mushroomed.

New York was a popular destination because of the employment opportunities, especially in garment factories (which currently employ some 20,000 people). By the 1980s New York's Chinese population had surpassed San Francisco to become the largest Chinese community in the Western Hemisphere, estimated at well over 200,000. No longer only working class, it includes many wealthy newcomers from Taiwan and Hong Kong, though the majority of Chinatown's residents remain Cantonese.

Chinatown has become a city within the city, with innumerable banks, pharmacies, lawyers, and health clinics that cater to its population. Nine Chinese newspapers are now published daily in the city. Asian immigrants from Vietnam, the Philippines, Malaysia, and Thailand also have begun to share the ever-expanding boundaries of Manhattan's Chinatown. It is estimated that there are one million Asian Americans in the Tri-State Area (New York–New Jersey–Connecticut), half of them Chinese.

The burgeoning Chinese population has formed new communities in Queens and Brooklyn, but the original Chinatown is still the cultural, social, and recreational crossroads for most new immigrants and visitors, as well as for its longtime residents.

A Shopping / Walking Tour

A Chinatown tour covers history as well as a world of wonderful shopping and dining. From the Canal Street subway station, walk east on Canal Street to Mott Street, the heart of Chinatown. You'll see food stalls everywhere, stores with piles of fresh fish neatly displayed on beds of ice, shops with roasted ducks hanging in the window, and many banks (attesting to the current prosperity of the community). Just past Mulberry Street is a supermarket, **Kan Man (1),** 200 Canal Street, an enormous introduction to what lies ahead. The store is laden with tonics, teas, jellies, ginseng root, and vegetables of every size and shape; row upon row of sauces (all the basic Chinese sauces can be bought ready-made); pork buns ready for the steamer; a big section of meats and fish; and dried oysters, shrimp, mussels, and mushrooms. Dried foods are popular because they need no refrigeration; soaking is all it takes to make them ready for cooking.

Downstairs are big stocks of kitchen and cookery items, preserves, tea sets, and fancy chopsticks. But with a long walk ahead, you may want to save purchases for the end of your visit.

To fortify yourself for the walk ahead, join the line at the busy **Tai Pan Bakery (2),** 194 Canal Street, (212) 732–2222, and choose one of the delicious soft buns filled with roasted pork or beef or sweets.

To go with your snack, turn right at Mott Street and walk ahead to **Ten Ren Tea Time (3),** 79 Mott Street, (212) 732–7178, and sample one of the current rages in Chinatown, cool fruit-flavored green tea concoctions with soft tapioca beads at the bottom. Oversize straws let you draw up the beads.

A few doors down is the main shop, the **Ten Ren Tea and Ginseng Company, Inc. (4),** 75 Mott Street, (212) 349–2286, an

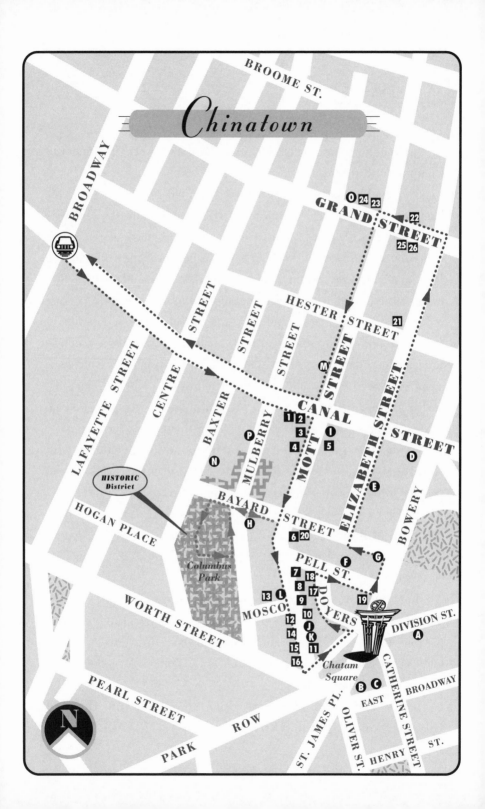

BACK SCRATCHERS

TEA

GOOD LUCK

SHOE HORN

CHOP STICKS

HERBAL

150 GRAMS

XIN QUN TEA

SLICES

GINSENG-D ROOT

attractive shop where you will find a generous sampling of Chinese teas as well as ginseng, the root that is thought to cure almost any ill.

Chinatown on a pleasant weekend is wall-to-wall with strollers and vendors. As you walk along Mott, you will pass scores of souvenir stands selling slippers, back scratchers, dolls, toys, even the miniature landscapes known as bonsai, and bamboo plants, which the Chinese consider good luck. For $1.00, you can buy a single mini-stalk of bamboo to bring a little luck home with you.

Across the street is a respite from the crowds, the **Eastern States Buddhist Temple of America (5),** 64 Mott Street, (212)

966–6229. Step into the incense-scented interior, where offerings are piled high and more than one hundred golden Buddhas gleam in the candlelight.

Next door, at 62 Mott, is the Chinese Consolidated Benevolent Association, a community center and an agency that has long helped newcomers.

Cross Bayard and you will find the **Ming Fay Book Store Corp. (6),** 42 Mott Street, (212) 406–1957, with many books in Chinese as well as English on tai chi, meditation, origami, feng shui, and traditional Chinese acupuncture.

If you have a yen for a special Chinese-style dress, the **New Age Designer (7),** 38 Mott Street, (212) 349–0818, will make one to measure in your choice of jewel-hued silks and satins.

Lamps are the specialty at the **Pearl of the Orient Gallery (8),** 36 Mott Street, (212) 267–5765, with many handsome choices in porcelain and cloisonné.

Lower Mott Street is part of the original Chinatown. The oldest of the shops, at 32 Mott, known as the **Mott Street General Store (9)** has closed, though efforts are being made to preserve the 1891 interior.

All manner of better quality, handsome gifts and home accessories can be found at **Wing On Wo & Co. (10),** 26 Mott Street, (212) 962–3577. Just down the block, at **China Silk & Handicrafts Corp. (11),** 18 Mott Street, (212) 385–9856, look for Oriental vases, statues, bowls, canisters, tea sets, and Buddhas by the dozens.

Just before the church across the street, at the intersection of Mott and Mosco Streets, you'll find a little red stand where Cecilia Tam, the **Egg Cake lady (12),** is usually on hand. She sells the best custard cakes in the neighborhood, as attested to by the constant lines.

Street vendors are found all around Chinatown—sometimes even an artist who will do Chinese lettering or brush paintings on the spot. And every other window seems to hold racks of roasted ducks. Their popularity began because most people didn't have ovens for roasting, so food shops took over, and the custom has persisted.

Anyone interested in Thai cooking will want to detour on Mosco Street for the **Bangkok Center Market (13)**, 104 Mosco Street, (212) 349–1979. It stocks everything from fresh galangal and lemongrass to seven kinds of fish sauce. Mosco also leads to Columbus Park (see page 174).

Back on Mott, cross the street and you'll find the **Church of the Transfiguration (14)**, 25 Mott Street, a Georgian-style church of stone with Gothic windows. Built in 1801, with a tower added in 1860, it has had an interesting history. It was originally an English Lutheran church but has changed with the nationalities of the community, becoming Catholic to serve first newly arrived Irish, then Italians. Now services are offered in Cantonese and Mandarin. The church is the focal point of the Chinese Roman Catholic community, offering classes and services to help newcomers.

Serious collectors will want to visit **Sinotique (15)**, 19A Mott Street, (212) 587–2393, a fine gallery dealing in antiques such as century-old altar tables and ceramics.

Near the end of the block is another big Chinese grocery store called **Kam Kuo Food Corp. (16)**, 7 Mott Street, (212) 349–3097, with produce of all kinds and more selections of Chinese sauces than you probably ever knew existed. Pearl River Soy Sauce, made without MSG, sells here for less than $1.00 for a huge bottle. Upstairs is a big selection of pots and kitchen utensils at good prices, including bamboo steamers in all sizes.

Mott Street ends at Chatham Square, a whizzing intersection where nine streets converge. The pagoda-shaped telephone booths and roofs on the bank, and the statues of Chinese heroes, tell you that this is without doubt Chinatown.

Head back on Bowery and turn left onto Doyers to walk another of the oldest streets in Chinatown. The **Nom Wah Tea Parlor (17)**, 13-15 Doyers Street, (212) 962–6047, was established in 1921 as a gathering place for the men of the community. It now shares the block with many newer establishments, but it still serves a tasty dim sum.

The curve in the road is the infamous Bloody Angle mentioned earlier.

Doyers runs into Pell Street, the last boundary of old Chinatown, with a chance for some delicious take-home vegetarian dim sum and other good things from **May May Gourmet Chinese Bakery (18)**, 35 Pell Street, (212) 267–0733.

Come back to Bowery for some local landmarks. To the right is the **Edward Mooney House (19)**, 18 Bowery, a brick Georgian-style home built in 1789, Manhattan's oldest row house.

Across Bowery, at the intersection with Division Street, is a statue of the Chinese sage Confucius, marking Confucius Plaza, the first major public-funded housing project built for Chinese residents, completed in 1976. The building of the plaza, with Chinese workers as part of the construction crew, showed that Chinatown had new political clout.

Turn left onto Bayard to find the **Chinatown Ice Cream Factory (20)**, 65 Bayard Street, (212) 608–4170, where you can sample such flavors as red bean, green tea, taro, and passion fruit.

A right onto Elizabeth Street will bring you back to Canal and the subway. Or, if you want see how Chinatown has grown, continue walking past Canal on Elizabeth Street to Grand Street, where a good sampling of shops is found.

On the way, at the corner of Hester Street, you'll pass the **Dynasty Supermarket (21),** 68 Elizabeth Street, (212) 966–4943, the most modern of the Chinese groceries, where you can shop in calm, heated or air-conditioned comfort. Here you'll find all the mysterious vegetables you've seen, neatly labeled. All the mystery isn't gone, however. When you see that the day's specials include things such as dried yuk jok and dried shark's fin, you'll know this isn't the typical neighborhood A&P.

At Grand, cross the street and head for the **Fay Da Bakery (22),** 214-216 Grand Street, (212) 966–8934, another place where

Columbus Park and a Chinese History Museum

The tranquillity of Columbus Park *running along Mulberry Street belies its beginnings. This used to be known as Mulberry Bend, one of the worst areas in the city, part of the severely overcrowded and infamous Five Points slum. Gangs with names like the Dead Rabbits and the Plug Uglies roamed the streets. A murder a day was commonplace; even the police were afraid to pass through. Reformer Jacob Riis called it "the foul core of New York's slums." Riis was instrumental in having the buildings razed in 1892, turning the dangerous neighborhood into Mulberry Bend Park, which is now known as Columbus Park, the only open space in all Chinatown.*

Across from the park is the Museum of Chinese in the Americas, *70 Mulberry Street, (212) 619–4785, (www.moca nyc.org), which has a permanent exhibit of photos and artifacts and changing exhibitions. It is open Tuesday through Sunday noon to 5:00 P.M.; admission is $3.00, under 12 free. Excellent walking tours of Chinatown are offered on Saturdays at 1:00 P.M. from May through September.*

Across from the museum, a sign of the growing multi-Asian presence in the neighborhood is the awning of the Asia Food Market Inc. *(27), 71½ Mulberry Street, (212) 962–2020, which advertises Thai, Indonesian, Philippine, and Chinese foods.*

you can munch on delicious soft buns or buy almond cookies, red- or black-bean cakes, custard tarts, and cream buns.

If you like Oriental fashions, you'll want to visit **Pearl River**

Chinese Products Emporium Inc. (23), 200 Grand Street, (212) 941–9373. They carry handsome silk tops, dresses, and pajamas with mandarin collars for children as well as women, along with lovely gifts like sandalwood and jasmine soaps, purses, dolls, and pillows.

The deli/grocery called **GT Trading Company (24),** 196 Grand Street, (212) 219–0519, sells a little of everything—squab, pig ears, squid, pig heads, cuttlefish, tofu, and lots of food to eat in or take out. Sesame balls, roast pork, and meat-filled pastries and dumplings are just a few of the choices.

Across the street, **Kamwo Herb and Tea (25),** 211 Grand Street, (212) 966–6370, can take care of what ails you with ginseng, herbs, teas, or maybe a dose of dried bugs. They claim to be the largest Chinese herbal pharmacy on the east coast.

Nearby is the **213 Grand Street Gourmet (26),** 213 Grand Street, (212) 226–4231. This humble place is not exactly gourmet, but the dim sum and snacks are tasty and extremely cheap.

At the corner of Mott, the DiPalo Dairy is a sure sign that you are walking in what used to be exclusively Little Italy. Turn left onto Mott and right at Canal for a last shot at shopping before you board the subway.

Chinese Cuisine

Chinese cuisine is familiar to most Americans, though we don't always get an authentic sampling. The styles of cooking are divided into four main regions.

Most common is Cantonese, from the south of China; it is a mild cuisine based on rice. Dim sum is typical Cantonese, along with stir-fried dishes cooked over very high heat in a wok (a round steel pan). Northern cuisine, centered in Beijing, often uses bread and noodles rather than rice and specializes in "sizzling" foods and sweet-and-sour dishes. Sichuan (sometimes spelled Szechwan) and Hunan, from the west of China, are known for hot and spicy flavors. The eastern region around Shanghai uses rice wine in cooking and produces a juicy specialty called soup dumplings, which are becoming increasingly popular. A less common cuisine from the east is from Fukien Province, which is known for "red-cooked" dishes in which ingredients are simmered slowly in soy sauce and wine until the liquid evaporates, leaving a reddish tinge to the food. Congee, a thick rice porridge, is another local specialty; the Chinese eat it for breakfast and sometimes at other times of the day topped with fish or meat. Many restaurants serve foods from more than one of these regions, but if you want to taste the best, choose a restaurant specializing in a particular region.

A TYPICAL CHINESE MEAL

Hot and sour (spicy) soup or wonton (bland) soup

Egg roll or pot stickers or scallion pancake

Peking duck or a choice of meats with black bean or garlic sauce

Dried sautéed string beans with chopped pork

Orange slices with cookies

The soybean is extremely important in the Chinese diet. Soybean extract is the source of the soy sauce used in so many dishes for salt, color, and flavoring; fermented soybeans are the basis for the widely used black-bean sauce. The bean curd called tofu is made by grinding soybeans with water into a cream that is cooked, strained, and coagulated. Tofu serves as a nutritious, inexpensive substitute for meat, which is scarce in many parts of China, one reason so many dishes use meat sparingly, as a flavoring with vegetables.

Dim sum, which means "touch the heart," is an array of small appetizers such as dumplings, steamed, sautéed, or fried, that are very popular among the Chinese, who generally eat them at tea-houses for lunch (and sometimes breakfast). They are served on rolling carts. You pick as many as you want as the carts go by, and the bill is determined by the number of small empty plates left on the table. Many Hong Kong–style dim sum restaurants are big and noisy, just as they are at home. In Chinatown dim sum is served all day.

A CHINESE SAMPLER

Chinese Sauces:
Chinese menus are usually divided according to main ingredients such as poultry, seafood, or vegetables, but all are served with much the same choice of basic sauces. These include:

Black-bean sauce: a savory sauce made from fermented, salted black soy beans, mixed with garlic, scallions, and ginger.

Garlic sauce: a Sichuan sauce that is hot, sweet, and tart.

Ginger sauce: a basic bean sauce flavored with fresh ginger.

Hoisin sauce: an all-purpose sauce, dark in color, made from soybeans, garlic, hot red peppers, and spices.

Hot-and-sour sauce: made with vinegar, hot chili peppers, sesame oil, and seasonings (the same ingredients that go into hot-and-sour soup).

Lobster sauce: a black-bean sauce enhanced with chopped pork and eggs. It doesn't contain lobster; it was originally developed to serve *with* lobster.

Oyster sauce: oyster extract reduced to a rich concentrate, mixed with soy, sugar, and cornstarch.

Sweet-and-sour sauce: a thick and syrupy sauce made with sugar, vinegar, cornstarch, and sometimes fruit juice.

Some Common Terms on Chinese Menus:
Most menus are quite descriptive, but here are a few terms to know:

Lo mein: dishes made with egg noodles.

Peking duck: a gourmet dish, the high point of a Chinese banquet. Duckling, roasted until the skin is golden and crisp, is cut into small rectangles and served with small pancakes similar to crepes in texture. The meat is placed on the pancake, topped with a dab of Hoisin sauce and a bit of scallion, and the pancake is folded over, forming a delectable tiny sandwich. This creates the ideal Chinese combination of taste, color, and texture—the crispness of the skin, the softness of the pancake, the spicy red sweetness of the sauce, and the crunchy bite of the scallion.

Pot stickers: dumplings filled with minced meats and/or vegetables, pan fried or steamed, served with a dipping sauce.

Scallion pancakes: scallion bits mixed with batter, and fried into crisp, chewy pancakes.

Soup dumplings: dough filled with a mixture of pork or crab and a flavorful mouthful of broth that spurts out when you take a bite. Sometimes listed on menus as xiao long bao or steamed buns.

Spring rolls: thin dough wrappers filled with shredded meats and/or vegetables and deep-fried. Egg rolls are similar, but usually larger and with thicker wrappers.

Wontons: small dumplings filled with minced shrimp, pork, and scallions, often served in soup.

R E C O M M E N D E D ¶◉¶ R E S T A U R A N T S

Canton (A) ($$), 45 Division Street, (212) 226–4441, is the Zagat readers' choice as the best in Chinatown for Cantonese food. The hostess will help you make the most of the menu.

Goody's (B) ($), 1 East Broadway, (212) 577–2922, long a favorite in Queens, has rated raves since it expanded to Manhattan with a tasty, authentic Shanghai menu and excellent soup dumplings.

Golden Unicorn (C) ($–$$), 18 East Broadway, (212) 941–0911, is typical Hong Kong–style, which means big, flashy, and noisy, and there are often waits to get in. The star here is the dim sum.

Grand Sichuan (D) ($), 125 Canal Street, (212) 625–9212, is a plain setting treasured by those who like it hot. It serves authentic versions of the peppery Sichuan dishes, often toned down for American tastes.

Jing Fong (E) ($), 20 Elizabeth Street, (212) 964–5256, the biggest and most authentic of the Hong Kong dim sum palaces, seats 1,000 and is a raucous scene. Share a table, try to get a waitress to come over, and see what things are like in Hong Kong.

Joe's Shanghai (F) ($), 9 Pell Street, (212) 233–8888, like the parent restaurant in Flushing, is best known for its soup dumplings, listed on the menu as "steamed buns." Join the crowd.

New York Noodle Town (G) ($), 28½ Bowery, (212) 349–0923, is a noisy, no-frills place that is great for soups, noodles, and roasted meat dishes.

Shanghai Cuisine (H) ($–$$), 89 Bayard Street, (212) 732–8988, has a stylish setting for Chinatown and many excellent Shanghai specialties, such as braised pork with brown sauce, a hot, gingery crab-bean-noodle casserole, and more of those delicious soup dumplings.

Sweet 'n' Tart Cafe (I) ($), 76 Mott Street, (212) 334–8088, spices food with tonics said to benefit the body, balancing your yin and yang. Lotus seeds in herb tea are recommended for the liver and kidney; double-boiled Oriental pears with almond are suggested to soothe the lungs. Come and take care of what ails you.

Sweet 'n' Tart Restaurant (J) ($–$$), 20 Mott Street, (212) 964–0380, has the same owner as the cafe listed above but is a much larger space with a formal dinner menu added to the soups, snacks, and drinks. The food is excellent.

Ping's Seafood (K) ($–$$), 22 Mott Street, (212) 602–9988, has a celebrity Cantonese chef, Chuen Ping Hui, who has a way with fish. Try the garlic-encrusted "Causeway Bay" lobster. This is the upscale location; there's a second at 20 East Broadway.

Vegetarian Paradise 3 (L) ($), 33-35 Mott Street, (212) 406–6988, has so many tasty dishes made with vegetables, soybeans, and tofu that you'll never miss the meat.

Joe's Ginger (M) ($), 113 Mott Street, (212) 966–6613, is the same Joe Si of Joe's Shanghai, this time pairing with his brother for a new venture that offers Sichuan and other regional dishes in addition to Shanghai fare. The famous soup dumplings are still on the menu, listed as "steamed buns," stuffed with pork or pork and crab.

Vietnamese and Malaysian restaurants are an ever-growing presence in Chinatown, offering excellent food at good prices. Here are a few that come highly recommended:

Nha Trang (N) ($), 87 Baxter Street, (212) 233–5948, one of the first, is still one of the best Vietnamese restaurants in Chinatown.

Nyonya (O) ($), 194 Grand Street, (212) 334–3669, has food described by one reviewer as "dazzling Malaysian flavors."

Pho Viet Huong (P) ($), 73 Mulberry Street, (212) 233–8988. Another plain setting for highly praised Vietnamese food.

A Taste of India in Curry Hill

Another Manhattan enclave that has survived despite changes all around it, this 3-block corridor just south of Murray Hill is filled with Indian shops and lined with restaurants that are a boon for diners in search of interesting food and reasonable prices. The food stores are a treasure trove of fragrant spices and grains, sure to intrigue cooks of all nationalities.

THE HISTORY

Taxi drivers, newsstand operators, doctors, professors, hoteliers and publishers. With an estimated population of 200,000, people from India are a visible and important part of every strata of life in New York City. Today you can find representatives of every Indian state and culture living in the city, speaking some twenty-six languages and even more dialects.

As with other Asian peoples, the influx of Indians did not happen until immigration laws were eased. Earlier immigrants from India were upper class, students, professionals and businessmen. They were well educated and English speaking but still suffered discrimination in this country. A 1946 law set an annual immigration limit of only one hundred.

In the 1950s there was a noticeable increase in the number of Indian students who came to this country, especially to Columbia University in Upper Manhattan. Those who remained settled in this

How to Get There

Take the #6 Lexington Avenue Train or the 102 or 103 Lexington
Avenue Bus to 28th Street.

neighborhood. One enterprising retailer, Kalustyan, began to import
and sell Indian foods and spices along with its Middle Eastern foods,
and though the location was much farther downtown on Lexington
Avenue, an Indian commercial corridor grew up around this store.

With the abolishment of the quota system in 1965, the numbers
of Indians has grown dramatically, with the newcomers tending to
settle in Queens along with their South Asian neighbors from
Pakistan, Bangladesh, and Nepal. But for those living in Manhattan,
the shopping and dining center remains on and around Lexington
Avenue from 26th to 29th Streets. The restaurants represent the variety of sects living in New York, with many vegetarian choices for
Hindus who do not eat beef and Muslims who eschew pork, and
Kosher Indian fare popular with Jews, Indian or not.

• • • *A Shopping / Walking Tour* • • •

From the subway stop on Park Avenue South, walk east on 28th
Street and on the downtown side you will pass **Little India
Emporium (1),** 128 East 28th Street, (212) 683–1691, with exotic
displays of statues, including the elephant god Ganesh, and all

manner of gifts, clothing and foods, incense, teas, and cooking equipment. There is also a good supply of Ayurvedic herbs and beauty products. Turn downtown on Lexington and make a left turn on 27th Street for **Om Saree Palace (2),** 134 East 27th Street, (212) 532–5620, a small shop with a dazzling array of saris and fabrics. If you want to see more saris, as well as colorful fabrics scarves and jewelry, you can detour later to Royal Sari House, 264 Fifth Avenue, (212) 679–0732.

For now, walk uptown on Lexington Avenue for foods galore. At **Foods of India (3),** 121 Lexington Avenue, (212) 683–4419, you can pick up big bags of fragrant basmati rice and more spices than you ever dreamed existed, as well fine chutneys, relishes, and Indian breads to take home. The stock includes Ayurvedic herbs and beauty products. Upstairs you will see Swapna Trading, (212) 684–3450, with a window filled with saris and signs advertising appliances, fabrics, and Punjabi suits. Next door is **Kalustyan's (4),** 123 Lexington Avenue, (212) 685–3451, founded in 1944. This was the first store to cater to Indians, but its wares are not limited to any one nationality. Recently renovated and enlarged, this bright and inviting space, scented by its huge stock of spices, features foods from thirty nations around the world—thirty-one kinds of rice, dozens of grains, teas, coffees, and a big selection of dried fruits. Another feature is specialized cookware such as couscous pots, Indian tahli trays, and Turkish coffeepots. Upstairs is a counter selling lunches to go. The variety of sandwiches in pita bread includes the vegetarian mujaddara—pita stuffed with a mixture of lentils, bulgar wheat, and crisply browned onions.

At the corner of 29th Street is **Spice Corner (5),** 135 Lexington Avenue, (212) 689–5182, offering a large selection of Indian, Lebanese, and Pakistani foods, everything from flavored pickles to barfi, an Indian-style fudge, plus fresh vegetables and many frozen entrees from samosas to chicken tikka.

On this brief walk you've passed many enticing restaurants; now it's time to make your choice.

Indian Cuisine

(See page 146)

RECOMMENDED 🍽 RESTAURANTS

The menus are similar in most of these restaurants. Expect a choice of dishes baked in a tandoori oven, curries, a variety of lamb entrees, vindaloo dishes in a hot and spicy sauce, biryani entrees of saffron-flavored basmati rice cooked with chicken, lamb, or vegetables, and exotic spices. Many restaurants offer vegetarian dishes from Southern India, such as dosas—pancakes made with rice flour, often rolled around vegetables and spicy stews. All have a selection of delicious Indian breads, including fluffy nan. Platters are an economical way to taste many dishes.

Baluchi's (A) ($–$$), 111 East 29th Street, (212) 481–4545, is part of a chain of Indian restaurants found around the city, where the food is dependable and the prices fair. This location has an appealing open-air section when the weather is agreeable.

Curry in a Hurry (B) ($), 119 Lexington Avenue, (212) 683–0900, a popular outpost since 1975, has counter service on the first floor, table seating upstairs. Platters come with basmati rice and fresh hot nan.

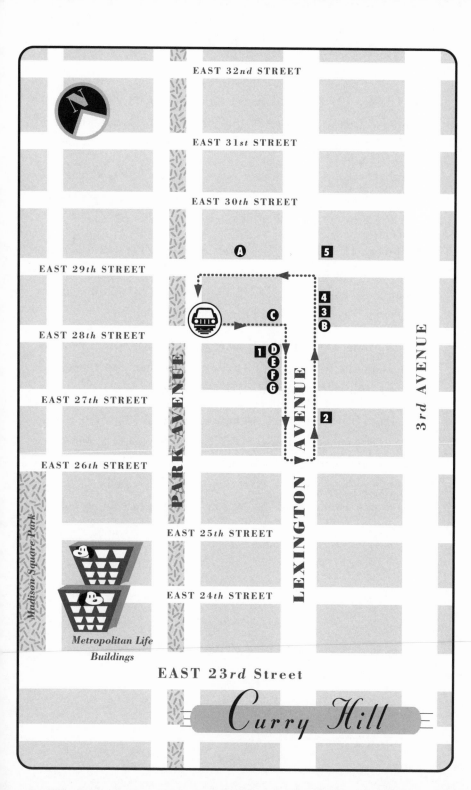

Joy (C) ($), 127 East 28th Street, (212) 685–0808. Stuffed breads are among the specialties of this unpretentious neighborhood standby. All-inclusive dinner specials are a bargain.

Pongal (D) ($), 110 Lexington Avenue, (212) 696–9458, caters to a Kosher clientele and is among the best-rated vegetarian restaurants in the area. The combo platter offers eight different dishes.

Annapurna (E) ($), 108 Lexington Avenue, (212) 679–1284, has an all-around menu that features a few unusual dishes like Goan Shrimp Curry and Lamb Shahjahani, cooked in the traditional way dating to the Moghul kitchen of Emperor Shahjahani.

Madras Mahal (F) ($), 104 Lexington, (212) 684–4010, one of the first restaurants to serve southern Indian cuisine, still ranks high with food critics. This is another Kosher kitchen.

Dosa Hut (G) ($), 102 Lexington Avenue, (212) 725–7466, a modest cafe, specializes in the dosa, an Indian version of a thin crepe made with rice and lentil batter that may be served plain or filled with potatoes, peas, or nuts. Over a dozen varieties are on the menu. If you choose the plain variety, you can add sauce or chutney and roll it up.

Eastern Europe in the East Village

The East Village neighborhood is a blend of hip and history, the restaurants a wide spectrum, Mexican to Italian to Thai. But also tucked within the streets of the neighborhood is the rich culture of a large Ukrainian population. Come and share their heritage and discover an area with a crazy-quilt past, from Peter Stuyvesant to Kleinedeutschland, from Jewish theater to the flower children of the 1960s.

THE HISTORY

Peter Stuyvesant, the governor of Dutch New York, built his country estate, or "bouwerie," in what is now the East Village in 1651, when this area was still farmland. The street we now call Bowery ran from downtown to his farm. Saint Mark's in the Bowery Church is on land where Stuyvesant's private chapel once stood; he is buried in the churchyard.

Development began in the 1700s, when Petrus Stuyvesant, Peter's great-grandson, began subdividing the land into plots. The finest town houses in this area were built in the early to mid-1800s.

Germans were already a sizable population in New York by 1840, and the next twenty years brought another 100,000 immigrants, fleeing hard times and religious oppression in their homeland. Many of them settled in the East Village, which became known as Kleinedeutschland, the major German-American center in the

How to Get There

By subway/bus: Take #6 Subway to Astor Place;
take the #15 Second Avenue Bus Line downtown and the
First Avenue Line uptown.

United States for almost the rest of the century. It was the wealthiest German families who first began to move uptown to Yorkville. A tragedy hastened a mass movement to join them—the sinking in 1904 of the pleasure boat *General Slocum* killed more than 1,000 members of St. Mark's German Lutheran Church, located on Sixth Street, including many women and children who were on board for their annual picnic outing. Many people moved away from the neighborhood to erase the memory of this terrible loss.

Their places were filled by Jewish immigrants moving up from the neighboring Lower East Side. In the 1920s the area developed as the "Yiddish Rialto," a center for Jewish theater. As the Jewish residents also began moving away in the 1960s, things changed radically. Intellectuals, artists, musicians, and writers, who were being priced out of Greenwich Village, were attracted by cheap rents and began moving east. The East Village became a center for radical politics and art and was known for its avant-garde theaters, bookshops, and coffeehouses where poets held forth. Hippies and flower children followed, and punk rock was born at clubs such as CBGB. But the drug scene of the 1970s brought a general decline to the neighborhood.

Conditions improved in the 1980s, attracting newcomers, but their arrival brought protests from those who could not afford the rising rents. Squatters occupied abandoned buildings and fought with the police who sought to evict them. Tompkins Square Park became a shantytown inhabited by the homeless. In 1990 police responded to complaints about drug dealing in the park by evicting the homeless and razing the shanties they had built there, setting off a series of marches and riots.

Things are calm today. The East Village is now a thriving neighborhood with a wide mix of residents, though it remains a favorite area for young counterculture types, particularly in "Alphabet City"—avenues A to C— the blocks east of First Avenue.

Through all the recent changes, a large community of Ukrainians have remained stable, staying near their church, St. George's, a religious and social center established in the early 1900s. When the Ukraine came under Polish rule after World War I, immigration to the United States grew dramatically. The population increased again after World War II, as Ukrainians who were displaced during the war refused to return to a homeland under the Soviet regime, where their culture and religion were forbidden. By the 1990s the Ukrainian population of New York numbered 80,000, the largest community of Ukrainians outside the Ukraine. Many of them live and worship in the East Village.

A number of the later arrivals were well-educated professionals, who helped to establish scholarly societies such as the Shevchenko Scientific Institute and the Ukrainian Academy of Arts and Sciences. Preserving their heritage is doubly important to Ukrainians, because their culture was nearly snuffed out during the long Soviet occupation. The Ukrainian Museum, founded in 1976, plays a vital role in promoting their culture and traditions.

The Polish population of the East Village is smaller, but it has been growing ever since the political protests of the 1970s. Polish eating places and food stores are now a visible presence along First Avenue.

• • •   *A Shopping/Walking Tour*   • • •

From Astor Place, walk to Third Avenue and turn right. On your right, you can't miss the imposing home of **Cooper Union for the Advancement for Science and Art (1),** 41 Cooper Square. It was established in 1859 by philanthropist Peter Cooper to provide a free technical education for promising students in engineering, architecture, and art, a mission it still fulfills. A statue of the founder stands in Cooper Square. The school's handsome Great Hall has been a platform for many prominent speakers, from Abraham Lincoln to William Cullen Bryant, and it continues to host many lectures and seminars.

A modest Ukrainian Baptist church stands on the corner of Third Avenue and Seventh Street, and a Ukrainian Orthodox church is at Third Avenue and 11th Street. But for the heart of the Ukrainian community, turn left onto Seventh Street to **St. George's Ukrainian Catholic Church (2),** 33 East Seventh Street, (212) 674–1615. The domed sanctuary was completed in 1978, replacing the original church on the site. It is a copy of an old-world Ukrainian church, with striking stained glass windows.

For Ukrainian crafts, there is no place like **Surma (3),** across the street at 11 East Seventh Street, (212) 477–0729. Established in 1918, the shop is filled with treasures including wooden clocks and candlesticks, mugs with black and red geometric folk designs, embroidered blouses, sashes, flowered scarves, religious icons painted on wood, black trays lavishly decorated with painted flowers,

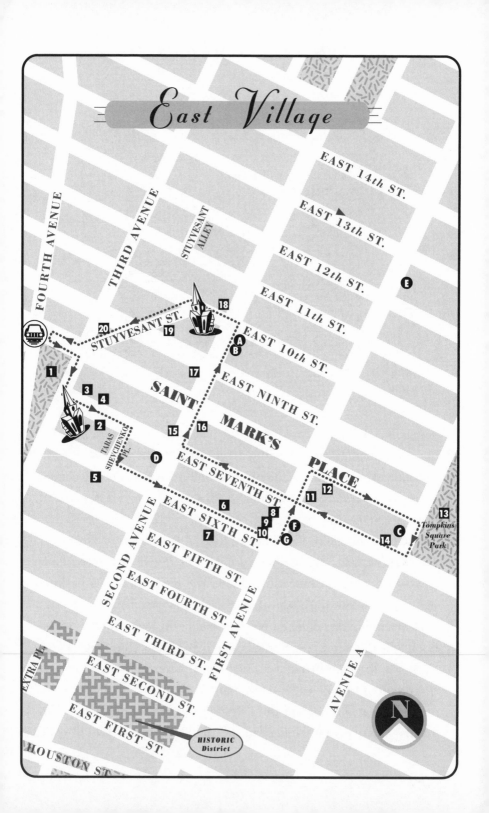

pottery, beads, figurines, inlaid boxes, and lots of intricate *pysanky,* the traditional Ukranian painted Easter egg. There's also a wide selection of music; this is the place to find a recording of the classic Ukrainian instrument, the bandura, with a sound somewhere between a guitar and a harp.

A few doors down is a different kind of neighborhood landmark, **McSorleys Old Ale House (4),** 15 East Seventh Street, (212) 473–9148, a fixture here since 1854. The current patrons packing the place are mostly college students, but the establishment doesn't look much different from an old Irish pub, still with sawdust on the floor and the same venerable wooden bar. Everyone from Peter Cooper to Brendan Behan has lifted a mug here, and the setting was immortalized by painter John Sloan in 1912.

A sign at the edge of the sidewalk tells of the pub's place in history, when women demanded the right to drink in the all-male establishment. They pressed their case with a lawsuit, Seidenberg vs. McSorley, which resulted in "McSorley's law," prohibiting sex discrimination in bars, hotels, restaurants, airplanes, golf clubs, and other public accommodations.

Cross back to the downtown side of the street and look for Tara Shevchenko Place just past the church. It takes you through to Sixth Street and the fine new home of the **Ukrainian Museum (5)**, 222 East Sixth Street, (212) 228–0110, opening in 2004. (The museum was not quite finished at press time, so phone for current hours and prices. Until the museum opens, limited classes and activities will be held at the old location at 203 Second Avenue, between 12th and 13th Streets.) The new building provides ample space for a beguiling collection of Ukrainian costumes—lavishly embroidered peasant blouses and colorful sashes, fancy sheepskin and fur vests, wedding wreaths of yarn and ribbons, and other garments worn in villages early in the past century. Displays also include ceramics, metalwork, brass and silver jewelry, decorative wood objects, and an outstanding collection of the intricately designed Ukrainian Easter eggs known as pysanky.

The museum also shows paintings and sculptures created

FESTIVE
WOMAN'S   Early 20TH
COSTUME   Century
THE UKRAINIAN MUSEUM.

by Ukrainian artists, one of the best known being Alexander Archipenko, as well as regularly changing exhibits. Classes are offered in traditional crafts such as embroidery and pysanky painting. The gift shop has books, blouses, wooden candlesticks, pottery, and "how to" books on embroidery and pysanky.

Walk east on Sixth to see the ill-fated German St. Marks Lutheran Church, now the **Community Synagogue (6),** 325 East Sixth Street, (212) 473–3665. You are also now on the street known as **Little India (7)** because of the line-up of inexpensive Indian restaurants that fill the south side of the block from Second to First Avenues. These were started by Bangladeshi entrepreneurs during the hippie days of the East Village to provide cheap eats; most reviewers don't think much of the food. In fact, the standard rumor is that one kitchen serves all the restaurants, so it hardly matters where you eat. If you have an appetite for Indian food, however, the best choices by most accounts are Mitali East, 334 East Sixth Street, (212) 533–2508, Haveli, 100 Second Avenue, (212) 982–0533, and Banjara, 97 First Avenue, (212) 497–5956.

If you want to buy Indian foods and spices, the **Spice Corner Grocery (8),** 113 First Avenue, (212) 475–4144, on the corner of Seventh Street, has a good supply of basmati rice and spices from curry to coriander.

Back to things Ukrainian (and Polish), between Sixth and Seventh Streets you will have passed a pair of food stores. **B&M Meats (9),** 111 First Avenue, (212) 677–1210, is more than meats—you'll see tempting breads, vegetables, and imported beers. **Bella's Mini-Market (10),** 109 First Avenue, (212) 982–7893, has a little of everything—breads, cold cuts, preserves, and canned goods. The first store is Polish, the second Ukrainian, but they cater to both nationalities.

Underground Landmarks

History buffs may want to check out a couple of unexpected finds in the East Village: two landmark graveyards. The New York Marble Cemetery can barely be seen through a gate on Second Avenue between Second and Third Streets. Founded in 1830, it was New York's first nonsectarian cemetery, and it consists of 156 underground marble vaults. There are no gravestones or markers, just plates set into the walls identifying those buried here, including such prominent New York names as Scribner and Auchincloss. Just around the corner, on Second Street between First and Second Avenues, is the New York City Marble Cemetery, established just a year later. This one can be easily seen from the sidewalk. Among those beneath the stone markers are members of the Fish and Roosevelt families.

The acknowledged "king" of the meat shops is **Kurowycky (11)**, 124 First Avenue, (212) 477–0344. The family came from the Ukraine over forty years ago, bringing their old-world recipes with them. They offer all kinds of uniquely good things: mazurka, a soft salami flavored with caraway seeds and garlic; krakowska, a ham sausage seasoned with garlic and pepper; kabanosy, a hunter's sausage, long and thin and spiced with paprika. If you're not sure what you want, they'll gladly give you tastes.

A couple of doors down is **First Avenue Pierogi and Deli (12)**, 130 First Avenue, (212) 420–9690, a tiny shop selling excellent take-out foods. The ready-to-cook pirogi comes with a variety of stuffings, from potato to carrot-mushroom; all you have to do at home is pan-fry or boil them for a tasty treat. Another good choice is the bigos stew, which has a delicious smoky flavor.

Turn right on St. Mark's Place to Avenue A and **Tompkins Square Park (13).** The playground where children are romping today seems calm, but you can still see a cluster of homeless people on the benches at the other side of the park, a sign that not everything has changed here.

Come back down Seventh Street, a street with many attractive townhouses, and you will pass **St. Stanislaus Church (14),** 101 Seventh Street, (212) 475–4576, a Polish church. If the church is open, go inside to see the many statues and paintings.

Turn uptown again on Second Avenue and you'll see some landmarks of the past, including the ornate red brick building with terracotta trim that is now the **Ottendorfer Branch of the New York Public Library (15),** 135 Second Avenue, (212) 674–0947. A German-American philanthropist built the library and the adjacent German Dispensary from 1883 to 1884 to improve the lives of his fellow German immigrants; it became the oldest operating branch of the New York Public Library.

The **Orpheum Theater (16),** across the street near the corner of Eighth Street is a former Yiddish theater that is still operating as an off-Broadway theater.

At Ninth Street is the best of the Polish butcher shops, **East Village Meat Market (17),** 139 Second Avenue, (212) 228–5590. The kielbasa is delicious. The store also has a nice selection of breads.

At the corner of Tenth Street and Second Avenue is **St. Marks's in the Bowery Church (18),** the second oldest in New York, with the original fieldstone portion dating to 1799. As the neighborhood became more stylish, a tower was added in 1828. The church has been restored in recent years. In the 1960s it served as one of the city's most socially and politically committed congregations. It continues to host poetry readings, experimental theater, and modern dance performances.

Continue heading west and you are entering the Saint Marks's Historic District, the area that was once Peter Stuyvesant's "bouwerie" or farm, and Stuyvesant Street, one of the first streets that was developed by Petrus Stuyvesant late in the 18th century. Two significant homes are the **Nicholas William Stuyvesant House (19),** at #44, circa 1795, and at 135, the **Nicholas and Elizabeth Stuyvesant Fish House (20),** built from 1803 to 1804. This street and development on Tenth Street formed what became known as the Renwick Triangle, a handsome group of buildings with uniform facades created by a noted architect of the day, James Renwick, Jr., in 1861.

Stuyvesant Street will lead you back to Third Avenue, where you can head for the subway or detour back up Saint Mark's Place, the headquarters of the remaining counter-culture of the East Village. The shops are the epitome of funk, filled with vintage clothing, sixties memorabilia, beads, posters, and lots of black leather. If you're interested, there's almost no body part you can't have pierced here.

Eastern European Cuisine

All Eastern European cuisines have much in common, so with slight variations, the dishes you'll find in Ukrainian restaurants are similar to the cuisines of Poland (see page 67), southern Russia (page 50), and Hungary (page 272).

This is hearty, solid, stick-to-your-ribs food, and nowhere in Manhattan will you find more generous meals at more reasonable prices, as scores of students from nearby colleges will attest.

An Eastern European Sampler

Here are some of the classic dishes offered in both Polish and Ukrainian restaurants in the East Village. Order a combination plate to taste soup, salad, stuffed cabbage, and pirogi with sour cream, all for under $10.

Blintzes: crepes filled with fruits and/or cheese, served as an entree or dessert.

Borscht: prepared Ukrainian-style, this beet soup is made with tomatoes, potatoes, cabbage, and meat, and served with sour cream. Comes hot or cold.

Kasha: buckwheat grains, known as groats, cooked into a cereal-like texture and served as a side dish.

Kasha varnishkes: kasha mixed with small, bow-tie noodles and sautéed onions; sometimes served with mushroom sauce.

Pirogi: packets of dough filled with cheese, meat, or potatoes, boiled or fried with onion sauté; served with applesauce or sour cream.

Potato pancakes: grated potato and onion mixed into patties with matzo meal or flour and egg, and pan-fried; served with applesauce or sour cream.

Stuffed cabbage: ground beef and pork mixed with cooked rice, onion, and herbs, rolled into cabbage leaves that have been cooked just enough to soften, and baked. Filling may also be a meatless mix of mushrooms, onion, rice, and herbs.

Ukrainian meatballs: ground pork and beef, onion, mushrooms, eggs, and spices formed into balls and oven-roasted, served with mushroom sauce.

Veal goulash: veal braised in a creamy herb sauce.

Vareniki: dumplings, usually stuffed with potato.

R ECOMMENDED 🍽 R ESTAURANTS

Veselka (A) ($), 144 Second Avenue, (212) 228–9682, has a funky coffeehouse air that attracts a lively young clientele for big portions of Eastern European specialties at small prices. A selection of draught beer is another plus. Walk past the counter section to the back for a quieter table.

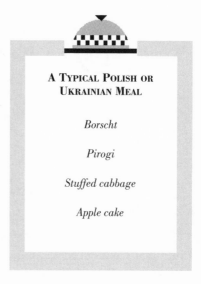

A TYPICAL POLISH OR UKRAINIAN MEAL

Borscht

Pirogi

Stuffed cabbage

Apple cake

Ukrainian East Village Restaurant (B) ($), 140 East Second Avenue, (212) 529–5024, is the most formal neighborhood dining room, with paneled walls, chandeliers, and waitresses in Ukrainian dress. But don't be put off—there's a full lineup of classic dishes, and the Chicken Kiev is the only item on the menu over $10.

Odessa (C) ($), 117 Avenue A, (212) 473–8916, is part-coffee shop/cafe, part–Eastern European restaurant, both open twenty-four hours a day. Come in for coffee and a cheese blintz or pastry, or a full meal.

Cafe Kiev (D) ($), 117 Second Avenue, (212) 420–9600, looks like a busy luncheonette in front, and does a thriving take-out business, but there's a quieter dining room in back where you can savor the day's line-up of homemade soups and have a tasty meal of stuffed cabbage or Ukrainian-style goulash.

Polish Restaurants (Menus are similar to Ukrainian):

Christine's (E) ($), 208 First Avenue, (212) 254–2474.

Polonia (F) ($), 110 First Avenue, (212) 254–9699.

Teresa's (G) ($), 103 First Avenue, (212) 228–0604.

Seeking Soul
in Harlem

"I'll be shouting, I'll be singing, my troubles will be over . . ."

They were, indeed, shouting with gusto, singing and clapping with jubilance on a recent Sunday morning in Harlem, delivering a hymn that I felt sure must be reaching clear to heaven. I was in one of hundreds of churches large and small holding gospel services all over Harlem. Attending these services is one of the most joyful ways to share in the rich traditions of America's best-known African-American neighborhood and to experience the love of music, religion, and zest for life that sets this community apart.

Services are social as well as religious gatherings for members of the congregations, who dress up in their Sunday finest for the occasion. And they are happy to welcome visitors. My tour group was greeted with hugs from congregants and welcomed from the pulpit at the Beulah Baptist Church, a small congregation on West 130th Street.

Peaceful Sunday mornings and early afternoons are also ideal for seeing the surprises of Harlem—the many fine buildings and historic sights of the area—not to mention enjoying a delicious soul-food brunch or lunch, sometimes with a gospel accompaniment. You can join a tour or enjoy a stroll on your own, as I did after the tour, with no feeling of uneasiness.

How to Get There

By subway or bus: For a full tour take the A, B, or C Train to
155th Street and St. Nicholas Avenue. Harlem is large, so if your
time or energy is limited, you may prefer to take the #2 or 3 Subway to
135th Street and begin this tour at number #3 or #4. The #102 and
the #7 Bus Lines run up and down Lenox Avenue between
116th and 145th Streets, ready to give a lift if
you get tired.

THE HISTORY

When a railroad was built down Park Avenue in 1837, Harlem
was divided into east and west, and it was the west side that attracted
the wealthy, mostly German-Jewish businessmen moving up from the
Lower East Side, who built substantial brownstone homes. The construction of the IRT Line along Lenox Avenue in 1904 brought a
building boom—overbuilding, in fact, with many apartments standing
vacant. This was just about the time when commercial development
was pushing the black population out of their neighborhoods, what
are now the Herald Square and Lincoln Center areas. An alert black
real estate agent, Philip A. Payton, Jr., saw an opportunity and took
over management of many buildings by promising premium rents to
landlords. He thus was able to move black tenants into this very
desirable housing. By 1914 Harlem's black population had swelled
to 50,000; by 1930 it was over 200,000.

Harlem's heyday came after World War I, a period that came to be known as the Harlem Renaissance. Literature flourished, with a core of fine writers, including W.E.B. Du Bois and Langston Hughes. Artists like Romare Bearden established distinctive painting styles. Jazz was at its peak. Clubs like the Cotton Club, the Savoy, and Small's Paradise featured greats like Duke Ellington and Cab Calloway, who brought white patrons flocking uptown. Marcus Garvey's Black Nationalist "Back to Africa" movement of that period failed, but it spawned a revival of black pride. (The Mt. Morris Park was renamed to honor Garvey in 1973.)

The Depression hit hard in Harlem, however, ending this glorious period. Unemployment was widespread, rents were high, and homes were divided into ever smaller units.

Harlem has many problems today, and many of its streets are not pretty, yet handsome middle-class neighborhoods remain. There are three historic districts, a number of fine blocks of homes, and many beautiful churches to be admired, and the spirit of vitality remains.

The entire area is enjoying what many believe may be a second renaissance, with new renovation and construction everywhere and stylish new shops and restaurants opening, gaining attention from the media. The Dance Theater of Harlem and the Black National Theater are well known, and jazz clubs are flourishing once again. Foreign visitors frequently include Harlem in their list of must-see neighborhoods in New York.

••• *A Walking Tour* •••

Some Harlem streets have been renamed for important past residents. To make things clearer, they are referred to here by their original numbers.

Frederick Douglass Boulevard = Eighth Avenue
Adam Clayton Powell Jr. Boulevard = Seventh Avenue
Malcolm X Boulevard = Lenox Avenue (equivalent to Sixth Avenue)

From the subway at 155th, walk east a short distance and turn right onto Edgecombe Avenue to **Sugar Hill (1),** along Edgecombe Avenue between 155th and 145th Streets. The privacy of this enclave on a hill high above Harlem made it a highly desirable location, a prized setting for the handsome three- and four-story stone row houses built for the wealthy between 1886 and 1906. From the 1920s to the 1950s, the residents were Harlem's elite—Supreme Court Justice Thurgood Marshall; jazz musicians Count Basie, Duke Ellington, and Cab Calloway; and later former New York City Mayor David Dinkins. The location became known as Sugar Hill, a symbol of the sweet life for those who had made it. Still in fine condition, many homes in Sugar Hill are now occupied by faculty members of nearby City College.

At 145th Street turn right and go 2 blocks, then make a left onto Convent Avenue to explore the **Hamilton Heights Historic District (2),** running from 145th to 141st Streets. This was once a rural area favored by the wealthy for their country homes. Among them was Alexander Hamilton, whose Grange (today a National Memorial) was built here in 1801. It was moved 2 blocks from its original site to Convent Avenue and 141st Street, where it is still poorly located, squeezed between other buildings. It has been closed awaiting a move by the National Park Service to a more suitable location. The Grange is largely overshadowed by the neighboring St. Luke's Episcopal Church, built in 1892–1895, the oldest of three impressive churches marking the boundaries of the area. Most of the housing dates from 1886 to 1906, after the elevated and subway lines were extended into the neighborhood.

Continue down Convent Avenue to detour through the impressive Gothic campus of City College, between 141st and 138th Streets. Or if you prefer, turn left onto 141st Street and walk 4 blocks to Eighth Avenue, then turn right to West 139th and **The St. Nicholas Historic District (Striver's Row) (3),** 202-250 West 139th and 138th Streets. These row houses, known as the King Model Houses (after their developer, David King), were built in 1891, at the height of real-estate speculation in Harlem. They were designed by three separate architects, but with care so that their varied architecture would fit into a harmonious whole. Successful blacks were attracted here in the 1920s and 1930s, giving rise to the nickname "Strivers Row." Among the prominent residents were lawyers, physicians, and musicians W. C. Handy and Eubie Blake.

If you continue down Eighth Avenue, you will pass signs of the rejuvenation of Harlem, rows of newer townhouses in a style so appropriate for the neighborhood it is hard to tell them from the old. Near 135th Street are some of the fashionable new shops, such as **Moshood (4),** 2533 Eighth Avenue (212) 507–2532, featuring the flowing African-inspired clothing of the Nigerian-born designer for whom the shop is named, and **Grandview (5),** 2531 Eighth Avenue, (212) 694–7324, a stylish boutique featuring contemporary clothing and accessories, much of it by African-American designers.

Turning east on 135th Street, **Sole Kitchen (6),** 236 West 135th Street between Seventh and Eighth Avenues, features the showroom of Harlem custom shoe designer Etu Evans, whose creations can also be seen at Bergdorf Goodman. A bit further down the block is a popular spot for an informal lunch, the Home Sweet Harlem Cafe (see page 216).

At Seventh Avenue, turn uptown once again and go right on 138th Street to the **Abyssinian Baptist Church (7),** 132 West

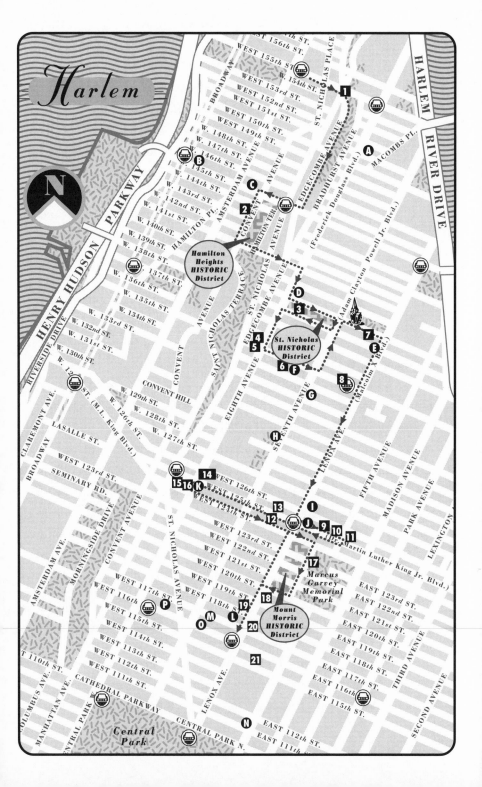

138th Street, between Seventh and Lenox Avenues, (212) 862–7474.
Lines often spill out onto the sidewalk waiting to hear the magnificent choir and organ at the popular services of this church at 11:30
A.M. each Sunday. This is one of the oldest and most influential congregations in the city. The original church was founded in 1808 by a
few free black parishioners who left the First Baptist Church of New
York City because they were unwilling to accept racially segregated
seating. Under a charismatic leader, Adam Clayton Powell Sr., an
elaborate church with imported stained-glass windows and an Italian
marble pulpit was dedicated on this site in 1923. Adam Clayton
Powell Jr., a fiery preacher, congressman, and civil-rights leader,
brought the church to national prominence when he took over the
pulpit in 1937. This impressive leadership continues under the
Reverend Calvin Butts III.

After church, vendors cluster on the corner of Seventh Avenue,
selling souvenirs such as turbaned African dolls and fresh produce,
including soul-food favorites like collard greens and okra.

Continue to Lenox Avenue and turn right to reach to the
**Schomburg Center for Research into Black Culture, The
New York Public Library (8),** 515 Lenox Avenue at 135th
Street, (212) 491–2200. This contemporary complex, completed in
1991, is the largest research center of black and African culture in
the United States. It doubles as a cultural center, with a theater and
two art galleries with changing exhibits. The nucleus of the enor-
mous collection was assembled by one man, the late Arthur
Schomburg, to preserve his people's legacy. It was purchased by the
New York Public Library in 1926.

The original library at 135 West 135th, between Lenox and
Seventh Avenues, was designed by McKim Mead & White in 1905. It
was the unofficial meeting place for writers during the black literary

renaissance of the 1920s and hosted many literary gatherings and poetry readings.

Turn downtown once again on Lenox Avenue to 126th Street to find the most famous restaurant in Harlem, Sylvia's—easy to spot by the spiffy purple awning that proclaims QUEEN OF SOUL. Sylvia's serves traditional Southern food and attracts many visitors to the neighborhood, though its popularity has made it grow large and somewhat commercial, with many tour buses lined up for the famous Sunday gospel brunch.

The next block, 125th Street, is the main shopping street and the nerve center of Harlem. The Starbucks on the corner of Lenox Avenue is a sign of the upscaling of the street and the neighborhood. Record shops here are great sources for rap and soul music, with all the latest hits.

For a more down-home touch, turn left at 125th Street to **Wimp's Southern Style Bakery (9),** 29 West 125th Street between Lenox and Fifth Avenues, (212) 410–2296, for take-home desserts like made-from-scratch sweet potato pie, peach cobbler, and custard pies—treats that are too good to miss. The cakes are also delicious; Wimp's baked the cake for Bill Clinton's welcome festivities when the former president moved his offices to Harlem.

Walk on to Fifth Avenue to find **The Brownstone (10),** 2032 Fifth Avenue between 125th and 126th Streets, (212) 996–7980. This is one of Harlem's most delightful stores, an eclectic, handsome, high-style collection of women's clothing, scarves, jewelry, and accessories housed in a brownstone. Across the street is **Harlem Underground (11),** 2027 Fifth Avenue, (866) 585–5005, offers shirts, jackets, caps, and other gear with a unique Harlem logo.

Turning west, again on 125th Street, proceed to the **Studio Museum in Harlem (12),** 144 West 125th Street between Lenox and Seventh Avenues, (212) 864–4500, with galleries on two levels for changing exhibits, three galleries showing a permanent collection of works by major black artists, and a small sculpture garden. The museum holds many special events and has a small shop with books and African crafts.

Across the street is the famous **Apollo Theater (13),** 253 West 125th Street, (212) 864–0372, where so many great enter-

tainers got their start. It was a whites-only opera house until 1934, when Frank Schiffman, a white entrepreneur, took over and opened the theater to all. It came to feature legends such as Bessie Smith, Billie Holiday, Duke Ellington, and Dinah Washington. The Wednesday-night amateur nights were legendary; Sara Vaughn, Pearl Bailey, James Brown, and Gladys Knight are among many whose careers were launched here. After World War II a new generation of musicians, including Charlie "Bird" Parker, Dizzy Gillespie, Thelonius Monk, and Aretha Franklin, continued the tradition. The beat has changed to rap and hip-hop, but the Apollo still features top black entertainers, and the Wednesday-night amateur night still packs them in.

The tall building on the northeast corner of Seventh Avenue is the Harlem State Office Building, built as a symbol to the community that the state had not forgotten them.

The big white building across the street in the middle of the block between 124th and 125th is Theresa Towers, once the elegant 1910 Hotel Theresa, where Fidel Castro stayed when he visited New York, and where Nikita Khrushchev came to call on him. In 1971 it was converted to an office building.

Keep walking to Eighth Avenue for another great place to hear gospel services in elegant surroundings, the **United House of Prayer for all the People (14),** known as the **"Daddy Grace" Church,** 2320 Eighth Avenue, (212) 864–8795, on the second floor of a modern building on the southeast corner. Across the hall from the sanctuary is a cafeteria with some of the best fried chicken and corn bread and the lowest prices to be found in the neighborhood. They'll pack it for you if you want to take some home.

Across the street is the big **Harlem USA (15)** development, with a Disney Store, HMV Records, Old Navy, and other national chain stores new to this area, plus a ten-screen Magic movie theater, financed by former basketball great Magic Johnson. This new competition has spawned a lot of upgraded facades on 125th Street, as local merchants fight to keep their customers.

One stop not to be missed within the complex is the **Hue-Man Book Store (16),** 2319 Eighth Avenue between 125th and 124th Streets, (212) 665–7400, one of America's largest African-American specialty book retailers, with a stock of over ten thousand titles. Proprietor Clara Villarosa, the first African American to serve on the board of the American Booksellers Association, was a pioneer when she opened a store in Denver in the 1980s. Now a grandmother and retired, she had come back to be near her family in Harlem when she was approached about opening a store in Harlem. She would help to fill a conspicuously empty space between the Sports Club and the Disney Store that booksellers like Barnes & Noble had declined to occupy. To finance the project, Villarosa found two forward-thinking female partners, Rita Ewing, former wife of basketball star Patrick Ewing, and Celeste Johnson, wife of former New York Knick Larry Johnson. The three women combined their own money and secured a $475,000 loan from the Upper Manhattan Empowerment Zone to make the store a reality. Readings are a regular feature and children's story hours are held on Saturdays at 2:00 P.M.

Walk east again for 2½ blocks on West 124th Street to reach Marcus Garvey Park and the **Mount Morris Historical District (17),** extending to 120th Street between the park and Lenox Avenue. This was a favorite neighborhood for German Jews moving up in the world from the Lower East Side, and you can plainly see that these late nineteenth-century town houses were once grand.

This is also the perfect area to admire a few of the finest Harlem churches and appreciate the layers of history they represent. The Ephesus Seventh-Day Adventist Church, 267 Lenox, at the northwest corner of 123rd, is housed in the former Reformed Low Dutch Church of Harlem, circa 1887.

At the Ethiopian Hebrew Congregation, a black congregation housed in a former mansion at 1 West 23rd Street, the choir sings in Hebrew on Saturday, while the Bethelite Community Baptist Church is housed in the original Harlem Club, 36 West 123rd, built for the white elite in 1889.

The columned Mount Olivet Baptist Church at 201 Lenox Avenue, at the northwest corner of 120th Street, was once Temple Israel, one of the most imposing synagogues in the city.

On the opposite corner of 120th Street is another harbinger of change in Harlem, **Settepani (18),** 196 Lenox Avenue, (917) 492–4806, an upscale bakery/coffee shop offering Italian pastries, cakes, and fresh-baked bread. You can find dishes such as a tasty quiche if you want to make this a lunch stop, but it's the desserts that are the real lure.

Cross the street and proceed to the next block for **Xukuma (19),** 183 Lenox Avenue at 119th Street, (212) 222–0490, a home design store that is a first for Harlem, stocked with the kind of stylish home accessories that would be right at home in trendier Manhattan neighborhoods.

Harlemade (20), 147 Lenox Avenue, (212) 987–2500, on the next block, is a little gift shop with locally made or inspired memorabilia, crafts, and unusual souvenirs, like 3-D Harlem street scenes and funky T-shirts.

The final stops are on 116th Street. This section of Harlem has become known as "Little Senegal" for the large number of West

African immigrants who have settled here, and several small no-frills restaurants serve this very distinctive cuisine.

It is also a hub for the Islamic community. The corner of Lenox Avenue is the site of the Malcolm Shabazz Mosque No. 7, where Malcolm X worshipped. The mosque is easy to spot, marked with a green dome.

Walk west to see some of the restaurants, and stop at the corner of Eighth Avenue and 116th Street to admire a particularly attractive intersection of broad boulevards and handsome buildings. On the northeast corner is Harlem's grandest apartment building, Graham Court, built by William Waldorf Astor at the turn of the century. Behind the iron gate is an arch clad in Guastivino tile (like that in Midtown's Oyster Bar), leading to a landscaped inner courtyard. On the southwest corner, the ornate, Moorish-style First Corinthian Baptist Church was originally one of America's first movie palaces, covered in rich terra cotta. The building was preserved when the church bought it in 1964.

On the north side of the street beyond Eighth Avenue are small shops with colorful African clothing in the windows and shops such as the Abyssinia Deli & Grocery, 225 West 116th, (212) 663–0553, and Touba Khassa, 243 West 116th, (212) 280–0827, selling books and tapes.

Further east on 116th Street between Lenox and Fifth Avenues is the most interesting shopping stop in Harlem, the **Malcolm Shabazz Harlem Market (21).** Past the gates of gaily painted minarets are more than one hundred neat stalls selling African art, drums, masks, dashiki shirts, hats, and a wonderful array of African fabrics sold by the yard. It's the perfect place to pick up a final souvenir of your trip.

Soul Food Cuisine

A mix of Southern and African heritage, soul food is hearty country fare with little concern for calories or cholesterol. Many consider it "comfort food"—like you wish your mother used to make. More sophisticated restaurants also serve Louisiana specialties, like blackened catfish and jambalaya. Corn bread and biscuits are the standard breads served with most Southern meals.

A SOUL FOOD SAMPLER

Here are some of the favorite dishes:

Barbecue: Southern-style barbecue means a large cut of meat slow-cooked over an open pit; hickory wood is usually used for fuel. Depending on the region, it may be served in slices or "pulled," meaning shredded, and the sauce may be vinegar- or tomato-based. Open-pit ribs are cooked in the same fashion.

Black-eyed peas: dried beans, named for their single black spot, often cooked with ham hocks or slab bacon. Superstition says it is good luck to have them on New Year's Day.

Chit-lins or **chitterlings:** pigs' intestines, carefully cleaned and stewed, and then often fried. Usually served with collard greens.

Collard greens: greens with a slightly bitter taste, usually cooked with smoked pork or a ham bone. Mustard or turnip greens are equally popular side dishes, prepared the same way.

Country gravy: similar to red eye; a white gravy made of milk and flour and pan drippings from chicken or pan-fried steak.

Fried catfish: another Southern staple, a whole fish or fillets, usually dipped in cornmeal, fried in a skillet and served with coleslaw and hush puppies.

Fried chicken: this best-known Southern dish needs little description, but there's a big difference between ordinary and great. The best is dipped in seasoned flour and deep fried until it is golden, flaky, and crispy with little grease on the outside, moist and tender inside. You'll taste it at its best in Harlem.

Grits: dried, hulled, ground corn cooked into a bland, creamy cereal with a slightly gritty texture; it is usually lavished with butter or gravy to give it flavor. Often served with eggs for breakfast in the South as well as for a side dish with dinner.

Hush puppies: cornmeal batter seasoned with chopped onions and/or garlic and deep fried by the spoonful into little round balls. Served as a side dish with many Southern entrees.

Oven-barbecued ribs: more tender than open-pit barbecue, these ribs are first baked plain, then baked a second time with a sauce made of tomato, vinegar, and brown sugar.

Pan-fried or **chicken-fried steak:** thin or cubed steaks, dipped in egg, dredged in flour and then sautéed, usually served with country gravy.

Red-eye gravy: ham gravy made from flour and water or coffee with the drippings from the pan in which ham has been fried.

Spoon bread: similar to a soufflé, made with milk, eggs, and butter and eaten with a spoon.

Sweet potato pie: mashed sweet potatoes, sweetened and blended with eggs, milk, and spices such as cinnamon, cloves, and nutmeg, then baked in a crust. The taste is similar to pumpkin pie.

R E C O M M E N D E D 🍴 R E S T A U R A N T S

Charles' Southern-Style Kitchen (A) ($), 2841 Eighth Avenue at 151st Street, (212) 926–4313, has a chef/owner, Charles Gabriel, who cooks only a few dishes each day, but whatever is served in this unpretentious storefront is delicious. Some possibilities: pork chops, fried chicken, or chicken smothered in gravy, pork ribs.

Copeland's Country Kitchen (B) ($), 549 West 145th Street, between Amsterdam Avenue and Broadway (212) 234–2356, known for sophisticated Southern food, has brought in celebrities like Bill Cosby, Ruby Dee, and Danny Glover. Along with traditional dishes, the menu lists Louisiana gumbo and jambalaya, Maryland crab cakes, and broiled lobster tails. Dinner only.

Sugar Hill Bistro (C) ($$), 458 West 145th Street, between Amsterdam and Convent Avenues, (212) 491–5505, is a classy cafe housed in a brownstone, with dining on the first two floors and an art gallery above. There's a little garden out back for sunny days. Eclectic cuisine with a Southern accent and live jazz on weekends bring an upscale crowd.

Londels (D) ($), 2620 Eighth Avenue at 140th Street, (212) 234–6114, offers upscale dining with all the Southern basics, plus Louisiana dishes. This spot is known for its Sunday gospel brunch.

Miss Maude's Spoonbread, Too (E) ($), 547 Lenox Avenue, between 137th and 138th Streets, (212) 690–3100, is a cheerful setting for Southern favorites like smothered pork chops, short ribs, fried shrimp, or fried chicken with sides of collard greens, candied yams, and the like.

A TYPICAL SOUL FOOD MEAL

Fried or smothered chicken or fried catfish with hush puppies

Mashed potatoes

Collard greens

Sweet potato pie

Home Sweet Harlem Cafe (F) ($), 270 West 235th Street, between Eighth and Seventh Avenues) is a funky coffee shop with mismatched chairs and tables, always crowded for its excellent, inexpensive home-made soups, sandwiches, and burgers.

Jamaican Hot Pot (G) ($), 2260 Seventh Avenue at 133rd

Street, (212) 491–5270, offers West Indian specialties for a change of pace, including curried goat and garlic shrimp.

Jimmy's Uptown (H) ($$), 2207 Adam Clayton Powell Boulevard, (212) 491–4000, is Harlem's swankiest dining spot.

Sylvia's (I) ($), 328 Lenox Avenue at 126th Street, (212) 996–0660, has gone from modest beginnings to becoming a legend, especially for Sunday brunch. The crowds mean that other restaraunts offer better food and ambience, but people still stand in line for specialties like stewed chicken and dumplings, meat loaf with Sylvia's special sauce, smothered steak, and chicken giblets. Sylvia's serves three meals a day.

Bayou (J) ($$), 308 Lenox Avenue, (212) 280–8779, 125 New Orleans North, is a Cajun-Creole winner with a chef who whips up delicious gumbo and crayfish étouffée, drawing fans from all over the city.

Daddy Grace Church Cafeteria (K) ($), See **(14)** page 210.

Native (L) ($$), 116 Lenox Street at 118th Street, (212) 655–2525, is an upscale newcomer with casual ambience and a change-of-pace French-Moroccan menu. The outdoor cafe is crowded on sunny afternoons.

Amy Ruth's (M) ($), 113 West 116th Street, (212) 280–8779, is open for all three meals and is one of the most pleasant places to enjoy delicious favorites from breakfast chicken and waffles to dinners of ribs or spicy shrimp over rice.

Emily's Restaurant (N) ($), 1325 Fifth Avenue between 111th and 112th Streets, (212) 996–1212, serves all the usual specialties with a welcoming ambience and affordable prices.

AN AFRICAN CUISINE SAMPLER

African meat dishes are often stews or casseroles since the available meat was usually not of high quality and required long cooking. Fish is also widely used. Most of these restaurants are Senegalese, one of the best of African cuisines.

A few typical dishes are:

Cheb: chunks of fish, usually bluefish, cooked with vegetables in a tomato sauce and served with rice.

Mafe or **mafee:** chicken or lamb stewed with vegetables and ground peanuts or peanut butter.

Tieboudienne: whitefish, eggplant, carrots, cassava, and cabbage, stewed in tomatoes with spiced rice.

RECOMMENDED 🍽 RESTAURANTS

The Baobab (O) ($), 120 West 116th Street, between Lenox and Seventh Avenues, (212) 864–0081, is an informal cafe decorated with folk paintings of African village life and portraits of heroes like Nelson Mandela and Martin Luther King Jr. French is the language of choice here, but the menu has helpful English descriptions of each of the chef's dishes of the day, which include chicken, fish, vegetable, and lamb, prepared Senegalese style, and often served with scented Jasmine rice.

Keur Sokhna (P) ($), 225 West 116th Street, between Seventh and Eighth Avenues, (212) 864–4700, a tiny cafe with just ten tables, has a typical Senegalese menu including mafe, a spicy lamb stew. An interesting dessert is thiaky, a pudding made with finely ground couscous mixed with yogurt, vanilla, honey, and fruit.

HARLEM JAZZ CLUBS

St. Nick's Pub, 773 St. Nicholas Avenue at 149th Street (212) 283–9728.

Strivers Lounge and Café, 2611 Eighth Avenue at 139th Street, (212) 491–4422.

Showman's, 325 West 125th Street (between St. Nicholas and Morningside Avenues), (212) 864–8941.

Robin's Nest, 457 West 125th Street, between Amsterdam and Morningside Avenues, (212) 316–6170.

Lenox Lounge, 288 Lenox Avenue between 124th and 125th Streets, (212) 722–9566.

HARLEM ART GALLERIES

The gallery locations are not on the walking tour route, but Harlem's growing art scene is worth seeking out. Phone to check hours.

Triple Candie, 461 West 125th Street, between Amsterdam and Morningside Avenues, (212) 864–4500

The Project, 427 West 126th Street, (212) 662–8610

Storefront 1838, 1838 Seventh Avenue at 111th Street, (212) 866–1838

P.C.O.G. Gallery, 1902 Seventh Avenue, between 115th and 116th Streets, (212) 932–9669.

A Hidden Slice of Seoul

Walking on the east side of Broadway near Macy's, if you look up around 31st Street, you'll notice that the street signs begin to say KOREA WAY. It's the first hint that you are about to discover a surprising slice of Seoul in the middle of Midtown Manhattan. Koreans may live in Flushing, but much of their business takes place in Manhattan. The business area spreads over several blocks, but the heart of things for food lovers is on 32nd Street, between Fifth Avenue and Broadway, easy to spot by the many Korean signs decking the buildings and easy to explore if you are shopping in the Herald Square area.

THE HISTORY

Read about the Korean community in New York on page 134, (Flushing).

How to Get There

Take the B, D, F, N, or R Train to 34th Street, Herald Square; M34, the 34th Street crosstown bus, or M6, Sixth Avenue Bus to 34th Street.

... A Shopping Tour ...

Though it is compact, this block includes two large Korean banks, four hotels, a Korean book and gift store, a giant supermarket, and some fifteen restaurants, many of them open twenty-four hours and still going strong at 2:00 A.M. Stroll both sides of the street to take it all in.

Starting from Broadway on the north side of the street, walk past the flashy Holiday Inn and the smaller Stanford Hotel to **Koryo Books (1)**, 35 West 32nd Street, (212) 564–1844, a store that is packed with books in Korean as well as English titles on Korea and Korean cooking. The store also sells Korean CDs, videos, greeting cards, and religious objects, and a selection of gifts including toys, dolls, games, vases, and wooden lanterns.

A few doors farther you'll spy the **Koryodang Bakery (2)**, 31 West 32nd Street, (212) 967–9661, with a variety of buns and sweet treats.

Farther on, the sign reading SUPER MARKET leads to a food store that is probably unlike anything in your neighborhood. **Han Ah Reum (3)**, 25 West 32nd Street, (212) 695–3283, is an intriguing Korean supermarket where you can pick up jars of kimchi, bean sauce, quail eggs, dumpling wrappers, packages of sweet marinated beef ready to be grilled for bulgogi, giant bags of rice or noodles, and dried everything, from seaweed to cuttlefish. The large take-out department offers many of the salads and appetizers served in restaurants, including kimchi. There are lots of cakes and sweets near the front of the store, and you can pick up a Korean newspaper at the checkout.

Keep walking past more restaurants and a few shops selling anything from cell phones to jewelry. At the end of the block, cross the

A Hidden Slice of Seoul

N

WEST 38th STREET
WEST 37th STREET
WEST 36th STREET
WEST 35th STREET
WEST 34th STREET
WEST 33rd STREET
WEST 32nd STREET
WEST 31st STREET
WEST 30th STREET
WEST 29th STREET

BROADWAY
AVENUE OF THE AMERICAS
FIFTH AVENUE
SIXTH AVENUE
BROADWAY
MADISON AVENUE

Macy's

Empire
State
Building

A B 1 2 3 C D
I 8 H 7 6 G F 5 4 E

street and work your way west once again. **Natural Oriental Herbs (4),** 2 West 32nd Street, (212) 594–6929, may have just what you need to cure whatever ails you. Herbs or not, you can have a soothing cup of ginger citron or ginseng tea and a Korean sweet in the same building at **Cafe Metro (5),** 2 West 32nd Street, (212) 244–2217, a small pleasing modern teashop. They also serve the chilled "bubble tea" with tapioca balls in the bottom that is the current rage in Chinatown.

A bit of everything can be found at **Sun Elt Plaza (6),** 22 West 32nd Street, (212) 564–3397, a Korean "general store" with books, music, cosmetics, and clothing.

If you want to learn tai chi, the **H. Won Tai Chi Institute (7),** 30 West 32nd Street, sixth floor, (212) 226–1836, invites visitors to come up and see how it is taught and practiced and to have a free trial lesson.

Should you have a desire to learn a bit of Korean, the **Korean Language Center of New York (8),** 38 West 32nd Street, Suite 1112, (212) 563–5763, will oblige.

These are examples of the many businesses occupying the upper floors of the buildings of the block. As you walk, you'll see dozens of signs advertising everything from body scrubs at a spa to karaoke clubs. They may not be places you want to patronize, but they add up to authentic ambience and a fascinating look into another culture. And when your stroll is over, you can choose among the many restaurants that pack the block.

Korean Cuisine

For descriptions of foods commonly used in Korean cuisine, see page 138.

RECOMMENDED 🍽 RESTAURANTS

Kum Gang San (A) ($–$$), 49 West 32nd Street, (212) 967–0909, a gleaming addition to the Holiday Inn, this restaurant boasts a two-story faux mountainside, complete with mini Shinto temples, cascading waterfalls, and a white grand piano improbably perched on a mountain. House specialties include go choo pajon, a kind of Korean pancake made with scallions and hot peppers and hae mool pajon, a similar dish prepared with seafood.

Gam Mee Ok (B) ($–$$), 43 West 32nd Street, (212) 695–4113, has a spare Japanese look with tables set on a polished wooden platform, walls with the look of shoji screens, and black and white photos. They claim to be famous for their kimchi, but you can enjoy a fine meal here even if you don't care for the classic Korean side dish.

Won Jo (C) ($–$$), 23 West 32nd Street, (212) 695–5815, an enormous menu and servings to match bring a steady stream of customers to this unpretentious spot.

Dae Dong (D) ($–$$), 17 West 32nd, (212) 967–1900. This is one of the handsomest restaurants on the block, tastefully decorated with murals of temple scenes and hammered copper chimneys over the grills. Even the soy sauce comes stylishly served, in green antique clay jars. The side dishes are delicious, from potato salad to marinated shrimp with greens. If you ask for tea, it will come in a tall glass. The jap chae, pan fried vermicelli noodles, comes highly recommended. The bulgogi is excellent.

Hangawi (E) ($$), 12 East 32nd Street, (212) 213–0077. The room is serene, the music other-worldly; remove your shoes and come inside for an unusual Zen-like experience. This restaurant serves vegetarian meals featuring "temple food" a diet favored by Buddhist monks, featuring roots, grains, and potatoes. It's so healthy, you'll emerge feeling cleansed.

Mandoo Bar (F) ($), 2 West 32nd Street, (212) 279–3075. Mandoo is the Korean version of dumplings; you can watch the ladies in the window making the tasty bite-sized treats, then go in and order a plate of ten for under $10. Soups, noodle, and rice dishes are also on the menu.

Woorijip (G) ($), 12 West 32nd Street, (212) 244–1115, offers a buffet where you can choose whatever pleases you among thirty-two dishes, hot and cold, and pay $5.49 per pound, making for a most reasonable and varied informal meal. Or you can choose the noodle bar with its choices of hot soup and noodle dishes, priced from $5.00 to $7.00 Like many of the restaurants on the block, Woorijip is open twenty-four hours.

New York Kom Tang Kalbi House (H) ($–$$), 32 West 32nd Street, (212) 947–8482, looks like a cafeteria, but wins high praise from diners who appreciate the barbecue grills fired by wood rather than the gas used in most restaurants. The grilled offerings range from beef to short ribs to eel to shrimp. If you don't want barbecue, the first-floor dining room has a full Korean menu.

Kang Suh (I) ($–$$), 1250 Broadway at 32nd, (212) 564–6845. Having received two stars from *The New York Times,* this very plain restaurant is often packed, smoky from the many grills going at once—and noisy. The food, however, is delicious, and the staff is used to explaining things to novices. If you order the favorite dish, bulgogi, waiters appear with boxes of live coals to fill the grill in the center of the table, where the sweetly marinated beef is cooked using long handled tongs, tended by you or by the staff, as you wish. The beef comes with rice and half a dozen small side dishes.

Savoring Little Italy

Pizza from a coal brick oven . . . a hearty glass of Chianti . . . perfect pastas . . . a sinfully rich cannoli . . . you'll find them all in New York City's Little Italy, along with some of the best take-home Italian breads, sausages, pastas, and cheeses sold in the city.

"Little" is an unfortunately apt description these days, with Chinatown taking over so much of the old neighborhood. But while it is a lot smaller than it used to be, the Italian stretch of Mulberry Street and its environs still holds plenty of Old World flavor and some wonderful eating and shopping. Many of the landmarks have been here for nearly a century. It is best to come on a warm summer evening, when the restaurants turn into sidewalk cafes, songs about Napoli fill the air, and the old neighborhood seems new again.

THE HISTORY

New York City's Italian population was small in the early years— fewer than 20,000 people in 1880. That changed dramatically when hard times in the Old Country brought a huge surge of people from southern Italy, raising the numbers to 220,000 by 1900 and 545,000 by 1910. Most of these newcomers had little education, and they did not have an easy time. Many worked on construction sites and in factories, often exploited by Italian bosses, known as *padrones*. Some settled in Greenwich Village and the boroughs, but the greatest number made their homes in the squalid tenements of the Lower East Side, in quarters so small and unsanitary that diseases such as tuberculosis were rife.

How to Get There

Take the #6 Lexington Avenue Train to Spring Street.

To add to their woes, the first wave of Italians found discrimination in the Catholic Church, which was then predominantly Irish. They were banned from the old St. Patrick's; and at places such as the Church of the Transfiguration, on Mott Street, they were relegated to the basement for worship. As the Irish eventually moved on, the first Italian pastor arrived in 1902, and his Italian parishioners were able to move into the main section of the church. Reflecting the waves of immigration in the neighborhood, the church today is predominantly Chinese.

A sense of solidarity and family helped the immigrant Italians. They stuck together, formed societies to help one another find work, and began to prosper and to grow in numbers. By 1930 the Italian population of New York was well over one million—17 percent of the city's population—and they were having a strong impact on city politics, as demonstrated by the election of Fiorello La Guardia as mayor in 1933. Leaders like Frank Costello and Carmine DeSapio became powers in Tammany Hall, the city's potent political machine.

Italian racketeers were also gaining wealth and notoriety at the time. The crime syndicates of the American Mafia were composed of families modeled on secret societies in Italy. Their image is often

The San Gennaro Festival

Eat, drink, and be merry! That might well be the motto during the festival of San Gennaro, *which transforms Mulberry Street for nine days each year in mid-September, honoring the patron saint of Naples. It is an event now shared by over one million visitors patronizing more than 300 vendors, who provide a feast of zeppole, ziti, pastries, and the sausage and peppers sandwiches that are the signature street food of the festival.*

Gennaro was a bishop of Naples in the third century who died a martyr during religious persecution. He became the patron saint of the city, where the people prayed to him for protection in times of crisis.

The annual feast in New York is the carryover of a Neapolitan tradition, begun more than seventy years ago by Neapolitan immigrants who missed their home. They strung lights on the street, cooked up sausage and peppers and zeppole, and paraded the statue of their patron saint, according to the custom in Italy. They still parade, and people still pin money on the statue, hoping for good luck, health, and fortune. The procession usually follows a mass at the Most Precious Blood Catholic Church, *113 Baxter Street, (212) 226–6427, where the statue is housed.*

The festival features rides and games for kids, plus live bands, with music ranging from opera to Frank Sinatra. One activity missing from recent years is gambling. Games of chance were eliminated in 1996, after the city cracked down on alleged mob infiltration into the organization that previously ran the feast. The current sponsors turn over all net proceeds from the feast to local schools and charities.

glorified in movies, but the crime associated with them plagued hon-est Italians, who formed organizations such as the Italian American Civil Rights League in the 1960s in order to fight stereotypes and prejudice against Italians.

As their position in the world improved, young Italians moved out of the old neighborhood, and the vacancies they left were filled by Chinese merchants, for the first time moving north of Canal Street, the traditional boundary between Chinatown and Little Italy. Seeing their turf dwindling, Italian merchants and restaurateurs have formed an association dedicated to maintaining Mulberry Street north of Canal Street as an all-Italian enclave, which it remains, at least for now.

• • • A Shopping Tour • • •

Spring Street is an excellent place to start. Walk east from the subway and you'll spy Lombardi Pizza, at this location since 1905, turning out coal-oven pizzas that many consider the city's best.

A short detour to Mott Street brings you to a traditional Italian bakery, **Parisi's (1),** 196-198 Mott Street, (212) 226–6378, a standby in the neighborhood for many years.

While it is not Italian, you may well want to look into Lale, the shop right next door at 200 Mott Street, (212) 941–7461, for its attractive displays of pottery, crystal, and rugs from Turkey.

Proceeding down Mott Street, turn right on Broome Street. At the corner of Mulberry you will see the Cafe Roma, busy serving up cap-puccino and espresso with biscotti or rich Italian cheesecake (see page 242). Across the street is Umberto's Clam House, 386 Broome Street, (212) 431–7545, known less for food than for the celebrity

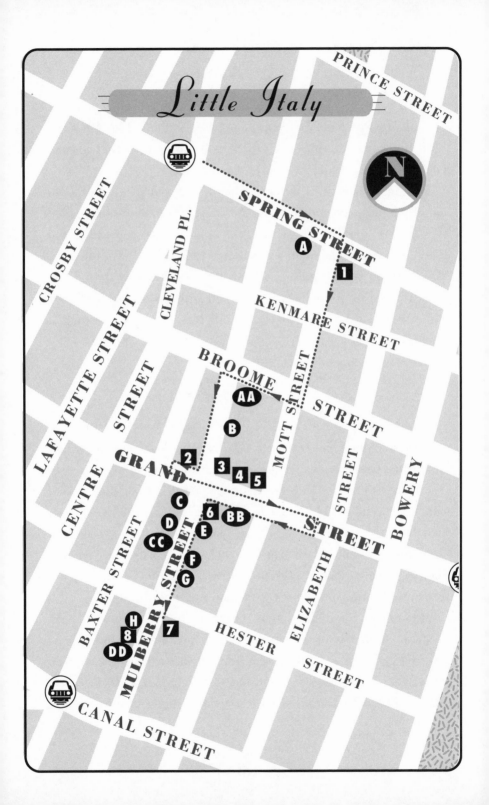

photos on the walls and the memory of 1972, when Mafia figure Joey Gallo was gunned down here during a family dinner.

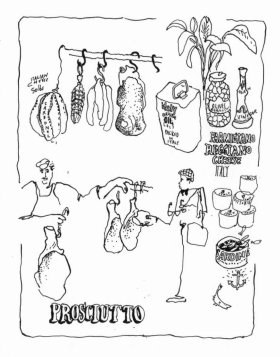

Mulberry's restaurant row continues for 3 blocks to Canal Street, with T-shirt and souvenir vendors all along the way—but Grand Street calls for food shopping.

Two prime candidates are across the street from each other on the corner of Mulberry and Grand. The **Italian Food Center (2),** 186 Grand Street, (212) 925–2954, usually has a few people sitting on the bench out front munching sandwiches. For good reason—this place makes the best in the neighborhood, served hot or cold on the shop's own baked hero rolls. Genoa salami, prosciutto, marinated mushrooms, provolone; have any or all. There's a wide range of imported Italian foods as well—olive oil, pastas, Italian fruit cakes—and prepared foods such as eggplant parmigiana or lasagna to take home.

The old-fashioned, tile-floored **Alleva Dairy (3),** 188 Mulberry Street (at Grand Street), (212) 226–7990, has been a haven for cheese lovers for nearly a century. There's smoked or fresh mozzarella, Romano, and other, less familiar cheeses you'll definitely want to taste and probably buy. It sells pasta and homemade tomato sauce, as well.

Next door is **Piemonte Homemade Ravioli Company (4)**, 190 Grand Street, (212) 226–1033, where ravioli is only one of the two dozen shapes and varieties of homemade pastas. The cannelloni, ravioli, and tortellini also come stuffed with wonderful meat or cheese or spinach.

At the corner of Grand and Mott is a "newcomer," here just seventy or so years, **DiPalo Dairy (5)**, 200 Grand Street, (212) 266–1033, where you can watch them making the mozzarella fresh every day and buy creamy ricotta and gorgeous Gorgonzola. DiPalo moved to the corner across the street from its original location recently, losing a bit of its old-world aura, but allowing more room for the many customers who used to stand in line to get into the old store.

Cross the street and walk back toward Mulberry and you'll spy perhaps the best-known cafe in Little Italy, Ferrara's (see page 242). It's big and fancy and some say it has gone commercial, but it's still hard to beat the cannoli here or the wide selection of sweets and endless boxes of Italian candies.

At **E. Rossi's (6)**, 191 Grand Street at the corner of Mulberry, (212) 226–9254, you'll find the tools to make your own fresh pasta or espresso plus serving bowls for your spaghetti, aprons, T-shirts, Italian cassettes, religious statuary, and whatever else you may need.

A similar variety of wares in a more spacious and attractive setting is found at **Forzano Italian Imports (7)**, 128 Mulberry Street, (212) 925–2525, with everything from CDs to cruets to pepper grinders.

Across the street is **Carosello Italiano (8),** 119 Mulberry Street, (212) 925–7250, a shop with a large stock of quality Italian ceramics.

If the day is warm, you may want to stop for a gelato a couple of doors down at the outdoor stand at Cha Cha's in Bocca al Lupo (see page 242). The cafe, which boasts Little Italy's only outdoor garden, also offers espresso, cappuccino, and all kinds of tempting desserts, plus mini-pizzas, sandwiches, and salads. The list of "Drinks of the Stars" reflects some of the many show biz friends of proprietor Johnny Cha Cha, including Danny Aiello, Tony Danza, Danny Devito, Robert De Niro, and Michael Douglas, all of whom have been spotted at the cafe. Cha Cha has appeared in several films himself.

From here you can wander down to Canal Street and back, reading menus, stopping at a cafe if the spirit moves you, and finally making the tough decision of where to eat.

Guaranteed, by now you'll be in the mood for an Italian dinner.

Italian Cuisine

Italian food needs little introduction in New York, where there are literally thousands of Italian restaurants.

The basic differences are regional, but most Little Italy restaurants serve the basic hearty southern Italian menu of Naples, featuring tomato sauces. The principal seasonings are basil, oregano, and garlic. Appetizers, known as antipasti, are an important part of the meal, served both hot and cold.

AN ITALIAN SAMPLER

Pastas are a staple in any Italian menu. Spaghetti surely needs no explanation, but some other common shapes of pasta include:

Cannelloni: large tubes, usually stuffed.

Cappelli or **angel hair:** super-thin, round strands.

Cavatelli: small snail shapes.

Farfalle: butterfly shapes.

Fettuccine: long, thin, flat ribbons.

Fusilli: long curly strands.

Lasagne: long, wide, flat ribbons with ridged edges.

Linguine: long, flat, very thin strips.

Pappardelle: medium-width flat ribbons.

Penne: short, hollow tubes cut diagonally.

Ravioli: small squares with various fillings.

Rigatoni: ridged tubes.

Shells: literally, shell shapes, usually stuffed.

Tortellini: small, stuffed rings.

Ziti: narrow, hollow tubes.

Popular sauces include:

Alfredo: a sauce made with butter, cream, and Parmesan cheese.

Bolognese: a tomato sauce with ground beef, green peppers, garlic, and onion.

Carbonara: a cream sauce with eggs, olive oil, cheese, and bacon.

Marinara: a tomato sauce with olive oil, garlic, and basil.

Pomodoro: simple sauce made with fresh tomatoes.

Other popular dishes include:

Antipasto misto: a selection of appetizers that may include grilled red peppers, salami, prosciutto, anchovies, beans, and a variety of salads.

Baked clams oreganate: clams on the half shell topped with a mixture of breadcrumbs with minced garlic, parsley, olive oil, and oregano and put under the broiler. A classic appetizer.

Bruschetta: bread that is toasted, brushed with olive oil (and sometimes garlic), and covered with chopped tomato.

Calamari: squid, usually served deep fried.

Caponata: a cold-relish appetizer made of fried eggplant that has been cooked with onions, zucchini, celery, and black olives.

Carpaccio: an appetizer dish of raw beef pounded paper-thin and drizzled with oil.

Fra diavolo: a spicy tomato sauce often used with seafood.

Gnocchi: dumplings made of flour or potatoes.

Lasagna: a well-known dish of large, flat pasta layered with meat sauce and ricotta and mozzarella cheeses. Vegetarian lasagna uses a light cream sauce, a mix of vegetables, and the same cheeses.

Minestrone: a thick, hearty vegetable soup.

Osso Buco: braised veal shank.

Pancetta: an Italian bacon used for flavoring sauces and pasta.

Prosciutto: smoked Italian ham, usually served in paper-thin slices; often served with melon as an appetizer.

Risotto: rice that is browned in butter and oil before being slowly simmered in stock, making it both creamy and firm. Usually a main dish, it can be served with many combinations of meats, seafood, or mushrooms.

Saltimbocca: thinly sliced veal wrapped in a thin layer of ham and usually braised in wine.

Scampi: shrimp, usually broiled and flavored with garlic, oil, and white wine.

Scungilli: steamed conch.

Veal or **chicken parmigiana:** a familiar dish made with breaded sautéed cutlets topped with tomato sauce, grated Parmesan and mozzarella cheeses, and put under the broiler to melt the cheese.

Veal or **chicken piccata:** thin cutlets dredged with flour and sautéed with white wine and lemon juice.

Veal or **chicken marsala:** cutlets pounded thin, dredged in flour, and sautéed with Marsala wine.

Italian Desserts:

Biscotti: twice-baked cookies with firm texture that are ideal for dipping in coffee.

Cannoli: crisp pastry shells filled with whipped cream, chocolate cream, sweetened ricotta cheese, or other ingredients.

Panettone: yeast coffee cake studded with raisins and dried fruits, a traditional Christmas cake, but served year-round.

Spumoni: a molded frozen dessert with several flavors of ice cream studded with candied fruit.

Tartufo: chocolate-coated vanilla ice cream.

Tiramisu: sponge cake soaked in brandy and espresso and layered with sweetened mascarpone, a soft rich cheese, and chocolate.

Zeppole: fried dough coated with powdered sugar.

R E C O M M E N D E D ¶◉ R E S T A U R A N T S

Plain or fancy, you'll find good, mostly southern Italian food everywhere in Little Italy. If you come for lunch, proprietors likely will be out on the sidewalk touting the virtues of their menus—"no pasta over $5.50."

Lombardi's (A) ($), 32 Spring Street, (212) 941–7994. Is this the best pizza in New York? You'll have a wonderful time deciding. Don't miss the white clam pie.

Da Nico (B) ($–$$), 164 Mulberry Street, (212) 343–1212, is an old-fashioned, family-run restaurant that everybody seems to like, serving celebrities and no-names with the same warmth. The

LITTLE ITALY N.Y.C. spring ST.

baked clams and rotisserie dishes are fine. The antipasto bar and the delicious pizza are pluses, and there's a nice garden in warm weather.

Il Palazzo (C) ($$), 151 Mulberry Street, (212) 343–7000, rivals Il Cortile for the title of "classiest in Little Italy," and some fans say the food is even better.

Taormina (D) ($$), 147 Mulberry Street, (212) 219–1007, a local landmark with reliably good food; used to be a favorite of mob boss John Gotti.

Angelo's (E) ($–$$), 146 Mulberry Street, (212) 966–1277, seems to have been here forever, with no changes to the red-sauce menu. But tourists love it, and so do many loyal New Yorkers who've been coming for years.

Il Fornaio (F) ($–$$), 132A Mulberry Street, (212) 226–8306, is praised for home cooking, homey decor, and good prices.

A TYPICAL ITALIAN MEAL

Antipasto

Pasta with a pesto or tomato sauce

Veal or chicken Marsala

Tiramisu

Pellegrino's (G) ($$), 138 Mulberry Street, (212) 226–3177, is not much on decor, but the homemade pastas and sauces are praised.

Il Cortile (H) ($$–$$$), 125 Mulberry Street, (212) 226–6060, offers excellent food, including northern Italian selections, in a handsome setting with an indoor garden. A class act.

Italian Cafes:

Four top stops for coffee in all varieties and tasty Italian pastries:

Cafe Roma (AA) ($), 385 Broome Street, (212) 226–8413.

Ferrara's (BB) ($), 195-201 Grand Street, (212) 226–6150.

Cafe Biondo (CC) ($), 141 Mulberry Street, (212) 226–9285.

Cha Cha's in Bocca al Lupo Cafe (DD) ($), 113 Mulberry Street, (212) 431–9755.

Memory Lane on the Jewish Lower East Side

The Jewish Lower East Side is alive with memories—of immigrants crowded into squalid tenements, worshippers at prayer in the synagogues, peddlers hawking wares from pushcarts, and children playing ball in the streets, the only open spaces to be found.

The spirit of these doughty newcomers remains, along with a sampling of the foods that provided them with a longed-for taste of home, plus some bargains that have long lured savvy shoppers to the Lower East Side. Come and walk into the past in this fascinating neighborhood.

How to Get There

Take the J or M Train to Delancey Street, the B or D Train to Grand Street, the F Train to Second Avenue, Delancey/Essex Street, or East Broadway. The M15 Bus travels through the Lower East Side on Allen Street.

THE HISTORY

The Lower East Side exemplifies the layers of history that tell the immigrant story of New York City. The first religious buildings were churches, used successively by Dutch, English, Irish, Germans, Italians, and now Chinese. The neighborhood's first synagogue, built in 1850, was erected by German Jews, the first Jews to arrive in large numbers, who constructed their temple to resemble the Cathedral of Cologne.

Between 1880 and 1920 some 1.5 million Eastern European Jews came to New York, most of them fleeing Polish and Russian pogroms. By 1910 they made up almost a quarter of the city's population. Many of them moved into the teeming tenements of the Lower East Side and eked out livings as peddlers on Orchard Street or working in garment factories. By 1920 they had founded some 500 synagogues and religious schools. A few synagogues were grand, but most were small, their congregations formed by immigrants from the same area banding together. Many of the neighborhood Christian churches, deserted by those who had moved uptown, were adapted for use as synagogues.

Some of the Jews who had come to America earlier and had made their way successfully reached out to help the newcomers. Their motives were not always altogether altruistic, however; some were embarrassed by these awkward newcomers.

The Educational Alliance was founded in 1889 by philanthropist David Sarnoff to help the immigrants assimilate and Americanize. It offered training in English, courses in business and civics, and hygiene—not to mention such rare amenities as hot showers.

A greater spirit of compassion motivated Lillian Wald, a middle-class German-Jewish woman, who in 1893 established a nursing service that provided medical care at home for the indigent. Two years later, financier Jacob Schiff purchased a building for the group. It became the Henry Street Nurses' Settlement, America's first visiting-nurses association.

The settlement evolved into a neighborhood center for civic and social work. It provided educational facilities, a playground and gymnasium, a loan fund and cooperative food store, summer camps for children, and concerts and plays for everyone. In 1944 the nursing service moved out and became an independent organization, The Visiting Nurse Service of New York.

Gradually the newcomers learned the ways of their new land and began to leave the neighborhood. In 1940 Mayor Fiorello La Guardia outlawed pushcarts in the city and Orchard Street became lined with shops (though many stores still like to put their wares out on the sidewalk to lure customers, especially on Sunday, when the street becomes a pedestrian mall). Only a small Jewish population remains in the neighborhood today, many of them Orthodox, and only a few food shops survive to serve them compared to the old days. But they still have their following; it isn't unusual to see a Mercedes double-parked on East Houston Street while someone runs in for smoked salmon and hand-made cream cheese.

In recent years Latinos and Chinese have moved into the Lower East Side, continuing the neighborhood's role as a haven for new arrivals. In another typical New York turn of events, the neighborhood has turned into a favorite site for trendy after-hours clubs, and young people are moving into some of the old tenement buildings.

... *A Shopping / Walking Tour* ...

This tour starts from the J and M Subway stop on Delancey Street. If you come via other stations, just follow the arrows.

From the Delancey Street stop, walk 2 blocks south, then cross the street and turn left onto Grand. **Kossar's Bialystocker Kuchen Bakery (1),** 367 Grand Street, (212) 473–4810, is a must for tasting what may well be the world's best bialys. These are chewy, flat, round rolls with a slightly depressed center with onions, lighter than bagels and absolutely delicious toasted. Kossar's also sells good bagels (though not baked here) and hearty breads by the pound—they'll cut off as much as you need.

This block also offers a sampling of the low-key kosher eateries of the area, selling everything from knishes to pizza to egg rolls. Not part of the kosher tour, but too good to miss, is the Doughnut Plant at 379 Grand Street. Don't mind the $2.00 price; these oversize, yeasty cakes are beyond compare. Both Martha Stewart and Emeril Lagasse have featured the creator, Mark Israel, on their shows.

From here, the first part of this walk covers history, landmark synagogues, and a couple of galleries, vital to understanding the neighborhood. If shopping is your main goal, head the other way on Grand Street.

To follow the tour, continue east on Grand and detour left on Norfolk Street for the **Congregation Beth Hamedrash Hagodol Synagogue (2)**, 60-64 Norfolk Street, (212) 674–3330. The small, picturesque white building with two square towers was home to America's oldest congregation of Orthodox Russian Jews, formed in 1852. The building began in 1850 as the Norfolk Street Baptist Church and was converted into a synagogue in 1885 after the church members moved north, eventually forming Riverside Church. The original Gothic woodwork and iron fence remain. It isn't unusual to find an artist across the street, capturing the church on canvas.

Back on Grand, walk east to the **Louis Abrons Arts Center/ Harry De Jur Henry Street Settlement Playhouse (3)**, 466 Grand Street, (212) 598–0400. The Playhouse was founded in 1915 by two sisters, Alice and Irene Lewisohn, for productions by youthful dramatic groups. It grew into an important experimental theater, the first in the United States to present a play written by a black author and performed by a black cast to a mixed audience. Among the important premieres here were James Joyce's *Exiles* and S. Ansky's *The Dybbuk*. The center has changing exhibitions of paintings and photography.

At the corner, Willett Street, turn left for the **Bialystoker Synagogue (4)**, 7-11 Willett Street, (212) 475–0165. The fieldstone building was constructed in 1826 as the Willett Street Methodist Episcopal Church. It became the Bialystoker Synagogue in 1905, housing a congregation who came to New York from the community of Bialystok, the second-largest city in Poland at that time. It is an active congregation for the Orthodox Jews of the neighborhood. A two-year restoration has made the interior into a beauty, ornately painted in glowing colors with Moorish motifs, biblical scenes, and the signs of the zodiac, which are found in some Jewish scriptures. The building is open for services on Saturday morning and may sometimes be seen by phoning in advance. Remember that during services women are allowed only upstairs.

A few more kosher stores are ahead on Grand Street, including **M&L Bake Shop (5)**, 504 Grand Street, (212) 673–5832. One of the last kosher butchers in the neighborhood, **Goldberg Meat Market (6)**, 500 Grand Street, (212) 475–6915, has meats high in quality, but no bargains. **Lega Kosher Foods (7)**, 510 Grand Street, (212) 505–5758, sells kosher cheeses, smoked fish, and salads as well as chocolate, nuts, and candies.

When you turn back down East Broadway, you'll see the last mikvah in the neighborhood, the Ritualarium at 311 East Broadway. According to Orthodox custom, women must use the bath as a ritual prior to marriage and once a month afterward. Men also may use the mikvah before the Sabbath. A shower or bath is taken before a quick immersion into the very small mikvah, which is symbolic, not cleansing.

Nearby is the **Henry Street Settlement (8),** 281 East Broadway and 263-267 Henry Street, (212) 766–9200, housed in three original, beautifully restored late Federal buildings that are now landmarks. A model for neighborhood settlement houses throughout the country, it has adapted to the changing community and continues to offer many important programs.

Farther on East Broadway you'll pass many remnants of the old Jewish community. The building at 235 East Broadway was the home of the *Lower East Side News,* the community newspaper. One of the current occupants is the United Jewish Council of the East Side, an organization that helps the elderly poor and sick of the neighborhood. Across the street is the Bialystoker Home for the Aged, built in 1929.

The blocks ahead are filled with small synagogues, past and present, tucked into the buildings of the street. Some of these small storefronts, known as *shtieblechs,* now belong to Ultra-Orthodox Hasidic groups. The Young Israel Synagogue, 225 East Broadway, was formed in 1913 to fight the growing movement toward Reform Judaism.

The next stop is the **Educational Alliance (9),** 197 East Broadway, (212) 780–2300, still an active participant in the community, providing services as well as art classes and performances in the Mazer Theater. The gallery in the building has worthwhile exhibits, such as contemporary photos of Lower East Side synagogues.

The eleven-story Forward Building, 175 East Broadway, was built in 1912 as the home of the *Jewish Daily Forward,* the most important Yiddish-language newspaper in the United States. It was

Bargain Shopping

The Lower East Side stores are a mixed bag. Some are modern shops where you can comfortably browse; others are old-fashioned, with the stock in boxes behind the counter. It helps to know designers and your size in all the stores.

How big are the discounts? Roughly equivalent to a department-store sale, 20 to 30 percent below list price.

For guidance, visit the Lower East Side Visitor Center, *261 Broome Street, (888) 825–8374 (www.lowereastsideny.com), Sunday to Friday 10:00 A.M. to 4:00 P.M. It offers free introductory shopping tours, meeting at* Katz's Delicatessen, *205 East Houston Street, every Sunday at 11:00 A.M., April through December. Free parking for shoppers is available at a lot on Broome Street between Suffolk and Norfolk Streets.*

All stores are shut tight on Saturday, the Jewish Sabbath; Sunday is the big shopping day.

A few old-timers worth mentioning are Lismore Hosiery, *334 Grand Street, (212) 674–3440, where name brands for men and women at bargain prices are stored in boxes stacked floor to ceiling. Farther down the street is* Harry Zarin, *318 Grand Street, (212) 925–6112, with a wide selection of fabrics to be bought by the yard or custom made into*

known for its liberal views, closely allied with Jewish labor organizations. The building now has Chinese owners and is being converted to condominiums.

Nathan Straus Square was named for the Jewish merchant–philanthropist, a partner in Macy's and Abraham and Straus. Among his many activities to help the poor, he sponsored a pasteurization laboratory in 1892 and set up depots to distribute free *slipcovers, curtains, and bedspreads.* Fishkin Knitwear Co., *314 Grand Street, (212) 226–6538, is a longtime discount retailer selling women's sportswear and specializing in cashmere; while Harris Levy, 278 Grand Street, (212) 226–3102, is one of the last survivors of what used to be rows of discount stores with linens for table, bed, and bath.*

Orchard Street is wall-to-wall stores, beginning with Sheila's Decorating, Inc., 66 Orchard Street, (212) 777–3767, another source for fabrics, wallpaper, and window treatments. The rest is mainly clothing and accessories.

Some longtime standbys are Salwen, 45 Orchard Street, (212) 226–1693, selling umbrellas and leather goods since 1902; Forman's, 82 Orchard Street, (212) 228–2500, with brand-name women's clothing and two additional nearby locations, Missy (large sizes), at 78 Orchard, and Petites, at #94; Klein's of Monticello, 105 Orchard Street, (212) 966–1453, stylish ladies' wear; and Fine & Klein Handbags, 119 Orchard, (212) 674–6720, with discounts on designer bags. Some choices for men are G & G International, 62 Orchard Street, (212) 431–4530, and Cougar Italian Clothing with a more-youthful, hip look, at 96 Orchard Street, (212) 475–0692. Next door is MicheleOlivieri, 94 Orchard Street, (212) 505–9664, with high-style Italian shoes for men.

milk to needy children.

Zigzag in the shadow of the Manhattan Bridge to see the imposing, Moorish-inspired **Eldridge Street Synagogue (10),** 12 Eldridge Street, (212) 219–0888. A National Historic Landmark, built in 1887, it was the first house of worship built in the United States by Jewish immigrants from Eastern Europe, mainly Russia and Poland, from whom 80 percent of American Jews descend. As many as 1,000 people attended services here at the turn of the century; during High Holy Day services, police patrolled on horseback to keep order in the streets.

Membership began to decline as congregants left the neighborhood in the 1920s and new immigration laws stemmed the tide of newcomers. The temple closed in the 1950s. The Eldridge Street Project has been at work for several years restoring the magnificent sanctuary. Tours are offered every Sunday on the hour, 11:00 A.M. to 3:00 P.M., and Tuesday and Thursday at 11:30 A.M. and 2:30 P.M.; the $4.00 admission fee goes toward further restoration. Many concerts and special events are also held here.

The old tenement across the street, at 19 Eldridge, is where singer/comedian Eddie Cantor was born.

Walk north on Eldridge Street and turn right onto Hester Street to begin a brief food-shopping tour—brief because only a handful of food shops are left in this area.

Visitors with a sweet tooth can visit **Sweet Life (11),** 63 Hester Street, (212) 598–0092, a pretty little shop filled with candies, from gummy bears to ten kinds of halvah, plus nuts and dried fruits. If sweets are what you're after, make a detour when you are walking near Wolsk's Gourmet Confections, 81 Ludlow Street just below Delancey Street, (212) 475–7946, a store past its fiftieth anniversary and a setting out of a movie.

Down Hester at **Gertel's Bakery (12),** 53 Hester Street, (212) 982–3250, are baked treats such as rugelach, jelly doughnuts, coffee cake, and apple strudel, along with breads and traditional dishes such as potato kugel.

Turn left onto Essex for a reminder of the old days. Guss' Pickles stood here for over eighty years, until a dispute with the landlord sent them over to Orchard Street. Taking advantage of the long-familiar location, **The Pickle Guys (13)** opened at 49 Essex Street (212)

656–9739, with a set-up similar to the original, but a bit more sterile since most of the barrels are now inside instead of on the sidewalk.

Sharing the building at 41 Essex Street are **Rabbi Eisenbach Hebrew Religious Articles (14),** (212) 982–4217, a somewhat musty shop with Judaica, antique and modern, and **G & M Kosher Caterers (15),** (212) 254–5370, where you can buy a ready-cooked roast chicken dinner with all the fixings to feed the family.

Turn left at Grand Street for one last Judaic shopping stop, with elaborate silver goblets, candlesticks, and menorahs at **Grand Sterling (16),** 345 Grand Street, (212) 674–6450.

Now the street signs will tell you that you are in the famous HIS-TORIC ORCHARD STREET BARGAIN DISTRICT, which includes part of Grand Street. Where to go depends on what you are seeking. (See "Bargain Shopping" on pages 250–51 for shopping tips.)

Just before Broome Street, you'll come to the new location for the original **Guss' Pickles (17),** 85–87 Orchard Street, (516) 642–2634.

Detour left on Broome Street for an unusual survivor, the **Kehila Kedosha Janina Synagogue and Museum (18),** 280 Broome Street, (212) 431–1619. This small but very interesting synagogue, over one hundred years old, is a landmark and has received a grant for renovation of the building exterior and roof. It was founded by a tiny group of Jews whose ancestors on a slave boat bound for Rome were shipwrecked off the coast of Greece two thousand years ago. The small, obscure community—speaking Greek with a Judeo accent —survives with a few dedicated members who enjoy telling visitors their story. The little upstairs museum has some fascinating pieces of Judaica, including handmade shofars, old marriage contracts, torah ornaments, and alephs, delicately hand-painted birth certificates for boys. The synagogue is usually open Sunday only from 11:00 A.M. to 4:00 P.M., and for Saturday service.

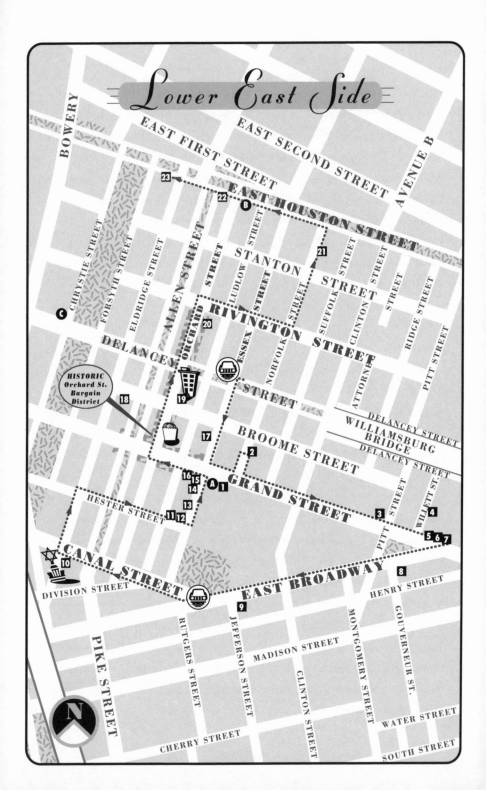

Back on Orchard Street, if you want to learn about the immigrant experience in New York, plan to spend a fascinating hour touring the **Lower East Side Tenement Museum (19).** Tours begin at the Visitor Center, 90 Orchard Street, (212) 431–0233. The guided sixty-minute tours are offered hourly Tuesday to Friday 1:00 to 4:00 P.M., Saturday and Sunday every half hour from 11:00 A.M. to 4:30 P.M.; admission $8.00. Special hands-on tours designed for families are held Saturday and Sunday noon to 3:00 P.M.

The "museum" is an actual tenement at 97 Orchard Street that was home to about 10,000 people from twenty-five countries between 1863 and 1935. Visitors see an untouched apartment and three apartments that have been restored to represent different periods. The stories of actual families who lived here have been researched to bring these quarters alive. They allow you to see firsthand what it was like to live with a family in a typical tenement flat—three small rooms averaging 300 square feet, with light from only two living-room windows. Newcomers living in similar buildings on the Lower East Side and in Chinatown have no more space today, but they do have more light.

The front hall is deliberately left unlit for a few moments to show you what it was like to come home and walk up several flights of stairs in darkness.

In 1874, when Nathalie Gumpertz, a German-Jewish dressmaker, was the sole support of her four young children, the plumbing consisted of an outhouse five flights down from her apartment. Her sewing machine was set at the living-room window, the only source of daylight. The 1918 apartment of the Rogarshevskys, an Orthodox Jewish family from Lithuania, has no more space but seems considerably larger. An 1879 law had required a center airshaft in each building to give ventilation and some small added light. Windows were cut on the airshaft and, in 1901, between rooms, considerably brightening things. Flush toilets were required on each floor in 1905, a huge step forward, though each floor held four apartments, each often housing a large family. The 1930s apartment of the Baldizzis, Catholic immigrants from Sicily, mirrors the hardships of the Depression years, when this family was evicted. The actual voice of daughter Josephine Baldizzi, who lived here as a child, brings their travails and small pleasures vividly to life. This unique museum sends you back to the streets with new understanding of your surroundings.

Follow Orchard Street north to Rivington Street for another notable synagogue, the **First Roumanian American Congregation (Shaari Shamoyim) (20)**, 89 Rivington Street, (212) 673–2835. It was built as the Allen Street Methodist Church in 1888 and purchased by the Hebrew congregation four years later. The lovely pulpit in the sanctuary is set against glowing stained-glass windows. Farther west down Rivington is the factory of the Streit Matzoth Co., 150 Rivington Street, (212) 475–7000, the last of its kind in Manhattan.

Walk to the corner of Norfolk and turn right for the last of the landmark synagogues, now known as the **Angel Orensanz Foundation (21)**, 172-176 Norfolk Street, (212) 420–0364. Formerly the Anshe Chesed Synagogue and later the Anshe Slonim Synagogue, it is the oldest synagogue on the Lower East Side, built in 1850 by German Jews and modeled after the Cathedral of Cologne, with seating for 1,300. The congregation became Hungarian, then Orthodox, and the building closed down in 1977, when all its members had moved away. It was bought by Orensanz, a sculptor, who uses the soaring spaces as an avant-garde gallery and concert hall. Mandy Patinkin and Tyne Daly are among those who have performed here.

If you want to see some of the trendy restaurants, such as 71 Clinton, Alias, and WD-50, detour over to Clinton Street between

Rivington and Stanton Streets. Walk up to East Houston Street and turn left for some choice food buying at **Russ & Daughters (22)**, 179 East Houston Street, (212) 475–4880. Known for their smoked salmon, they also have delicious herring, not to mention pickles and sauerkraut, bagels, dried fruits, and nuts, and are noted for their caviar selection. This is a third-generation family business with roots in a pushcart, circa 1900.

Now comes the final big decision: whether to walk back for a corned-beef sandwich at Katz's Delicatessen, or have a warm knish at **Yohna Schimmel's Knishes Bakery (23)**, 137 East Houston Street, (212) 477–2858. The bakery has been turning out this favorite Jewish treat since 1910, and it has the tin ceilings and antique food cases to prove it.

Jewish Cuisine

Jewish cuisine is as much a cultural as a geographic tradition. As Jews have lived under the rule of many countries, their dishes are greatly influenced by other cuisines, especially those of Russia, Poland, and other Eastern European countries. This can be seen in dishes such as borscht, blintzes, stuffed cabbage, and sour pickles. Smoked fish, corned beef, and pastrami are Jewish favorites that have created the great tradition known as the New York deli. Middle Eastern dishes from Israel, such as hummus and falafel, are also popular, though not as common on the Lower East Side. The kosher tradition of separating milk and meat carries over into the restaurants of the neighborhood.

To read more about kosher traditions, see page 38.

A JEWISH FOOD SAMPLER

Here are some common Jewish foods:

Babkas: slightly sweet yeast coffee cakes; excellent served toasted with coffee. May be seasoned with cinnamon.

Bagels: a Jewish contribution to modern mainstream American cuisine. A proper bagel is made using malt rather than sugar for slight sweetening, formed by hand, sunk into boiling water, then baked in a hot oven. It may be plain or topped with poppy seeds, sesame seeds, crushed garlic, or minced onion. It is chewy, but never tough. Today most bagels are machine-made, and the quality varies considerably. Many are no more than round rolls. Most shops on the Lower East Side sell traditional bagels.

Blintzes: crepes filled with sweetened cottage or farmer's cheese and/or fruit and sautéed. Served with sour cream or apple sauce.

Borscht: the Jewish version is a clear beet soup without meat, served with sour cream.

Brisket: the Jewish version of pot roast, made from the brisket cut of beef, which is very easy to slice.

Challah: an egg bread with an oval, braided shape and poppy-seed topping. Traditionally eaten for the Sabbath and for holidays.

Cholent: a filling meat-and-potato stew, simmered for many hours over a very low heat.

Chopped liver: chicken livers mashed with minced onion, hard-boiled eggs, and the secret ingredient: rendered chicken fat, known as schmaltz.

Gefilte fish: ground whitefish, pike, and carp, mixed with egg, grated onion, and enough bread to hold the mix together, formed into oval dumpling shapes and boiled in fish broth. When the fish is chilled, the broth gels. It is served with horseradish. A traditional dish for holidays.

Gribenes: thin strips of chicken skin, onions, and chicken fat, the leftovers from making schmaltz. Also known as cracklings.

Hamantachen: a three-cornered pastry filled with sweetened poppy seeds, traditionally associated with the holiday of Purim.

Honey cake: a sweet pound cake made with honey and cinnamon, traditionally served on the Jewish New Year to symbolize wishes for a sweet year.

Kasha: buckwheat grains or groats; can be cooked like cereal or shaped into small pancakes and fried.

Kasha varnishkes: kasha mixed with small, bow-tie pasta and sautéed onions; sometimes served with mushroom sauce.

Kishka: a Jewish "sausage" stuffed with matzo meal, onions, and schmaltz.

Knishes: the classic knish is a soft dough shell filled with oniony mashed potatoes. They may also be stuffed with kasha and modern variations such as fruit and cheese.

Kosher pizza: the difference is in the cheese, which contains no retsin, considered an animal product.

Kreplach: dumplings of chopped meat or chicken encased in dough, boiled or fried. Can be served as a side dish or in soup.

Kugel: a baked pudding with many variations, usually a sweet dish served with the main dish. It can be made with noodles and a sweet-ened cream-cheese sauce, sometimes with raisins or grated potatoes added, or with softened matzos, mixed with apples and preserves.

Matzo: an unleavened, unseasoned bread baked in flat sheets, with a consistency similar to crackers. It is served at Passover as a symbol of the bread the Jewish people baked in the desert in their flight from persecution in Egypt.

Matzo brei: an omelet incorporating softened matzo, served with preserves.

Matzo meal: a matzo flour used in baked dishes at Passover. The best-known dish made from matzo meal is matzo balls or *knaidlach*, a mix of meal and egg formed into balls, which are boiled and served in the famous cure-all chicken soup known as "Jewish penicillin."

Potato latkes: grated potatoes mixed with matzo meal and grated onion and fried in oil; served usually with apple sauce or sour cream.

Rugelach: small pastries made with rich cream-cheese dough, filled with jam, chopped nuts, and raisins. Chocolate may be used instead of jam.

Schav: green borscht, made with spinach or sorrel.

Schmaltz: rendered chicken fat, the kosher answer to lard, and a flavor that makes for great chopped liver and other favorites. It is used as a spread, as a seasoning, and for cooking. Schmaltz is made by sautéing chicken fat, grated onion, and slivers of chicken skin; the liquid is strained off as schmaltz; the rest becomes gribenes.

Stuffed cabbage: a chopped meat, rice, grated onion, and egg mixture, spooned into cabbage leaves, and rolled and cooked in tomato sauce.

Tsimmes: a vegetable casserole, usually sweet and containing carrots, sweet potatoes, and prunes, cooked for a long time over very low heat until the vegetables are quite soft. The Yiddish word *tsimmes* means a "big fuss" or "to-do," translated in food terms to mean a dish with many ingredients.

R E C O M M E N D E D R E S T A U R A N T S

The choices are dwindling, but here are a few spots where you can sample Jewish fare:
Shalom Chai Pizza (A) ($), 359 Grand Street, (212) 598–4178, isn't much to look at, but if you want a snack and want to know how pizza tastes made with strictly kosher cheeses, this is the place.

A Typical Jewish Meal

Chicken soup with matzo balls

Roasted chicken or brisket with kugel

Rugelach or sponge cake with fruit

Katz's Delicatessen (B) ($), 205 East Houston Street, (212) 254–2246, has been serving up classic Jewish deli foods since 1888, and the age shows, but never mind. Take a number and feast on the famous kosher hot dogs or hot pastrami sandwiches.

Sammy's Roumanian (C) ($), 157 Chrystie Street, (212) 673–0330, might also be known as "cholesterol city" for the giant portions of shmaltz-laden foods. After a dinner of rib steak and gribenes, you won't need dessert—though you may need Alka Seltzer. The festive decor and music give Sammy's the atmosphere of a perpetual Jewish wedding or bar mitzvah celebration, and most of the patrons do seem to be celebrating an occasion. Fans say you need to come here at least once in your life.

Middle Europe on the Upper East Side

The old German Yorkville is gone but not forgotten. Most of the landmarks have disappeared, it's true, but you can visit the last survivors of the food shops offering the best of German specialties, please your sweet tooth, and visit a couple of prize churches—and there's still the chance to savor an authentic, old-fashioned German meal. The Hungarian neighborhood nearby also survives in the form of charming churches and delicious foods.

While you're in the neighborhood, take a stroll on the river walk

How to Get There

By subway: Take the #6 Subway to Lexington Avenue
and 86th Street.

By bus: Take the #101/102 Bus running north on Third Avenue,
south on Lexington; #M15 running north on First
Avenue, south on Second Avenue.

in the park named for one of New York's most famous early German
residents, and pay your respects to Gracie Mansion, the eighteenth-
century country house that is the official residence of New York
City's mayor.

THE HISTORY

Germans were among the earliest immigrants in New York and
among the most numerous; by 1860 they numbered 200,000, one
quarter of the city's population.

As they prospered German families left their old neighborhoods
on the Lower East Side and the East Village to newer arrivals and
settled farther north, in Yorkville, traveling by horse-drawn cars that
carried passengers from Prince Street to the stagecoach terminus at
Third Avenue and 86th Street. The wealthiest families led the way—
people like the Rhinelander family and Jacob Ruppert, whose
Yorkville brewery was the eighth largest in the United States.
Ruppert's brewery occupied the blocks between 90th and 92nd

Streets between Second and Third Avenues, where Ruppert Towers, a high-rise apartment complex, now stands.

By 1850 this was already a predominantly German neighborhood, and 86th Street soon was lined with beer halls where people consumed

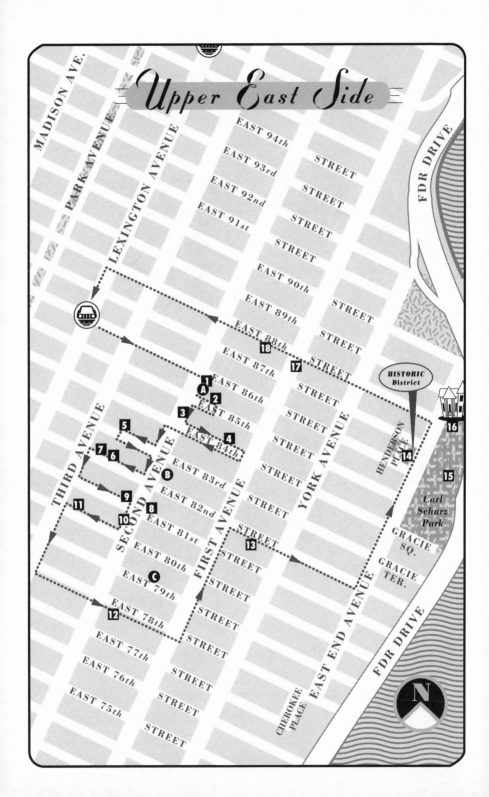

the local brews and listened to oom-pah bands. In 1877 Manhattan had seventy-eight breweries, many of them German-owned.

Development accelerated when the Third and Second Avenue elevated lines were completed in 1878 and 1879, respectively. The German population in New York City peaked in 1900 at 748,882, a number that made German-Americans an important political force. Two world wars with Germany as the enemy brought hostility, however, and Germans increasingly elected to live outside the city. The beer halls and German movie houses that lined 86th Street closed, and restaurants and shops serving German families began to fail.

The demolition of the Third Avenue El in 1955 hastened the gentrification of the neighborhood, as brownstones gave way to high-rise apartment buildings. Yorkville's German identity all but disappeared. The Rhinelander Mansion at 72nd Street and Madison Avenue, home to the most influential family in nineteenth-century Yorkville, is now occupied by a Ralph Lauren store.

The Hungarians came to the city as a prominent part of the great European immigration movement in the late nineteenth century. They settled mostly in the upper 70s and lower 80s, building churches and establishing their own shops and restaurants. The population peaked around 1940, topping 123,000—the largest Hungarian community in the nation. By the next influx in 1989, after the Eastern bloc governments collapsed, only a fraction of the newcomers could afford to live in the gentrified old neighborhood. But they still come to enjoy the churches, shopping, and other resources that remain here. You can see some of the old-timers enjoying each other's company and join them for a hearty dinner at the First Hungarian Literary Society (see page 273).

To appreciate the interiors of the lovely small sanctuaries in this neighborhood, plan your walk for Sunday, when services are held.

... *A Walking Tour* ...

From the subway walk east on 86th Street (now, sadly, without a single German landmark), until you come to Second Avenue, where a short turn to the right brings you to what remains of the old German Yorkville, **Schaller & Weber (1),** 1654 Second Avenue, (212) 879–3047. The collection of steins in the window and the notices on the bulletin board tell you that this is still headquarters for a German community. It is also the best spot in New York for anyone in search of German wursts, Westphalian ham, and more than one hundred other German meats and sausages. Almost next door is the last of the traditional German restaurants, Heidelberg (see page 272). It has been at this spot since 1939.

Make a quick detour east onto 85th Street to discover another old-timer, **M. Rohrs' House of Fine Teas and Coffees (2),** 303 East 85th Street, (212) 396–4456. The Old World shop is a delight, with its antique red and gold tins made in Yorkville at the turn of the century and the old-fashioned coffee grinder still used to get the blends just right. Whether you want Indian Mysore, Colombian Supremo, or Viennese Roast, you've come to the right place. They'll gladly supply you with a proper coffeepot, as well. If you're a tea person, there are some twenty kinds of loose tea for sale, along with teapots and strainers.

Come back to Second Avenue and continue to the next block to find **Elk Candy Company (3),** 1628 Second Avenue, (212) 585–2303, a spiffy new location for a company whose homemade chocolates and colorful marzipan have been part of the neighborhood for sixty-five years.

At the corner, walk toward First Avenue to see the **Zion St. Mark's Evangelical Lutheran Church (4),** 339 East 84th Street,

(212) 650–1648, built in 1888 as the Deutsche Evangelische Kirche von Yorkville and still offering services in German every Sunday at 11:00 A.M. The building is on the National Register of Historic Places.

On to a bit of old Hungary. Back on Second Avenue walk 1 block farther downtown and turn west for **St. Elizabeth of Hungary Roman Catholic Church (5)**, 211 East 83rd Street, (212) 734–5747, a 1918 structure almost hidden between the brownstones until you look up to see the neo-Gothic exterior and Old World spire. Walk up the steps and go inside to see the glorious painted ceiling.

Back on Second Avenue heading downtown, you'll come to the delightful Mocca Hungarian Restaurant (see page 273).

Turn west on 82nd Street to find the modern, attractive **Hungarian Reform Church (6)**, 229 East 82nd Street, (212) 734–3139, built in 1959. A few doors down are the **Hungarian House** and **Hungarian Library (7)**, 213-15 East 82nd Street, (212) 744–5298, a pair of brick houses devoted to Hungarian education and literature. A plaque marks the visit of Cardinal Mindszenty of Hungary in 1973.

Come back to Second Avenue and the corner of 81st Street for the most important Hungarian food shop in the neighborhood (and probably in the city), the **Yorkville Packing House (8)**, 1560 Second Avenue, (212) 628–5147. This is the place to find good Hungarian meats as well as specialties like goulash seasoning and fresh-cooked goulash to go. Meats include Hungarian sausage seasoned with paprika and many kinds of cold cuts and pork products. Rich Hungarian paprika (much better than the stuff we usually buy in tins), red cabbage, and bryndza, a Hungarian sheep's-milk cheese, are among many other specialties to be found.

Look across the street for **Molnar Travel Service (9)**, 245 East 81st Street, (212) 535–3681, and you'll find a window filled

Gracie Mansion

Gracie Mansion, *a two-story Federal-era home with a graceful porch and trellis railings, is a pleasant surprise in the middle of modern New York. It was built in 1799 as a country estate by Archibald Gracie, a Scottish shipping magnate. The site overlooks the turbulent waters of Hell Gate, where the Harlem and East Rivers meet.*

Gracie had financial reverses and was forced to sell the house in 1823. It was occupied by several owners before the city acquired the property in 1896, renaming the grounds Carl Schurz Park. It was restored in 1924 to become the Museum of the City of New York and again in the 1930s, when the museum moved to larger quarters and the mansion became a house museum. In 1942 Fiorello La Guardia made it the official mayor's residence. A reception wing was added in 1966.

The Gracie Mansion Conservancy was established in 1981 as a non-profit corporation with the goal of maintaining the home, one of the oldest surviving wooden structures in Manhattan. The first major restoration was undertaken between 1981 and 1984. In 2002 another major renovation took place. When Mayor Michael Bloomberg decided to maintain his own townhouse residence rather than move to Gracie Mansion, the house became more accessible to the public. It will accommodate visiting officials and dignitaries.

The main floor of the house is a showcase of early New York at its finest. At the center of the faux-marble floor of the entrance hall, a painted compass recalls the ships that made the Gracie fortune. The Conservancy offers fifty-minute tours on the hour on Wednesdays from 10 A.M. and Thursdays from noon; admission is $7.00. Tours are by advance reservation only, call (212) 570–4751 or (212) 570–0985.

with Herend porcelain figures, vases, and plates imported from Hungary and offered for sale. As you might have guessed, the company specializes in travel arrangements to Hungary.

Continuing down Second Avenue, you'll pass **Carpathian Travel (10),** 1543 Second Avenue, (212) 879–8003, with windows full of folders on Budapest, some of them in Hungarian. These agencies are good bets for the best rates on trips to Hungary.

Turn west (right) on 80th Street to see the **Hungarian Baptist Church (11),** 225 East 80th Street, (212) 288–0258, with terra-cotta trim, arched windows, and a doorway in a design of alternating shades of brick. The building dates to 1890.

Walk down Third Avenue to 78th Street and turn east to find **Orwasher's Bakery (12),** 308 East 78th Street, (212) 288–6569, another neighborhood standby since 1916, family-owned for three generations. Bread is still made by hand here and baked in an old-fashioned brick oven. The raisin pumpernickel bread and challah are legendary.

Now proceed up First Avenue, turn east on 82nd Street and you'll find the big **St. Stephen of Hungary Church and School (13),** 414 East 82nd Street, (212) 861–8500, a 1928 neo-Romanesque–style building in bright yellow with a tile hip roof.

Continue east to East End Avenue and turn north (left) for an intriguing complex, the **Henderson Place Historic District (14),** 549-553 East 86th Street. Once owned by John Jacob Astor, this block was acquired by John C. Henderson, a wealthy fur importer, who had a complex of thirty-two two-story Queen Anne houses constructed in 1882 as a self-contained community. Twenty-four of these picturesque homes remain, their well-preserved original gables, dormers, turrets, slate roofs, and many-paned windows intact.

Across the street is **Carl Schurz Park (15),** with an esplanade overlooking the river, named for the most prominent German immigrant of the nineteenth century. Schurz came to New York in 1852 and settled in Yorkville in 1881. His career included stints as an army general, U.S. senator, U.S. secretary of the interior, editor of the *New York Evening Post* and the *Nation*; and chief editorial writer for *Harper's Weekly.*

Near the end of the park is **Gracie Mansion (16),** East End Avenue and 88th Street, (212) 570–4751, the residence of the mayor of New York. (For more information see "Gracie Mansion" on page 268.)

Exit the park at 88th and walk west, making a downtown detour on First Avenue to find **Glaser's Bake Shop (17),** 1670 First Avenue, (212) 289–2562, a family business now in its third generation, still making its trademark Dobos tortes and "black and whites," big soft cookies with half vanilla and half chocolate icing. The blue-and-white, old-fashioned tile floor and wood-paneled walls tell of a company that has been in this spot for nearly one hundred years.

Come back to 88th and continue west for a final German landmark, the **Church of the Holy Trinity (18),** 316-332 East 88th Street, (212) 289–4100, built in 1889 of golden brick and terra cotta in French Gothic style, the arched doorway richly decorated with carved images of saints and prophets. The church complex, including a parsonage and Saint Christopher House, are set around a landscaped court with one of New York's loveliest bell towers, adorned with a handsome wrought-iron clock with brass hands. The church was donated by Serena Rhinelander in memory of her father and grandfather on land that was part of the Rhinelander Farm, which the family had owned since 1798. The church was intended for the poorer residents of Yorkville.

Now the only thing left is to decide whether to choose a German or Hungarian meal to end your excursion.

German Cuisine

Sausage, sauerkraut, dark bread, and beer are the most basic and familiar German foods, but many American favorites—including pot roast, meatloaf, breaded veal cutlets, and chocolate cake—also have

German roots. Other typical German dishes are pickled herring in sour cream, soup with dumplings, roast duckling, paprika sauces (borrowed from the Hungarians), potato pancakes (a favorite shared with Eastern European neighbors), and red cabbage. Westphalian ham is rightfully famous. Dill and caraway are frequently used seasonings in this cuisine.

A TYPICAL GERMAN MEAL

Marinated herring

Sauerbraten or schnitzel

Mashed potatoes, spaetzle, or dumplings

Apple strudel

A GERMAN FOOD SAMPLER

German cuisine is on the heavy side, with lots of dumplings and rich sauces—definitely not for weight watchers—but it can be delicious on a cold winter night. Typical dishes include:

Apfelstrudel: thin pastry layers alternating with sliced apples.

Dumplings: balls of dough cooked in boiling water, usually served in soups or with gravy; potato dumplings are also popular.

Kassler rippchen: smoked pork chops.

Sauerbraten: marinated beef similar to pot roast but in a sweet-and-sour gravy.

Schnitzels: cutlets, usually of veal. Popular preparations include wiener schnitzel, breaded veal cutlets; jaeger schnitzel, sautéed with mushrooms, cream, and wine; or paprika schnitzel, served with a creamy paprika sauce. Schnitzel a la Holstein is a breaded cutlet topped with a fried egg, anchovies, and capers.

Schwarzwalder kirschtorte: Black Forest cake, moist layers of chocolate with a filling of cherries soaked in brandy, frosted with whipped cream.

Schweinebraten: roast pork.

Spaetzle: tiny dumplings made with flour and eggs, a favorite side dish with meats, especially those made with gravies.

Wursts: German sausages come in several varieties, usually boiled and served with sauerkraut. Most common varieties include knockwurst, made of pork and beef; bauernwurst, a spicier pork-and-beef combination; bratwurst, pork usually pan-fried rather than boiled; weisswurst, a milder white sausage made of veal and beef; and leberwurst, sausage made with liver.

R E C O M M E N D E D 🍽 R E S T A U R A N T

Heidelberg (A) ($–$$), 1648 Second Avenue, (212) 682–2332, calls itself "Manhattan's favorite German beer garden," and there are few rivals left to dispute this claim. Come for four kinds of wurst, served with potato salad and sauerkraut, or home-style sauerbraten, wiener schnitzel, spaetzle, potato pancakes, homemade apple strudel and a big selection of imported German beers. Sausage platters and mixed-grill platters let you sample several specialties.

Hungarian Cuisine

The seasoning that distinguishes many Hungarian dishes is paprika, used to good effect in sauces and stews, sometimes thickened with sour cream. Even Hungarian sausage is made with paprika. Caraway and poppy seeds are also used a great deal. The schnitzel, dumplings, red cabbage, and creamed herring on the menu are similar to German dishes.

A HUNGARIAN FOOD SAMPLER

Here are a few Hungarian specialties:

Goulash: a rich beef stew with onions, tomatoes, and potatoes, generously seasoned with paprika.

Palacsinta: crepe pancakes rolled around a filling of fruit or sweetened cheese.

Paprikash: a cream sauce seasoned with paprika, usually offered with veal or chicken.

Red cabbage: shredded cabbage cooked with apple-cider vinegar and a bit of sugar.

Strudel: the familiar layered dessert using paper-thin dough similar to phyllo dough.

R E C O M M E N D E D 🍽 R E S T A U R A N T S

Mocca Hungarian Restaurant (B) ($), 1588 Second Avenue, (212) 734–6470, brings to mind a simple European cafe, with flowery china on the wall and old-fashioned lighting. Chicken paprikash, beef goulash, stuffed cabbage, schnitzels, and roast veal with cream of mushroom sauce are among the traditional choices. The prix fixe lunches and dinners are great bargains.

A TYPICAL HUNGARIAN MEAL

Soup with dumplings
Chicken Paprikash
Palacsinta

First Hungarian Literary Society (C) ($), 323 East 79th Street, (212) 288–5002, is home to a group formed in 1889 to preserve Hungarian culture. They have been at this address since 1925, ensconced in a small building with a sign so inconspicuous you might easily pass it by. Shelves of books remain, in both English and

Hungarian, but today this is primarily a setting for socializing. Card-playing and monthly movies in Hungarian are favorite activities for a mostly older group, many of whom still speak Hungarian. In 2003, a well-regarded Queens restaurant, A Touch of Hungary, took over the kitchen of the upstairs dining room/card room, where the heaping $16, four-course meal may be New York's best value. Visitors are welcome; just be sure to reserve at least a day in advance.

The menu is traditional, with starters such as herring or chopped liver, followed by a homemade soup—maybe cold sour cherry or hot bean flavored with smoky bacon. Main courses of stuffed cabbage on a mound of cooked cabbage, goulash, schnitzels, and the like are big enough to feed two, but the obliging waitress will gladly wrap the leftovers to take home. That way you can save room for desserts like delicious apple walnut cake, flaky jelly roll with apricot filling, or cheese cake, served with coffee or tea. As you waddle down the stairs, look at the annual group photos of past club members on the walls; one of them dates back to 1910.

United Nations on Ninth Avenue

Ninth Avenue isn't exactly a neighborhood, but when you talk about ethnic food in New York City, it can't be left out. It is the most densely populated food street in Manhattan, wall to wall with markets and restaurants that can take you from Sri Lanka to South America to the Deep South of the United States, all within about 20 blocks. One writer dubbed it "America's most mouthwatering street." So a stroll down Ninth Avenue seems a fitting ending to this book.

THE HISTORY

The surroundings used to be notorious, a slum so dangerous it was known as Hell's Kitchen, a name that is still used by many New Yorkers. This far-west neighborhood, which extended from Midtown into the 60s, was the inspiration for the ballet *Slaughter on Tenth Avenue* and the gang fights in *West Side Story*. But the uptown slums were razed to make room for Lincoln Center, and the lower part of the area is benefiting from the revitalization of 42nd Street. There are

How to Get There

By *subway:* Take the A, C, or E Eighth Avenue Train to
34th Street and walk 1 block west to Ninth.

By *bus:* Take the M34 Crosstown Bus.

still some rough patches as you head toward the river, but things are
definitely looking up. These days the neighborhood is being pro-
moted as "Clinton," after the De Witt Clinton Park west of 11th
Avenue between 52nd and 54th Streets.

Whatever else was happening around it, Ninth Avenue has
always been about food. When the El rumbled overhead, it was filled
with an army of pushcarts known as Paddy's Market. The food stores
are indoors now; it's a low-rise, low-rent district with a remarkable
diversity of fare. There are trendy newcomers, to be sure, especially
among the restaurants serving theatergoers, but many of the merchants have been here for years. A number of newer places are catering to a new wave of immigrants—Mexicans, Filipinos, Dominicans,
Pakistanis, Senegalese, and more who live or work in the area.

... *A Walking Tour* ...

Ninth Avenue is packed with temptations, whether you want to
have a meal right here or take home the fixings.

A good start is **Manganaro Grosseria Italiana (1),** 488 Ninth

Avenue between 37th and 38th Streets, (212) 563–5331, a family business founded in the 1890s, still with the old-fashioned tin ceilings and vintage showcases. This is a store loaded with Italian everything—prosciutto, sausages, olive oil. The provolone and smoked mozzarella are the favorites among a wide choice of cheeses. There's a restaurant in the back where you can order sandwiches, pasta, or veal and peppers; they'll pack up the foods to take home if you like.

Anything from game birds to whole suckling pigs to cows' feet to the best Smithfield hams can be found at **Giovanni Esposito & Sons (2),** 500 Ninth Avenue, (212) 279–3298, which caters to the diverse customers of the neighborhood. But the cognoscenti come for the homemade Italian sausage, made from a family recipe half a century old.

Some excellent stops await between 39th and 41st Streets. **Central Fish Company (3),** 527 Ninth Avenue, (212) 279–2317, has been a fixture for seventy-five years. From eels to sea urchins, Florida shrimp to Brazilian lobster tails, there are few fish varieties you won't find, all high in quality and low in price.

One block north is a repeat performance. **Sea Breeze Fish Market (4),** 541 Ninth Avenue, (212) 563–7537, is another great stop for fresh fish at refreshing prices, and **International Foods (5),** 543 Ninth Avenue, has all kinds of products and spices plus a lot of Greek specialties; look for fresh feta cheese, homemade yogurt, and dips such as taramasalata and tzatziki.

Another old-timer, in a new location, is **Empire Coffee & Tea (6),** 568 Ninth Avenue, (212) 586–1717, founded in 1908. The barrels here are laden with more than seventy kinds of coffee beans. There's a similar array of teas to choose from. This is also a good spot for a quick pick-me-up cup at the coffee bar.

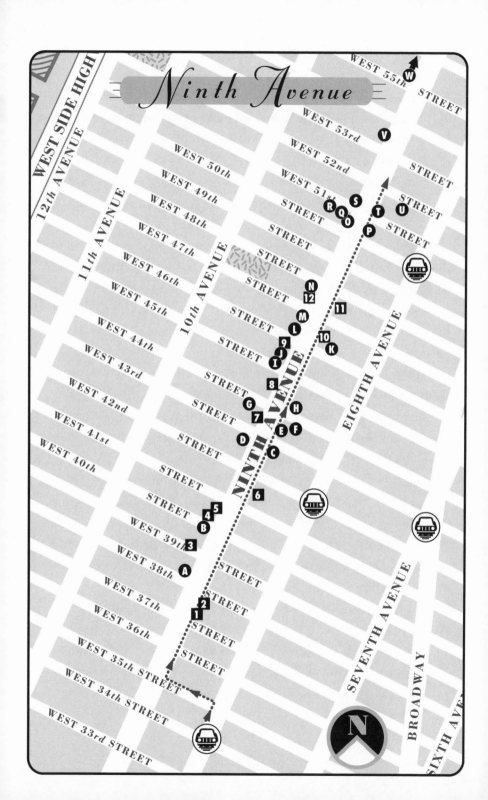

Cheese lovers will find Nirvana at the **Ninth Avenue Cheese Market (7)**, 615 Ninth Avenue, (212) 397–4700, offering a mind-boggling 420 varieties. Fortunately, the knowledgeable clerks can help you make a choice. There's more than cheese, like twenty-five kinds of olives and homemade babaghanouj, plus sandwiches and salads.

A family business for more than seventy years, the **Poseidon Greek Bakery (8)**, 629 Ninth Avenue, (212) 757–6173, offers baklava and other sweet phyllo pastries, plus pastry triangles filled with spinach, cheese, meat, or vegetables. It also sells its own home-made phyllo dough and frozen trays of miniphyllo appetizers, great to have on hand for unexpected guests.

The old Bruno, the King of Ravioli, has given way to **Tartare (9)**, 653 Ninth Avenue, (212) 333–5300, transformed with smart new decor by the grandson of the Bruno who founded the business in 1905. Geared to present-day New Yorkers, the specialty is delectable take-out foods, from soups, sandwiches, and salads to rotisserie cooked meats and complete dinner boxes. They even offer a family dinner for four—roasted chicken, mashed potatoes, spinach, and dessert. There is a butcher shop on the premises, as well.

Though not an old-timer, **Amy's Bread (10)**, 672 Ninth Avenue, (212) 977–2282, can hold its own with anyone, as attested to by the lines at the counter. Amy's sells a little of everything—scones, focaccia, sourdough, semolina with black sesame seeds, black olive bread, and a delicious walnut apple raisin roll. Thirty different items are baked daily using organic whole grains and unbleached flour. Each loaf is hand-formed and baked on a stone hearth, making for a crunchy, flavorful crust. The bread freezes nicely if you wrap it well. Amy's also serves a fine sandwich.

Pozzo Pastry Shop (11), 690 Ninth Avenue, (212) 265–7530,

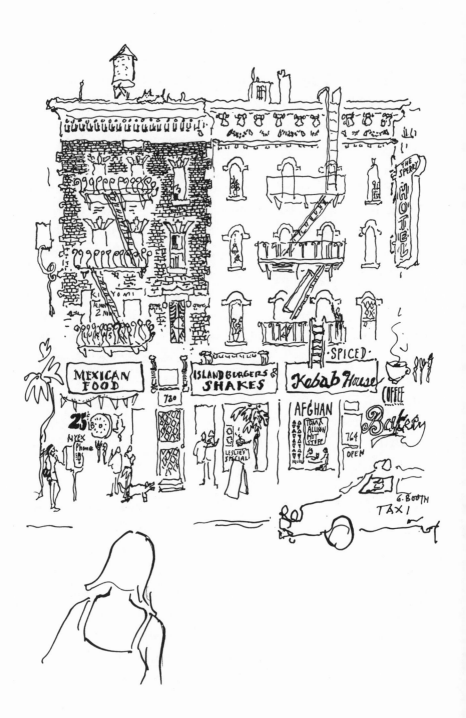

is an old-fashioned family bakery, a fixture on the Avenue since 1952. The proprietors, the Bianchi family, began their business in Italy over one hundred years ago. French and Italian cookies, pastries, and breads are delicious, and cakes for birthdays and other occasions are a specialty. Some of the Italian goodies include biscotti, focaccia, and panetone.

The treats at **Leon Bakery (12),** 695 Ninth Avenue, (212) 489–6677, are from south of the border. This tiny, spotless bakery has cookies, sweet rolls, flaky fruit turnovers, and other Mexican favorites. The store also sells Mexican herbs, cheeses, and chocolate to be used for cooking at home.

By now you are probably laden with packages. It's time to go home or to face the delightful dilemma of choosing a place to eat.

R E C O M M E N D E D **¶|◉|** R E S T A U R A N T S

Ninth Avenue has enough nationalities to please any palate. The settings may not be fancy, but the spices and the prices are right.

Here is a sampling of the range of cuisines, including some of the new, trendier favorites: (Numbers in parentheses following the address indicate cross streets to help locate restaurants).

Salon Mexico (A) ($), 507 Ninth Avenue (corner of 38th), (212) 868–7780, a very informal spot for soups, tacos, burritos, and a variety of platters at budget prices.

Tagine Dining Gallery (B) ($$), 537 Ninth Avenue (39th–40th), (212) 564–7292, adds Moroccan spice and ambience to the block. The restaurant is named for a Moroccan staple, a fragrant stew served in an earthenware dish with a cone-shaped top. Couscous and

The Ninth Avenue
International Food Festival

*New York City's biggest food festival began in 1974 to pro-
mote Ninth Avenue's bounty with a street fair. Shop owners and
restauranteurs responded with outdoor tables showing off their
wares and specialties. Now the vendors come from near and far.
The festival, held each year on a Saturday in mid-May, has
grown to attract more than a million people, who jam the streets
to savor the Italian sausage, burritos, egg rolls, samosas, and
other treats adding up to a United Nations of food.*

lamb dishes are also featured. After 8:00 P.M., musicians perform on
a small stage.

Zuni (C) ($$), 598 Ninth Avenue (43rd), (212) 765–7626, a cheer-
ful small restaurant, offers paintings of Ninth Avenue scenes and a
well-received eclectic American regional menu ranging from
Southwestern to Cajun.

Esca (D) ($$$), 402 West 43rd Street (west of Ninth), (212)
564–7272, is a gourmet choice, rating raves for its Italian seafood
specialties. The dinner tab is high, but lunches are more reasonable.

Chimichurri Grill (E) ($$), 606 Ninth Avenue, (43rd–44th), (212)
586–8655, specializes in Argentine grilled meats and empanadas,
served with chimichurri sauce, the country's most popular condi-
ment.

Lakruwana (F) ($), 358 West 44th Street (east of Ninth), (212)
957–4480, is one of the city's few Sri Lankan restaurants, with a

highly seasoned cuisine including curries similar to spicy Indian but with their own unique flavors.

Caribbean Spice (G) ($–$$), 401 West 44th Street (west of Ninth), (212) 765–1737, a few steps off the Avenue, serves authentic Jamaican foods, including a fine version of the famous jerk chicken, marinated in island spices and barbecued.

Marseille (H) ($$$), 630 Ninth Avenue (44th), (212) 333–2323, a new brasserie-style restaurant for a special night out, salutes its worldly namesake city with widely praised cuisine that fuses Mediterranean with French, Moroccan, and Turkish influences.

Cascina (I) ($$), 647 Ninth Avenue (45th–46th), (212) 245–4422, named for the owner's vineyard in Italy, is one of the newer Italian choices, serving foods from the Piedmont region. Many dishes are prepared in a dome-shaped, wood-burning, stone oven (including tasty individual pizzas). Brick walls, candlelight, and antique chandeliers add to the ambience.

Bali Nusa Indah (J) ($), 651 Ninth Avenue (45th-46th), (212) 974–1875, serves Indonesian specialties like nasi goreng, a fried rice dish and kare ayam, an Indonesian chicken curry.

Pomaire (K) ($), 371 West 46th Street (east of Ninth), (212) 956–3056, is a Chilean restaurant with interesting and tasty choices such as meat and corn pie, or shell steak broiled with onions. Chilean pottery brightens the walls.

Zen Palate (L) ($$), 663 Ninth Avenue (46th), (212) 582–1669, is a serene restaurant operated by Buddhists who know how to make the most of a vegetarian menu.

Hell's Kitchen (M) ($$), 679 Ninth Avenue (46th–47th), (212) 977–1588, offers "Nouveau Mexican" delights in an intimate setting of tile and brick. No reservations are taken, so there is often a line, but unless you have theater tickets, just have a margarita at the bar and wait your turn; fans say it's worth it.

Pietrasanta (N) ($$), 683 Ninth Avenue (47th Street), (212) 265–9471, is a standby for Italian home-style cooking and a reasonable tab. Both the excellent bread and pasta are homemade.

Dakshin (O) ($), 741 Ninth Avenue (50th), (212) 757–4545 is a no-frills Indian restaurant with interesting dishes at pleasing prices.

Rice 'n Beans (P) ($$), 744 Ninth Avenue (50th–51st), (212) 265–4444, specializes in Brazilian dishes such as feijoada, a hearty dish of black beans, pork, and beef served with rice.

Uncle Nick's (Q) ($$), 747 Ninth Avenue (50th–51st), (212) 245–7992, a Greek seafood taverna, is an old-timer on the block known for terrific appetizers and grilled fish specialties. The Ouzaria next door features a Greek version of a tapas bar.

Hallo Berlin (R) ($), 402 West 51st Street (west of Ninth), (212) 541–6248, a lively little German spot, serves all kinds of German sausages and sauerkraut, herring prepared half a dozen ways, and lots of German beers.

Chanpen Thai Cuisine (S) ($), 761 Ninth Avenue (51st), (212) 586–6808, is one of the more attractive of the avenue's Thai choices, with a long and interesting menu. Highly recommended are the shrimp soup and the coconut milk chicken curry.

Afghan Kebab House (T) ($$), 764 Ninth Avenue (51st–52nd),

(212) 307–1612, features grilled kebabs as well as tasty tandoori chicken and korma, a savory stew made with meat or vegetables in a creamy yogurt sauce.

El Papasito (U) ($), 370 West 52nd Street (east of Ninth), (212) 265–2225, is a no-frills cafe a few steps off Ninth with an authentic Dominican menu featuring good gumbo soups, traditional beefsteak dishes, and excellent roast pork and baked chicken served with fluffy yellow rice. Several seafood dishes are prepared Creole style.

Rinconcito Peruano (V) ($), 803 Ninth Avenue (53rd–54th), (212) 333–5685, brings the interesting soups and spices of Peru to Ninth Avenue. Try the papa a la huancaina, sliced potatoes in a spicy cream sauce, and almost any of the dishes seasoned with cilantro.

Puttanesca (W) ($–$$), 859 Ninth Avenue (56th), (212) 581–4177, is a little too busy at times, but that's because it is an always dependable choice for tasty Italian food at fair prices. Good to know about if Carnegie Hall or other upper 50s destinations are in your plans.

$\mathcal{A}$ $\mathcal{F}estival$ $\mathcal{C}alendar$

More than one hundred fairs, festivals, and parades are held each year in New York City, most between May and October. This list describes some of the major events celebrated by the city's ethnic groups. Everyone is invited to join the festivities!

If no information number is provided here, phone the New York Convention and Visitors Bureau, (212) 484–1222, for exact dates. To reach the Queens Tourism Council, call (718) 286–2667; for the Brooklyn Tourism Council, call (718) 855–7882, extension 51. For Flushing Meadows–Corona Park information, phone the City of New York Parks & Recreation Department, (800) 201–PARK.

JANUARY – FEBRUARY

Chinese New Year. Between January 21 and February 21. Ten days of celebrations starting on the first full moon after January 21, with parades and dragon floats on Mott Street in Chinatown and Main Street in Flushing.

MARCH

St. Patrick's Day Parade. March 17. Fifth Avenue. The traditional Irish parade, complete with bagpipers, draws one of the city's largest audiences.

Greek Independence Day. March 25. Fifth Avenue. A sea of blue

and white fills the avenue as bands and Greek-Americans in
native costumes join the march.

MAY

Norwegian-American Seventh of May Parade. Sunday in mid-
May. Bay Ridge, Brooklyn, (718) 851–4678. Ethnic costumes, floats,
and Nordic treats bring Scandinavians from all over to Bay Ridge.

Ukrainian Festival. Weekend closest to May 17, the anniversary of
Ukraine's adoption of Christianity. East Seventh Street. Traditional
foods, crafts, and folk dancing are offered.

Ninth Avenue International Food Festival. Mid-May.
Ninth Avenue between 37th and 57th Streets. A two-day food
extravaganza.

Czechoslovak Festival. Memorial Day weekend. Bohemian Hall,
29-12 24th Avenue, Astoria, Queens, (718) 274–4925. Traditional
music, dance, and foods.

JUNE

Puerto Rican Day Parade. First Sunday of the month. Fifth
Avenue. This colorful parade features floats, bands, and lots of
music celebrating the island's independence.

National Greek Heritage Folkloric Festival. Third weekend in
June. Bohemian Hall, Astoria, Queens, (718) 626–7896.
Traditional music, colorful folk dancing, and lots of Greek food
favorites.

St. Anthony of Padua Festival. Takes place around June 10 in
Little Italy. A smaller festival than San Gennaro, but another occasion when a statue of the saint is carried through the streets and
food stalls are set up along Sullivan Street.

JULY

Colombian Independence Day Festival. A Sunday near July 20. Flushing Meadows–Corona Park, (718) 699–4833. Colombian music, dance, and food mark the occasion.

Feast of St. Paulinus (The Giglio). Three Sundays in July. Our Lady of Mount Carmel Church, 278 North Eighth Street, Williamsburg, Brooklyn, (718) 384–0223. The legend of the saint is re-created by parading enormous replicas of a boat and a 65-foot spire representing the southern Italian town of Nola.

Irish Festival. Last weekend in July. Rockaway Beach Boulevard, Queens, (718) 634–1300.

AUGUST

Feast of Santa Rosalia. A weeklong event at the end of August. 18th Avenue, Bensonhurst, Brooklyn. Processions celebrating the patron saint of Sicily light up the avenue and bring out church auxiliaries and local food purveyors.

Hong Kong Dragon Boat Festival. Two weekends in mid-August. Meadow Lake, Flushing Meadow Park. Boat races, demonstrations of Chinese traditional arts, and vendors with Chinese food make for a festive setting.

Ecuadorean Independence Day Festival. Sunday close to August 10. Flushing Meadow Park. Ecuadorean music, dance, and foods mark the day. A parade is also held on 37th Avenue from 70th to 94th Streets, Jackson Heights, (718) 217–6532.

Festival of India. A Saturday in August. Flushing Meadow Park. The exotic foods, music, and dances of India are on display.

Ganesh Chathurthi. A nine-day festival honoring the Indian elephant-headed god Ganesh. Hindu Temple Society of America,

45-37 Bowne Street, (718) 460–8484. Special prayers, fruit, and flower decorations and performances by Indian dancers. At the end of the festival, Ganesh is carried around Flushing in a procession.

SEPTEMBER

West Indian Day Parade. Labor Day. Eastern Parkway, Crown Heights, Brooklyn, (718) 467–1797. West Indian heritage is celebrated with enormous floats, lavish costumes, contagious Caribbean music and stands offering calaloo, rotis, jerk chicken, and other Caribbean specialties. A million people turn out to watch.

Korean Harvest and Folklore Festival. Sunday in mid-September. Flushing Meadows–Corona Park, (718) 760–6660. This is both a religious ceremony and a celebration of music and dance and traditional cuisine.

Steuben Day Parade. Third weekend of the month. 86th Street, (516) 239–0741. German costumes and oom-pah bands, lots of wurst and Old World beer wagons.

Desfile Hispano de Queens (Hispanic Day Parade of Queens). Second Sunday in September. 37th Avenue beginning at 70th Street, Jackson Heights, (718) 286–3000.

Feast of San Gennaro. Ten days around the third week in September. Mulberry Street. Music, games, and tons of Italian food (sausage and pepper sandwiches are the trademark); a statue of the patron saint of Naples is paraded through the streets.

OCTOBER

Pulaski Day Parade. Sunday afternoon closest to October 5. Fifth Avenue between 31st and 52nd Streets, (877) 4PULASKI. Marching bands, floats, and folk costumes celebrate Kazimierz

Pulaski—the Polish hero of the American War for Independence—
and those who fought for freedom in their homeland. A cross of
flowers is formed as the parade passes St. Patrick's Cathedral.

Hispanic Day Parade. Early to mid-October. Fifth Avenue, (212)
242–2360.

$\mathcal{G}uided\ \mathcal{T}ours$

Guided tours can provide a wonderful introduction to a new neighborhood.

FOOD-ORIENTED AND/OR FOOD-INCLUSIVE TOURS

Here are a few reliable groups and individuals:

The New School, (212) 229–5690, is the one organization that regularly holds culinary tours. Some of the neighborhoods covered include Polish Greenpoint, Italian Bensonhurst, Indian Flushing, Russian Brighton Beach, and Jewish Borough Park. The tours are quite expensive but do include lunch.

Big Onion Walking Tours, (212) 439–1090, does numerous tours covering New York history and periodic "Multi-Ethnic Eating Tours" combining Chinatown, Little Italy, and the Lower East Side.

The 92nd Street Y, (212) 996–1100, gives excellent tours stressing Jewish history and visiting synagogues on the Lower East Side and in Williamsburg and Borough Park, with some discussion of foods.

CULTURAL AND ARCHITECTURAL WALKING TOURS

Among the best of the many groups offering tours are:

Lower East Side Tenement Museum, (212) 431–0233, offers

guided neighborhood heritage walking tours every Saturday and Sunday at 1:00 and 2:30 P.M. April through December.

Municipal Art Society, (212) 935–3960, presents well-informed architectural and historical tours throughout Manhattan and in Brooklyn.

The Hasidic Discovery Center, (800) 383–TOUR, does weekly Sunday-morning walking tours of the Lubovich Hasidic community of Crown Heights, with transportation from Midtown Manhattan by minivan. The tour includes a visit to a synagogue.

Jack Eichenbaum, (718) 961–8406, an expert in urban geography, does informative and enjoyable tours of Queens, on his own and in conjunction with the Municipal Art Society and the Brooklyn Center for the Urban Environment.

Queens Historical Society, (718) 939–0647, offers historical walking tours of the borough.

Brooklyn Center for the Urban Environment, (718) 788–8500, leads a variety of tours on a variety of topics in all sections of the borough.

Brooklyn Attitude Tours, (718) 398–0939, provides narrated journeys on Saturday, by bus and on foot, through a variety of neighborhoods.

Brooklyn Historical Society, (718) 222–4111, ext. 23, sponsors tours of a variety of historic neighborhoods in the borough.

$\mathscr{B}$ibliography

Ayto, John. *Food & Drink from A to Z: A Gourmet's Guide* (New York: Oxford University Press, 1994).

Brennan, Jennifer. *The Cuisines of Asia* (New York: St. Martin's Press, 1984).

Daly, Margaret. *Brooklyn Eats* (New York: Brooklyn Chamber of Commerce, 1997).

Dolkart, Andrew S. and New York City Landmarks Preservation Commission. *Guide to New York City Landmarks* (New York: John Wiley & Sons, Inc., 1998).

Ettlinger, Steve. *The Restaurant Lover's Companion* (Reading, Mass.: Addison Wesley Publishing Company, 1995).

Freudenheim, Ellen with Daniel P. Wiener. *Brooklyn: Where to Go, What to Do, How to Get There* (New York: St. Martin's Press, 1991).

Gabaccia, Donna R. *We Are What We Eat: Ethnic Food and the Making of America* (Cambridge, Mass.: Harvard University Press, 1998).

Gingold, Alfred, and Helen Rogan. *Brooklyn's Best* (New York: City Books, 1998).

Halvorsen, Francis. *Eating Around the World in Your Neighborhood* (New York: John Wiley & Sons, Inc., 1998).

Hyman, Gwenca L. *Cuisines of Southeast Asia* (New York: John Wiley & Sons, Inc., 1993).

Jackson, Kenneth T. *The Encyclopedia of New York City* (New Haven: Yale University Press, 1995).

Jaffrey, Madhur. *Indian Cooking* (New York: Barron's Educational Series, 1995).

Lambert Ortiz, Elizabeth. *The Book of Latin American Cooking* (New York: Alfred A. Knopf, 1994).

Leeds, Mark. *Ethnic New York* (Chicago: Passport Books, 1995).

Levine, Ed. *New York Eats (More)* (New York: St. Martins Griffin, 1997).

Manbeck, John B., Consulting editor. *The Neighborhoods of Brooklyn* (New Haven: Yale University Press, 1998).

Morgan, Lane. *The Ethnic Market Food Guide* (New York: Berkeley Books, 1997).

O'Neill, Molly. *New York Cookbook* (New York: Workman Publishing Company, 1992).

Papashvily, George and Helen Papashvily. *Russian Cooking* (New York: Time Life Books, 1981).

Queens Tourism Collaborative. *Queens: A World of Choices, A Complete Tour Planning Guide* (Woodhaven, N.Y.: Queens Council on the Arts, 1998).

Recipe Club of Saint Paul's Greek Orthodox Cathedral. *The Complete Book of Greek Cooking* (New York: Harper Perennial, 1991).

Sheraton, Mimi. *From My Mother's Kitchen* (New York: Harper Collins, 1991).

Smith, Jeff. *The Frugal Gourmet on Our Immigrant Ancestors* (New York: William Morrow and Company, 1992).

Teubner, Christian, Silvio Rizzi, and Tan Lee Leng. *The Pasta Bible* (New York: Penguin Studio, Penguin Books USA, 1996).

Weiss-Armush, Anne Marie. *The Arabian Delights Cookbook* (Los Angeles: Lowell House, 1995).

West, Karen. *The Best of Polish Cooking* (New York: Hippocrene Books, 1991).

Willensky, Elliot, and Norval White. *AIA Guide to New York City* (New York: Harcourt Brace Jovanovich, 2000).

Wolfe, Gerard R. *New York: A Guide to the Metropolis* (New York: McGraw Hill, 1993).

Zibart, Eve, Muriel Stevens, and Terrell Vermont. *The Unofficial Guide to Ethnic Cuisine & Dining in America* (New York: Macmillan USA, 1995).

General Index

$\mathscr{R}$estaurant $\mathscr{I}$ndex

Coffee and Dessert Cafes

ABOUT THE AUTHOR

Eleanor Berman is a widely published travel writer and the author of ten travel guides, including the *Eyewitness Travel Guide to New York* and the award-winning *Traveling Solo* (published by The Globe Pequot Press). She lives in New York City.

ABOUT THE ARTIST

John Coburn's drawings are featured in two books about New York City, one on Manhattan hotels and the other on Central Park. He exhibits in New York and Toronto, where he lives with his wife, Leslie, and their two children.

Help Us Keep This Guide Up to Date

Every effort has been made by the author and editors to make this guide as accurate and useful as possible. However, many things can change after a guide is published—establishments close, phone numbers change, facilities come under new management, and so on.

We would love to hear from you concerning your experiences with this guide and how you feel it could be made better and be kept up to date. While we may not be able to respond to all comments and suggestions, we'll take them to heart and we'll also make certain to share them with the author. Please send your comments and suggestions to the following address:

The Globe Pequot Press
Reader Response/Editorial Department
P.O. Box 480
Guilford, CT 06437

Or you may e-mail us at:
editorial@GlobePequot.com

Thanks for your input, and happy travels!